An Introduction to the Sociology
of Rural Development

NORMAN LONG

An Introduction to
the Sociology of Rural
Development

TAVISTOCK PUBLICATIONS
London and New York

First published in 1977
by Tavistock Publications Limited
11 New Fetter Lane, London EC4P 4EE
Reprinted 1982 and 1984

Printed in Great Britain by
Richard Clay (The Chaucer Press) Ltd,
Bungay, Suffolk

ISBN 0 422 74490 5

Contents

To
the memory of
Amy Louisa Long

Preface

This book was conceived and written for a course on problems of development and social change. As I developed my lectures, it became clear to me that there was a need for a general critical survey of relevant sociological and anthropological literature. Such a work should integrate the discussion of theoretical and methodological topics with an account of empirical findings so that the student might appreciate the interconnections between theory and research practice. This book tries to accomplish this difficult task.

It has not been possible within the space of this short introductory text to cover all relevant issues; nor have I been able to review more than a small sample of case-studies. I have instead attempted to achieve some sort of coherent focus and balance in the argument by juxtaposing contrasting theoretical orientations and by concentrating on studies of Third World rural populations. Even so there are some glaring omissions. For example, although I discuss problems concerning technological and social innovation, there is no treatment of the enormous (but, in my opinion, theoretically dull) literature on the diffusion and adoption of agricultural innovations written by American and Continental rural sociologists. Also I do not cover the literature concerning the renewed interest in peasant studies which has led to some exciting cross-disciplinary exchanges between sociologists, anthropologists, economic historians, and economists. Clearly the discussion that follows bears closely on the problems of understanding different forms of peasantry and on the changes that peasant societies have undergone with the impact of industrialization and increasing centralized state control. However, I have chosen *not* to get involved in diffusion or peasant studies *per se,* as both require more specialized treatment than can be attempted here. The same point holds for the study of rural markets and market behaviour which has attracted the attention of anthropologists and geographers.

My survey is also limited in two other important respects. There is no attempt to examine the processes and problems of rural social change in socialist societies like China. The Chinese case could in fact be regarded as a critical one, since it offers an alternative model of development to that of capitalism. But the paucity of detailed local-level rural studies, which might give substance to the many generalized statements made about Chinese development strategy, makes the task of evaluation especially tricky. The second limitation is likely to disappoint those who turn to the book for support for their own interest in developing an interdisciplinary approach to Third World development. The discussion is basically restricted to a review of sociological and anthropological work and only marginally deals with the contributions of economists, political scientists, and geographers. This decision to keep squarely within the bounds of sociological types of analysis does not commit me to a narrow disciplinary point of view, since I fully recognize the need to develop collaborative work. An appraisal of sociological perspectives can, I believe, add to our understanding of the general issues involved and possibly lead to more informed interchange between specialists of different backgrounds. It is hoped, therefore, that the discussion will be of interest to others besides students of sociology and anthropology.

The book is in no way original in terms of the materials or theories presented: its main claim is that it synthesizes the relevant literatures of sociology and anthropology in a world in which these disciplines, like others, are increasingly sealed off in separate departments.

My primary debt is to the students I have taught over the past three years. It was their continual probing for clarification on the different theoretical perspectives and on how they might be interconnected that drove me to put my thoughts down on paper. I would also like to acknowledge the stimulus of my friend and colleague, Dr Bryan Roberts of Manchester University, who was my co-director in a research project in Peru and with whom I have had numerous discussions concerning problems of development, especially in relation to the Latin American context. In addition, I have special debts of gratitude to persons who took on the onerous task of reading and commenting on the draft of this book: to David Winder of the Department of Administrative Studies, Manchester University; to Gavin Williams of St Peter's College,

Oxford; and to Professor Raymond Apthorpe of the School of Development Studies, the University of East Anglia. Each of them gave much needed encouragement at a time when my interest and energies were flagging and offered incisive criticism of the argument. Although I cannot claim to have adequately dealt with the many excellent points they made, I found their various suggestions and alternative interpretations most helpful in settling my own views. The exhausting business of getting thoughts to paper was also greatly assisted by Mrs J. McGough and Mrs C. Dowson, who typed the manuscript.

My final dedication must be to my wife, Ann, and to Alison and Andrew, who had some enjoyable weekends exploring the countryside of the North East of England, without me, so that I might finish the book. I thank them for their patience and support, and for recognizing that time estimates must be multiplied by a factor of ten.

Durham, July 1976.   Norman Long

CHAPTER 1

Introduction

This book examines perspectives and problems involved in analyzing the processes of rural development in the Third World. But in no sense is it a manual for development planners or for administrators and technicians concerned with the implementation of development programmes. Nor does it attempt a comparative study of neo-colonial or Third World economies, or of the differential impact of industrialization and urbanization on rural populations. Its aims are far less practical and ambitious in scope.

The discussion is primarily intended as a critical review of prevailing sets of ideas and analytical frameworks used by sociologists and social anthropologists in their studies of economic development and social change. However in order to avoid adding to the already voluminous body of rather abstract statements concerning the nature of development, I have interspersed this discussion with empirical examples designed to test the usefulness of the various theoretical approaches. This enables me to combine an account of general conceptual and methodological issues with an examination of specific field studies. I have chosen to concentrate on the rural sector because of its strategic importance for the poorer nations of the world, and because my own research experience and interests have been focused there.

THE SIGNIFICANCE OF THE RURAL-AGRICULTURAL SECTOR

Although rural phenomena cannot be understood without taking into account the wider socio-economic structure, the rural sector of Third World countries is distinctive in the kinds of practical and analytical problems it presents. It generally accounts for a large proportion of the national population, of which the overwhelming majority are engaged in agriculture and allied occupations; and contains about two-thirds of the poorest income categories of the country as a whole (Chenery *et al.*, 1974:19–21). Yet despite this, it is the source of primary products (agricultural produce and minerals) for export to the advanced industrial countries and of foodstuffs and labour for national urban and industrial centres. It exhibits a mixture of 'traditional' non-capitalist and newly-emergent capitalist forms of organization; and, unlike Western European industrial countries, has a large and persisting peasant population. This peasantry is frequently resistant to many changes introduced by the state, even if its policies are ostensibly aimed at improving agriculture and at redistributing productive resources on a more equitable basis. A large proportion of farmers use relatively simple forms of technology and, according to technical standards of efficiency, do not always maximize their use of available resources. These and other features, such as the apparent 'under-employment' of labour and the low rate of return from investment, are often singled out as constituting the 'agrarian problem'.

The significance that one attaches to these features and how one depicts the relationship of agriculture to national development, however, varies according to one's point of view. Several commentators, for example, have stressed the 'economic backwardness' and 'traditionalism' of the rural areas, suggesting that these are major impediments to national economic development and the source of ,many conservative attitudes towards modernity and economic growth (Boeke, 1953). Others have emphasized the dynamic role that agriculture can play in promoting industrialization through the capital it earns on export crops, which is then used to finance urban-industrial development; and through the provision of basic foodstuffs for expanding urban populations and of labour for factory production (Dorner, 1972:16–17; Mellor, 1966). Another view is that the rural sector is the main target for surplus extraction by more powerful metropolitan groups who siphon off essential resources (labour and capital) and who utilize them for the promotion of their own entrepreneurial interests to the detriment of rural populations (Frank, 1969a; Leys, 1975).

These differing views of course merely highlight different dimensions and are not necessarily incompatible. The first calls for an appreciation of the internal socio-cultural and economic conditions of rural society and of the ways in which particular systems of production and customary modes of behaviour may function to limit economic growth. The second focuses upon the interrelations of the agricultural and non-agricultural sectors of the economy. It hypothesizes that improved levels of agricultural production leading to increased exports will generate capital for industrial investment; and that the growth of industry will in turn create increased demand for foodstuffs and additional labour, leading to higher rural incomes and an enlarged demand for manufactured goods. This process seldom occurs as smoothly as predicted and so governments must frequently resort to more direct means of stimulating capital transfers (e.g. through taxation or by manipulating the terms of trade between rural and urban areas). The third point of view proposes a political economy approach to the problem. It stresses the importance of considering the economic inequalities and imbalances that arise from the control exercised by more powerful and strategically placed urban groups and their provincial allies. This approach attempts to relate internal socio-economic processes to the distribution of power at the national, and by implication also the international, level.

Several of these interpretations will receive fuller treatment later when we examine their sociological counterparts and theoretical elaborations. Suffice it here to have indicated the broad issues involved.

A perennial difficulty in attempting to deal with literature on economic development and social change is determining what is meant by that elusive concept 'development' which, together with its sister notion of 'growth', conjures up a whole range of organic metaphors (Nisbet, 1969:3–4). Most social scientists nowadays distinguish between 'economic growth', which is usually identified by reference to some quantifiable index like increase in per capita income or Gross National Product, and 'economic development', which implies some kind of structural and organizational transformation of society, although there would be considerable disagreement as to exactly what the latter entailed. Brookfield (1975:xi) suggests that 'The popular trend is to define development in terms of progress toward a complex of welfare goals, such as reduction of poverty and unemployment, and diminution of inequality'. Such a definition clearly involves the idea of structural change but it is value-laden in that it gives emphasis to the positive or beneficial consequences of socio-economic development. It does not allow for the concurrence of both negative and positive consequences. Indeed this objection forms a central issue in Marxist critiques of economic development literature. Marxist writers argue that development of the industrial nations of Western Europe in fact 'required' the 'underdevelopment' of the Third World; and in this way the non-industrial countries became dependent satellites of the more advanced nations, thus losing effective control over their own economic destinies (Frank, 1967a; Szentes, 1973).

The term 'development' is fraught then with numerous conceptual and ideological problems and it would be foolhardy in a work of this nature, which reviews a wide range of different theoretical positions, to attempt to arrive at some agreed definition. At this stage all that needs saying is that my basic subject matter is sociological work that deals with the processes by which rural populations of the Third World are drawn into the wider national and international economy and with the accompanying social transformations and local-level responses. Since none of the examples given are of established socialist economies, an alternative way of formulating this is to say that I am concerned with studies that analyze the outcomes of capitalist penetration and of state intervention in the rural sector.

SOCIOLOGICAL THEMES AND ORIENTATIONS

The main rationale for the presentation of materials is that of identifying and critically evaluating dominant theoretical orientations. By 'theoretical orientation' I mean the sets of ideas, assumptions, and methodological approaches that serve to guide or orientate the researcher in his examination of substantive issues. Hence it does not constitute what is normally thought of as a theory. An orientation offers ways of selecting, conceptualizing, categorizing, and ordering data relating to certain kinds of analytical problems. But it does not in itself form a consistent system of interrelated propositions which are capable of being tested empirically, although it may facilitate the formulation of such hypotheses or theories (Kaplan and Manners, 1972:32–4).

Theoretical approaches to the study of rural development have been formulated in response to specific types of questions and have themselves influenced the ways in which the problems have been posed. It is difficult to describe comprehensively the range of issues raised for they cover both questions of a very general nature concerning the evolution or transformation of rural society and more specific inquiries about the significance of particular factors or social categories in promoting socio-economic change.

On the most general level, first we have questions aimed at depicting the general consequences on rural populations of such processes as the commercialization of agriculture, urbanization, and industrialization; or that attempt to characterize the ways in which a capitalist market economy affects the social and economic structure of peasant villages. Several works have framed the problem more specifically in terms of the effect on particular social institutions, such as family and kinship systems or political and religious structures.

A second related question is whether one can identify particular local institutions or macro-level factors which might be said to inhibit the process of socio-economic development. And the obverse of this is the identification of facilitating factors or what some writers have called 'socio-cultural prerequisites'.

Other types of analysis have been more interested in the problem of why it is that within a cultural group or between groups placed in similar circumstances there has been marked variation in the responses to economic opportunities. Indeed the question of differential responses to change has been a major preoccupation of social anthropologists studying events at local community level and has led to a rapidly growing body of case studies on entrepreneurship, just as (in the United States) the adoption and diffusion of innovations has been a primary concern of rural sociologists (Rogers, 1962; 1969). Variability has also been explored from the point of view of why there apparently exist differences in the receptivity and rate of change between different institutional spheres; between, for example, family and political structures as against religion and ideology.

Some researchers have directed their attention to more pragmatic questions. Nowadays governments play a major part in shaping the kinds of structural changes that take place. It becomes pertinent therefore to ask how particular development policies are likely to affect rural areas and to examine the intended and unintended outcomes of specific rural development programmes. For example, one can explore how far the implementation of a land reform programme or the establishment of new rural co-operatives is affecting existing patterns of economic differentiation and leading to a re-distribution of productive resources. These and similar questions necessitate relating local-level processes and change to developments in the national economy and to the role played by the state.

The analysis of the articulation of local and national systems raises a host of complex problems which have been examined from different theoretical standpoints. These problems include questions concerning the mechanisms by which particular rural zones are linked into the national and international economy, the role and characteristics of brokers of various kinds, the relations between different modes of production, and the rather vexed issue of the differences (if any) between peasant and non-peasant cognitive systems. The latter point in fact links into a larger body of literature which deals with actors' perceptions and 'folk' models and which discusses the question of changing rationalities in situations of socio-economic development.

These, then, are some of the analytical issues covered by sociological and anthropological writers on rural development. Each writer comes to grips with them through the explicit or implicit use of certain theoretical concepts, metaphors, and frameworks, which enable him to order his data and develop particular explanations or lines of argument. Even the way in which problems are posed provides a clue to the kinds of theoretical and methodological predilections of the author, even if the latter claims to be merely interested in ethnographic description.

In the chapters that follow I differentiate between various types of theoretical approach. Although my choice is somewhat arbitrary in that I do not claim to cover all significant contributions (e.g. recent developments in the study of peasant economic systems or work on the diffusion of agricultural innovations), I do attempt to survey the more important paradigmatic ones which represent coherent traditions of research (Kuhn, 1962:10).

The first part of the book (Chapters 2 to 4) deals with two contrasting macro-orientations: the modernization approach and Marxist analyses of underdevelopment. The modernization approach subsumes a wide range of types of analysis based on such ideas as structural differentiation, the traditional/modern dichotomy, the rural-urban continuum, and the concepts of structural and cultural 'obstacles' or 'prerequisites' to development. These various formulations are discussed in Chapters 2 and 3. The Marxist framework has two major variants: the theory of structural dependency and the analysis of the articulation of different modes of production, which are the subject-matter of Chapter 4. The merits and shortcomings of these contrasting macro-orientations are examined and some attempt is made to determine how useful they are for the exploration of particular analytical problems.

The next chapter (Chapter 5) focuses upon the question of differential responses to change and discusses the transactional and decision-making models of entrepreneurship developed by an-thropologists. This literature attempts to understand the complex-ities of structural and organizational change at a local community or regional level of analysis from the point of view of interacting groups and individuals. It aims, that is, to relate the rural entrepreneur to his more immediate social and cultural environment and to isolate the factors affecting his economic and organi-zational decision-making. Although much of this work remains at a relatively micro-level of analysis, it does connect up at certain critical junctures with some of the more general issues raised by modernization theory and the dependency model. For example, modernization approaches have stressed the importance of iso-lating the values and attitudes that act as incentives for entre-preneurial behaviour: the anthropological model explores this by reference to specific cases of entrepreneurship and looks at the role of ideology and other factors in decision-making. Similarly, one can see a connection between the anthropologist's interest in the analysis of brokers who provide the points of intersection between local and national systems and the study of dependency structures, which treats the rural areas as satellites of metro-politan centres. Nevertheless anthropological studies of entre-preneurship derive essentially from the growth of actor-oriented perspectives in anthropology rather than from the literature on the sociology of development, and because of this they tend to concentrate on small-scale interactional processes and actors' perceptions and strategies rather than on the more general patterns of structural change.

The last part of the book (Chaper 6) discusses the sociological aspects of planned social change. Somewhat removed from the above themes, which take as given the economic and social planning inevitably involved in rural development, this chapter examines the relationship between government policies and socio-economic change. Here I discuss different approaches to planning, distinguishing between the 'improvement' and 'transformation' strategies, and illustrate these by reference to examples of community development programmes, settlement schemes, and land reform. Although much of the research dealing with planned change claims simply to document the intended and unintended consequences of policy or to describe the types of interaction between 'change agents' and the recipients, planners' and anthropologists' models alike make certain assumptions about the nature of development and the likely outcomes of particular policies, and give causal weighting to the factors involved. Hence both the planning process and the study of socio-economic change rest upon sets of ideas, assumptions, and methodologies which derive from the sorts of macro-theoretical orientations mentioned earlier. Indeed such frameworks as the modernization approach or structural dependency theory have been used to justify various strategic policy decisions. These and other related issues are explored in Chapter 6.

The final chapter offers an overview of the approaches and materials reviewed, attempts to reconcile micro with macro levels of analysis, and suggests future directions for research.

CHAPTER 2

The Modernization Approach

The search for a macro-theoretical framework capable of ordering the wide range of comparative observations on economic development and social change has been a major preoccupation of social scientists over the past two or more decades. Not surprisingly this has led to a revival of interest in problems concerning social evolution and the study of developmental processes first raised by such writers as Spencer, Tylor, Morgan, Durkheim, and Marx. Most contemporary writers fall broadly into one of two contrasting theoretical camps: those who adhere to a neo-evolutionary modernization approach and those who espouse a Marxist orientation. This chapter focuses upon the modernization approach and examines its analytical utility for comprehending the types of social transformations occurring among rural populations in the Third World.

MODERNIZATION AND THE PROCESS OF STRUCTURAL DIFFERENTIATION

According to Wilbert Moore, the concept of modernization denotes 'a "total" transformation of a traditional or pre-modern society into the types of technology and associated social organization that characterizes the "advanced", economically prosperous, and relatively politically stable nations of the Western World' (Moore, 1963:89). Such a view is predicated on the assumption that one can describe the general features of both 'traditional' and 'advanced' or 'modern' societies and thus treat development as the transformation of the one type into the other. Of the various attempts at formulating a model to depict this process, Neil Smelser's (1963) based on the idea of structural differentiation is perhaps the most elegant. For him a developed economy and society is characterized as a highly differentiated structure and an underdeveloped one as relatively lacking in differentiation: hence change centres on the process of differentiation itself. By 'differentiation' Smelser means the process by which more specialized and more autonomous social units are established. This he sees occurring in several different spheres: in the economy, the family, the political system, and religious institutions.

Smelser's model is not concerned with isolating economic determinants, but rather with describing the social transformations that accompany economic development, which, following Lewis, he defines as the growth of output per head of population. Economic development takes place through (a) the modernization of technology, leading to a change from simple traditionalized techniques to the application of scientific knowledge; (b) the commercialization of agriculture, which is characterized by the move from subsistence to commercial farming, leading to a specialization in cash-crop production and the development of wage labour; (c) the industrialization process, which depicts the transition from the use of human and animal power to machine power; and lastly, (d) urbanization, which consists of changes in the ecological dimension and is the movement from farm and village towards the growth of large urban centres. These processes, he suggests, sometimes occur simultaneously and sometimes at different rates. For example, in many colonial situations agriculture became commercialized without industrialization; or, as in the Guatemalan case described by Nash (1958a), industrialization developed with little urbanization.

Nonetheless, these four processes tend to affect the social structure of 'traditional' societies in similar ways. First, we find that structural differentiation occurs as more specialized and autonomous social units are formed. For example, as economic development takes place, several kinds of economic activity become separated from family institutions. Cash cropping leads to the separation of consumption and production activities normally associated with the household, and wage labour undermines the production system. Thus the nature and the functions of the family change. No longer the basic economic unit of production, the family's activities become 'more concentrated on emotional gratification and socialization' (Smelser, 1963:108). Apprenticeship within the family declines, pressures develop against the recruitment of labour along kinship lines, the pattern of authority is transformed as elders lose the control they exercised, and the nuclear family becomes differentiated from the extended family. Marriage norms may also change as more emphasis is given to personal choice in the selection of mates and as women become more independent economically, politically, and socially. Similar changes occur in other institutional contexts. For example, in the field of social stratification we find that recruitment to various occupational, political, and religious positions tends to depend more on achievement criteria than on ascription, and individual mobility increases. Also multi-functional religious and political roles are replaced by more specialized structures.

Second, a process of integration takes place whereby these differentiated structures are united on a new basis. This denotes, for example, the move from a 'pre-modern' political structure, where political integration is closely bound up with kinship status, tribal membership, and control of basic economic resources and of mystical sanctions, to a 'modern' type characterized by the existence of specialized political parties, pressure groups and a state bureaucracy.[1] We find similar integrative processes operating in other areas of social life: for example, in the economic sphere when peasants and tribesmen develop new types of social relationships through participation in capitalist or modern co-operative-type enterprises, trade unions, and labour recruitment agencies, or in the religious with the emergence of churches, sects, and religious bureaucracies separate from political institutions.

Accompanying both these processes of differentiation and integration is the spasmodic occurrence of social disturbances (e.g. outbursts of violence, the emergence of religious and political movements) which reflects the uneven rate of change. According to Smelser, discontinuities frequently occur because integration does not always keep abreast of differentiation, and this can lead to a disruption of the social order. He gives the example of colonial societies in which the economic, political, and educational structures may have been modernized but where a policy of indirect rule actively encouraged conservatism in family and local political affairs. This produced a situation where new activities and goals conflicted with existing traditional attitudes and institutions, as was the case with African tribal authorities under British colonial rule (Fallers, 1955; Gluckman, Mitchell, and Barnes, 1949; and Busia, 1951). He also mentions the fact that in the early stages of modernization we often witness the emergence of religious movements based on ascetic and this-worldly values and beliefs that legitimize the rejection of traditional ties and values, but which later may clash with the attempts at integration through national political structures and ideologies. This has happened recently, for example, with Jehovah's Witnesses in Zambia and Malawi (Long, 1968; and Wilson, 1973).

Although Smelser recognizes that differences in pre-modern conditions and in traditional structures may shape the impact that the forces of modernization have on particular social systems (and hence variations in the path of change), he claims that such a model depicts the general, ideal-typical features and processes of social development.

Such a view is not confined to Smelser but is also found among other writers. Hoselitz (1960), for example, applies Parsons's pattern variables,[2] which essentially underlie Smelser's differentiation model,[3] to the study of the development process. He argues that developed countries are characterized by universalism, achievement orientation, functional specificity, and underdeveloped countries by the opposite variables of particularism, ascription, and functional diffuseness. Like Smelser, Hoselitz conceptualizes the change from a traditional to a modern society as entailing the eventual modification or elimination of 'traditional' pattern variables. Hence modernization involves the structural shift from functionally diffuse economic roles (which are closely identified with other political or religious roles) to functionally specific roles that operate irrespective of the category of person with whom one interacts. This transformation is conceived by Parsons and Hoselitz as occurring by means of the differentiation process described by Smelser. Variations in the development of nations can then be explained by reference to the presence or absence of these structural elements, and indices constructed to measure the degree of modernization attained.

Later theorists, notably Eisenstadt (1966; 1970), have refined this approach to take account of the diversity of societal types subsumed under this single concept of a 'traditional' or 'pre-modern' society, and to distinguish between different processes by which modernization might be initiated:

'The process of modernization may take off from tribal groups, from caste societies, from different types of peasant societies, and from societies with different degrees and types of prior urbanization. These groups may vary greatly in the extent to which they have the resources, and abilities, necessary for modernization. They may differ in their capacity to regulate the more complex relationships between different parts of the society which are attendant on social differentiation and in the extent to which they are willing or able to become integrated into new, wider social frameworks.' (Eisenstadt, 1970:25)

Another aspect that must be considered is the nature of the initial impetus to modernization. This can vary enormously. In some cases it has been provided by various groups internal to the society, like the Protestant entrepreneurs of Western Europe (Weber, 1904) or the Meiji oligarchs of Japan (Bellah, 1957), but more usually in the Third World it has been the result of the impact of various external forces such as colonial expansion, and the spread of technical innovations or cultural movements. Also, depending on the factors operating, we find differences as to which institutions are first affected by structural differentiation and normative change. Furthermore, Eisenstadt holds that the sequence of development and the problems encountered are significantly influenced by the policies and strategies adopted by the more active elites of the society who have a major role to play in the 'institutionalization of modernization'; and he looks to detailed socio-historical analysis for explanation of the variations in the paths and sources of change. While acknowledging that the core characteristics are more or less as described by Smelser and Hoselitz, he argues, in addition, that modernization can only be sustained if the society develops a certain degree of structural flexibility whereby it becomes 'capable of dealing with new, changing problems and of absorbing, within its central institutional sphere, new social groups and strata with their problems and demands' (Eisenstadt, 1966:49). Thus he would add to the concepts of 'differentiation' and 'integration' a third term – 'adaptation' – to emphasize that, unlike traditional societies, the modern or modernizing society possesses an institutional structure which is capable of absorbing changes beyond its own initial premises and of dealing with structural dislocations, protest movements, and elements of disorganization. The modes for handling such problems, and how prevalent they are, will of course vary according to the type of social system, but a firmly based, relatively stable, political structure and ideology seems a necessary prerequisite. Hence modernization signals 'the establishment of new, broader political and social entities, whose symbols of identity are couched in non-traditional terms and whose institutional frameworks cut across narrower parochial units and emphasize more general, universalistic criteria' (Eisenstadt, 1966:16).

PROBLEMS OF EMPIRICAL APPLICATION

Some anthropologists have been attracted by Smelser's formulation. For example, Dalton writes:

'The transformation sequence we call modernization is an interaction process in two senses. Not only do economic and socio-cultural activities and relationships interact, but also *old* economic activities, social relationships and cultural practices change in reaction to *new* ones becoming instituted . . . Smelser characterized the process of changing the old as "differentiation", and instituting the new as "integration". These are central ideas . . [which have] power in an anthropological context . . . The structure of traditional village society becomes undermined because its traditional functions become displaced once superior economic and technological alternatives become available.' (Dalton, 1971:26,29)

In point of fact, however, the approach does not appear to have been used to any great extent by anthropologists as a comprehensive framework for the analysis of field data. In part this is due to the fact that anthropological research is normally confined to a relatively short time-span and often to the earlier phases of the development process, where continuity with previous structural forms and unevenness of structural change between institutional spheres are likely to be more apparent than the establishment of new 'integrative' institutions. Because of this a more circumstantial analysis (perhaps along the lines advocated by Eisenstadt) of the ways in which a traditional system has adapted itself to the new external forces impinging upon it has seemed more appropriate. Moreover, rural systems, as Redfield (1956) and others have forcefully demonstrated, are essentially 'part-societies' which become increasingly dependent upon the wider system as modernization is stepped up. Modernization theory recognizes this but is primarily concerned with characterizing the overall patterns and processes occurring at the more global level of the nation, and may therefore be somewhat inappropriate as a conceptual framework for analyzing micro-processes at local level. Anthropological studies also suggest that traditional types of relationships and values may not be so incompatible with modern economic and political forms as some modernization theorists have assumed. Smelser, Hoselitz, and others would argue, of course, that ideal-type constructs are not supposed to be isomorphic with particular realities but should be used to isolate the more important variables and to suggest how these might be interrelated; it remains for empirical investigation to test their applicability.

To evaluate the usefulness of the approach we need to explore two different problems. Does it single out the crucial sociological variables and relationships associated with development in contemporary rural situations and thereby help us to understand more fully the dynamics of social change? And second, are the underlying assumptions of the model adequate for comprehending the complexities involved?

The first issue will be examined through a discussion of selected empirical work analyzing the social consequences of techno-economic change. I start with Epstein's study of *Economic Development and Social Change in South India* (1962) because the concepts it employs resemble closely those of Smelser, although its empirical findings are at variance with his model.

The Effect of Modern Irrigation Agriculture in South India

Epstein analyzes the impact of a Government-sponsored modern irrigation project on the economic and social structure of two, differently located, villages in Mysore State. She is particularly interested in tracing the effects of technological innovation and economic change on the institutional structures of the two villages. She finds that, although the development of modern commercialized agriculture had brought about a shift in the social and economic life of the communities, the pattern of development varied according to whether the village lay in the central zone of irrigation or on the fringe. In the case of Wangala village, which reaped the full benefits of irrigation and therefore expanded its existing agricultural economy, development was unilinear 'in the sense that the new opportunities were in line with the former mode of economic organization' (Epstein, 1962:9) and this resulted in relatively little change in social structure. On the other hand, Dalena village, which was on the fringes of the irrigation area and therefore could not participate directly in the cash-crop economy, exhibited a pattern of economic diversification as its inhabitants responded to increased employment opportunities in the nearby town, became contractors for the Public Works Department, and engaged in various small-scale commercial activities. Some of them even bought up irrigated land or worked as agricultural labourers in neighbouring villages. As a consequence of their greater involvement in a wider range of economic relations and of the impact of multifarious urban influences, Dalena social structure underwent considerable transformation.

In the concluding chapter of her book, Epstein sets out to distinguish between different types of structural and cultural change and to examine how they are functionally related. She categorizes structural change into economic, political, ritual, familial, and organizational, and attempts to isolate the specific changes in roles and relations pertaining to each of these.

Epstein explains the persistence of traditional relationships and institutions in Wangala by arguing that the body of techniques introduced was merely an improvement of an existing technology which did not result in a re-allocation of productive resources or in an increased range of economic relations. Farmers wishing to exploit the new agricultural opportunities did so by adapting various existing institutional arrangements to secure new economic ends. This, then, was a situation where such factors as the land tenure system, the hereditary relations between the Peasant caste and Untouchables, and the pattern of inheritance did not seriously hamper development. In fact, they provided an established framework within which growth could be initiated. This emphasized that caste relationships and values were not insurmountable obstacles to development as had often been assumed. She also found that there had been no change in formal political and ritual relations. The village council (*panchayat*) was still controlled by hereditary lineage elders who settled intra-village disputes. Also Peasant 'patrons' continued to function as arbitrators for their Untouchable clients as previously; and the relations between Peasants and Untouchables and other functionary castes were still determined primarily by their relative ritual status.

In contrast, in Dalena *panchayat* members were not necessarily lineage elders and many cases were now taken to the courts in the nearby market and administrative centre of Mandya. Ritual status was no longer 'the ultimate determinate of social status' (Epstein, 1962:321), since breakdown in traditional economic relations between Peasants and Untouchables had led to the re-structuring of their political and status relations. The Untouchables now displayed more awareness of their own economic and political interests as against those of the Peasants, and were more inclined to participate in regional activities through political parties.

These differences then were positively correlated with a change in economic roles and relations. Only in the case of familial change did this not hold true. In both villages joint family ties were becoming less important as brothers, fathers, and sons developed divergent and sometimes conflicting interests due to their involvement in the modern market economy.[4] Only with respect to conjugal roles was there a marked contrast. Somewhat paradoxically, Dalena had maintained its customary pattern, whilst in Wangala, women had become more independent economically from their husbands and therefore less subservient in their behaviour. This was explained by the fact that Dalena men had been drawn into the urban labour market, leaving the women as 'the pillars of the traditional village farming economy' (Epstein, 1962:323), with virtually no new economic opportunities. Wangala women, however, were freer to turn to other pursuits and became petty traders and moneylenders in the markets of Mandya. This gave them much greater bargaining power in their own households.

Structural Concomitants of Techno-Economic Change

Although Epstein's study was not originally conceived in terms of a structural differentiation model of social change and in fact reveals some of the limitations this approach has for understanding short-run changes and adaptations, her monograph nonetheless shares some of the same predilections. In the first place, like Smelser, Epstein is basically interested in analyzing the structural repercussions of externally-induced change. Here the analytical problem is to establish how far certain economic and technological innovations have brought about concomitant changes in existing social institutions (e.g. in family and kinship patterns, or political and religious institutions). Hence both writers operate with a structural view of social systems which gives priority to identifying the main social groupings, social positions, and institutional regularities, and to describing how these are functionally interrelated and may change over time with the influence of new external factors. However, while Smelser tends towards a unilinear view of development and writes of the change from multifunctional roles to more specialized structures, Epstein shows how 'economic development may occur without change in ['traditional'] economic roles and relations' (1962:318).

Elsewhere I have outlined the theoretical and methodological limitations that a strict structural or institutional approach has for the study of social change (Long, 1968:6–9; also Guessous, 1967; Smith, 1973:130–48; Van den Berghe, 1963:695–705). Structural analysis enables one to make *post hoc* statements about the types and magnitudes of institutional changes that have occurred between two or more time-periods or to formulate highly generalized propositions about the kinds of structural change expected to occur under the impact of certain external factors. But it cannot adequately deal with the variability and flexibility of social systems, with the problem of isolating the factors responsible for change, nor can it handle the question of the differential responses to change shown by different social groups or categories within a given population.[5] These questions are of crucial significance if one wishes to understand the complexities of change occurring in any one empirical situation. Indeed Epstein herself departs from an institutional analysis at points in her study where she wishes to probe more thoroughly into the variations in the overall pattern.[6] Moreover, as Wilbert Moore argues, these variations and flexibilities (demographic, structural, and normative) enable a social system to endure and to adapt to changing circumstances. But they also provide 'the possibility and indeed the probability of innovation' and lead to 'forms of selective adaptation with significant and enduring consequences' (W. E. Moore, 1963:13, 20).

Alternatives to the institutional approach will be discussed in later chapters. Suffice it here to have indicated its main limitations. Smelser's concern for institutional regularities limits the utility of his model for dealing with internally-generated change, and for understanding the differential responses to external factors shown by different groups within the same institutional or cultural setting. Obviously, therefore, it is unlikely to be of much value for analyzing the internal dynamics for specific empirical situations, particularly if the changes are of recent origin. If it is of value at all, then it is more likely to be of use for describing the broad patterns of socio-historical change over a relatively long time-period, as Smelser (1959) himself has attempted in his study of the social consequences of the British Industrial Revolution and Eisenstadt (1966) in his survey of the modernization process in Europe, the Dominions, and the Third World.

Epstein's study, however, directs our attention to other important aspects. Smelser's model suggests that the introduction of a modern technology and commercialized agriculture will tend to produce similar types of structural change in the countryside. He argues that it brings changes in the organization of production and consumption activities and in existing family and kinship structures. Patterns of social status, political relations, and even religious institutions may also be modified. These changes reflect the underlying processes of structural differentiation and integration that occur as more specialized social units are created.

Yet Epstein's analysis emphasizes that structural differentiation is by no means a necessary outcome of techno-economic change and that it generally takes place at an uneven rate within different parts of the social structure. Hence, although in both villages a breakdown in joint family ties was evident following the transition from subsistence to cash economy, the pattern of change in other aspects was quite different for Wangala and Dalena. In Wangala, which received the full effects of modern irrigation, traditional relationships were adapted to meet the demands of the new technology, whereas in Dalena these same relationships underwent modification due to its involvement in the wider non-agricultural economy. This leads Epstein to conclude that 'economic development may occur without any change in economic roles and relations, provided it does not result in a reallocation of resources or in an increased range of economic relations' (Epstein, 1962:318). And as a corollary, she states that this also explains why political and ritual roles and relations were unaffected. The fact that Dalena experienced the most thorough-going structural change in economic, political, and ritual relations, suggests that involvement in an urban wage economy may be more significant for generating social change than the production of cash crops for external markets. Only where a reallocation of existing agricultural resources (e.g. through land reform or land sales) occurs, or where the labour or capital requirements of the new technology cannot be met along traditional lines, can one expect major transformations in rural social structure.

In a later study of economic development and social change among the Tolai of New Britain, Epstein explores these same ideas in a different cultural context. She writes:

'The rate of social change will be inversely related to the ease with which new cash earning activities can be combined with the traditional way of life. The. low labour input of Tolai subsistence and cash crops [cocoa and coconuts] facilitated a high degree of continuity in social institutions ... The traditional social differentiation between elders, middle-farmers and single men re-asserted itself under the new economic activities and is still much more pronounced than the new differentiation between migrants and villagers. It would be interesting to compare and contrast the continuity in Tolai social life with the change in similar societies, where the newly introduced cash crops required so much labour that they could not be easily combined with the customary way of life.' (Epstein, 1968:171)

This emphasizes the importance of examining closely the technical and operational requirements of a new techno-economic system in order to identify how far it is compatible with existing modes of social organization, ecological circumstances, and cultural priorities.[7] Some types of new technology and commercial production tend to have more immediate and radical effects on production and consumption activities and, over a longer time-span, lead to substantial modification in the social structure and normative system. Depending on the situation this can produce more specialized forms of labour, a differentiation between cash-crop as against subsistence spheres, a separation of production from consumption units, and changes in family and social organization generally. But these changes are not automatic and not always immediate.

From Axe to Plough in Central Africa
In contrast to Epstein's studies, my own research among the Lala of Zambia (Long, 1968) illustrates a pattern of more marked social change resulting from techno-economic change. In the early 1950s

the Lala of Serenje District experienced a significant shift in their system of agriculture due to the introduction of ox-plough farming and Turkish tobacco as the cash crop. The new technology was designed partly to replace the mixed slash and burn (or swidden) and hoe-cultivated system, which was in a state of imminent collapse because of the growing pressure of population on the meagre resources available. But it was also hoped that the production of tobacco, a valuable export crop, would lead to an increase in rural incomes and to an overall improvement in the local economy whose main cash input derived from migrant labourers working in the Copperbelt mines.

The main results of this change, as I recorded them in the early 1960s, were as follows. It generated new modes of recruiting and organizing labour outside the household, leading in some cases to the use of wage labour, and reduced the sharp division of labour between the sexes characteristic of the traditional system, thereby promoting much more interchangeable production roles. It tended to undermine traditional attitudes towards land tenure which were founded upon an usufructuary system with the chief acting as custodian of the land, and encouraged farmers to seek more permanent rights over specific tracts, which they hoped would eventually enable them to acquire rights of individual ownership and inheritance. The production of a cash crop brought about a general increase in the economic prosperity of the area and led to the development of the non-agricultural sector, as successful farmers and returning urban workers invested their savings in the establishment of small shops and other small-scale businesses. This produced a more diversified and slowly expanding economic system.

These economic changes, together with other factors, such as the deteriorating ecological situation and certain reforms which took place in the local politico-administrative structure (for details see Long, 1968:96–8), played an important role in bringing about a fragmentation of the traditional village unit and a proliferation of numerous smaller settlements composed of single nuclear or small extended families instead of localized matrilineal descent groups. Matrilineal descent groups, it seems, were somewhat incompatible with cash-crop farming and the accumulation of wealth above subsistence needs: the new economic opportunities led to an increase in disputes between matrilineal kin for control over economic resources and contributed to the disintegration of corporate kinship groupings. Problems over inheritance and property holding became a major focus for conflict among kin:

> 'Under customary law only close matrilineal male descendants are eligible to inherit (i.e. uterine brothers and sisters' sons), though sons may receive a small bequest if the man leaves plenty of possessions . . . Many farmers and shopkeepers now wish to leave their property to their own children rather than their sisters' sons: but frequently they have maintained close contact with their own matrilineal kinsmen and have received considerable assistance from them in the establishment of their enterprises. This creates a potentially explosive situation which can erupt on the man's death, if not before . . . some farmers have tried to solve this difficulty through a form of anticipatory inheritance whereby they transfer during their life-time some of their material assets to their sons so that the sons are already in possession of them at their father's death.' (Long, 1968:193–4)

If this trend continued it seemed that one could predict a major shift in the Lala system of kinship and inheritance, and possibly also changes in land tenure and the pattern of local politics. Indeed, with respect to the latter, it was already clear that the new economic situation had contributed to the emergence of new criteria of status and power and had devalued the position of the village headman and that of the leader or 'Warden' of the matrilineal group (Long, 1968:144–5, 152–3). Wealth, education, and leadership in non-indigenous associations (e.g. a church or political party) were in many contexts more powerful factors for allocating prestige than traditional criteria.

This example shows the enormous complexities of identifying the key factors responsible for certain types of change, for at the same time as techno-economic innovation was taking place, so were other processes at work which were affecting the social structure and cultural regime. For example, the long-term effect of labour migration to urban areas had undoubtedly brought with it a widening of social and cultural horizons and had contributed in a major way to the implanting and expansion of the religious sect of Jehovah's Witnesses. This religious movement was important because it contained within it many individuals who responded early to the new opportunities and many who, for various reasons, were either disenchanted with traditional culture or wished to utilize resources in rather novel ways. It also offered some ideological justification for the taking on of new socio-economic roles and spoke out strongly against the existing system of matrilineal kinship which it regarded as contrary to the Christian ethic. Another set of factors producing changes of central significance was the deteriorating ecological situation and the gradual shift from axe to hoe cultivation, which was already noticeable prior to the introduction of the new technology, and which constituted an attempt to combat the disastrous effects of an overpopulated swidden system. Further changes resulted from the implementation of new arrangements for local government, which effectively undermined the position of the Lala village headman and made minor changes in the legal system (see Long, 1968:140–2 for details).

PROBLEMS OF CHANGE AND CONTINUITY

Any study of the social concomitants of techno-economic change must therefore confront the extremely complex problem of trying to estimate the effects of the new production system as against other change-producing factors. Obviously it is essential to treat technological innovation in relation to the total context of change and development. A simple but radical change in agricultural technology may itself lead to a re-structuring of production and non-production activities: Salisbury (1962) argues, for example, that the displacing of stone axes by steel ones among a New Guinea Highland people substantially reduced the time spent on subsistence production and led to an expansion of ceremonial and political activities. It did not, however, produce much change in the economy and social organization: food production went up only 4 per cent and the existing kinship and clan system remained unimpaired. It was not until the area was brought into closer contact with the outside, through the establishment of effective colonial rule and the export of wage labour, that significant structural changes occurred. Hence, technological change by itself will not stimulate the emergence of commercial production unless there also exists a viable system for marketing produce and for providing other necessary inputs. Moreover, as I have suggested, when we are dealing with situations that are already part of a wider economic and political structure we must face the added difficulty of attempting to isolate the possible different effects of various processes (e.g. changing technology, urbanization and labour migration, industrial development, and the spread of social and cultural innovation).

In addition we cannot assume that the results of similar types of economic development will be structurally the same everywhere. Beyond indicating the specific technical requirements of a modern technology, cropping system, and market structure, we are unable to predict confidently what the social consequences will be, for these will depend on the type and flexibility of institutional structures, on the availability of social and material resources, and on existing cultural orientations and prior conditions. We cannot even assume, therefore, as Smelser does, that the long-term effect of economic development will be the replacement of so-called traditional institutions by relationships and values of a more 'modern' type. Indeed, as Eisenstadt comments,

'Within any group, community, or organization that develops in modern society many particularistic, ascriptive, and diffuse orientations inevitably tend to persist and develop. Thus on the local community level the ties of friendship, often kinship and common residence, have many particularistic and ascriptive orientations that are perpetuated and often even restructured in modern settings.' (1966:153).

Moreover, as many anthropological analyses have shown (e.g. Geertz, 1963; and Belshaw, 1955), these particularistic relationships and values may be of strategic importance for the mobilization of resources in order that farmers or businessmen might expand their enterprises. At the same time of course they can be used by 'modernizing' elites to retain monopoly over the scarce means and benefits of development at local or national level.

The concepts of structural differentiation and integration may, as Dalton suggests, be central ideas for the analysis of rural development but we should be careful not to assume that the direction of change is always towards more specialized and autonomous social institutions and to the formation of new types of social groupings. Epstein's Indian study shows, for example, the considerable extent to which existing non-capitalist relationships and values were harnessed to the demands of the new economic system, and how traditional economic roles and relations remained largely intact and did not develop more specialized functions. There was also little evidence that the caste structure and village political institutions were affected by the introduction of commercial agriculture. In her later New Britain study she argues that structural continuity among the Tolai was high because,

> 'The traditional social and economic system embodied many of the features which are usually associated only with rapidly growing economies, such as a high degree of social mobility set in an extremely flexible political system with status achievement rather than ascription, specialization facilitated by a monetized economy [in this case it was based on shell money or *tambu*] together with emphasis on individual enterprise, thrift, and *tambu* accumulation. This favourable setting provided a fertile ground for the emergence of "big" men, who, like true capitalists, were employing their resources to maximize their profits ... [Later with European contact it] provided a fertile ground for economic development. (Epstein, 1968:32,xxii).

This interpretation is consistent with the point of view expressed by Hoselitz (1960) and Eisenstadt (1966) that certain traditional societies may already possess the so-called necessary socio-cultural prerequisites for economic growth. This theme will be discussed at length in the next chapter.

A more extensive survey of the literature than can be attempted here would, I believe, show that, implicitly at least, many anthropologists have conceptualized socio-economic development in terms of the idea of increasing structural differentiation and the rise of new integrative structures.[8] They have also been concerned to show the extent to which traditional or 'tribal systems have in fact absorbed *many* changes into their traditional equilibrium' (Gluckman, 1965:286). But such studies do not necessarily adopt a neo-evolutionary and functionalist model of the kind advocated by Smelser and, to a lesser degree, by Eisenstadt.

It may be generally valid to argue that, under the impact of larger scale economic and political structures, traditional rural systems experience an increase in the scale of their social relationships, tend to develop more differentiated institutions, and become involved in new types of social groupings, but seldom does this occur in the rather uniform and deterministic manner suggested by Smelser. Nor do pre-existing relationships and values simply become displaced by new modes: normally there is some accommodation between traditional and newer forms of organization. Traditional concepts and values may acquire new meanings, or, as Parkin (1972:5) suggests for the Giriama of Kenya, there may be 'an exaggeration of . . . culturally prescribed and publicly recognized forms' which may 'actually mask underlying developments of a new and radical nature'. The anthropologist or sociologist is interested in understanding development from both a structural and cognitive point of view and must develop modes of analysis capable of dealing with socio-cultural systems in which quite disparate systems of belief and social classification may co-exist (Mitchell, 1960:19). To frame one's analysis solely in terms of the ideas of structural differentiation and integration would seriously limit the range of interesting problems to be explored. Furthermore it is doubtful that such concepts have much explanatory power beyond being shorthand descriptions for some of the types of structural change associated with societies undergoing socio-economic development.

GENERAL THEORETICAL AND METHODOLOGICAL LIMITATIONS OF MODERNIZATION THEORY

The foregoing discussion of empirical studies has raised some of the difficulties of applying Smelser's model to the study of economic development and social change in contemporary rural situations. I now wish to outline its more general analytical weaknesses and assumptions.

In common with other traditional-modern formulations by Hoselitz and others, Smelser's model seems to rest on the idea of unilinear development along the lines of what appears to have happened in Western European capitalist countries. This impression is supported by the fact that he first developed it when analyzing the kinds of social change that accompanied the British Industrial Revolution. However, the model is not 'a distillation of actual Western experience, nor even an average of the several experiences of the Western nation-states', but rather an idealization of the main direction of certain social and cultural trends that proved so successful in the West (Smith, 1973:87). Hence, although it may not accurately reflect the processes of modernization as they occurred in Western Europe, it nonetheless extrapolates from an understanding of this particular historical sequence and posits the existence of similar structural processes arising under conditions of economic growth in the Third World. To this extent it is ethnocentric.

Eisenstadt's analysis is less open to a charge of this nature since he presents a more flexible view of modernization, which takes account of the variations in the structural and cultural characteristics and outcomes of different types of societies, including within his frame of reference both capitalist and socialist systems. However his attempt to identify the various integrative and adaptive mechanisms that lead to a pattern of 'self-sustained' growth (which he sees best illustrated by the early modernization of Western Europe and the United States), together with his concern for 'breakdowns' in modernization (which occur more readily in the newer states of Africa, Asia, and Latin America), convey the impression that he, too, is arguing from the standpoint of a Western model of development.[9] Moreover, as Wertheim has so convincingly argued,

> 'Eisenstadt's terminology reveals a distinct bias in favour of the western type of development, which he views as a more harmonious one than other patterns which he equally includes within the "modernization" concept. His stress upon "adaptation" and "integration" as basic requirements for "sustained growth", his view of political "eruptions" as symptoms of "unsuccessful adaptation", as external manifestations that the more normal smooth road towards modernity has been blocked, betray a preference for gradualism as evinced in the western type of growth.' (1971:92)

Nettl and Robertson (1968:45–50) make the further point that in much of the literature there is a tendency to equate modernity with Western liberal democracies. A main reason for this, according to them, is that 'the idea of structural differentiation owes much in its evolution to the economic concept of the division of labour in capitalist or neo-capitalist societies', where such notions as 'democratization' and 'participation' form the core of political ideology (Nettl and Robertson, 1968:45,49). In contrast to many other writers, Eisenstadt is less inclined to this view of modernization since he assigns a less central role to structural differentiation as a mechanism. He argues, for example, that in certain modernizing societies there is a trend towards a simplification of roles and organizations as one dominant institution is able to extend its power over other institutional domains, as happens in military or totalitarian regimes. He calls this process 'dedifferentiation'.

The point remains, however, that modernization theorists often construct their models on the basis of an understanding of the social concomitants of Western economic development; and such models are probably largely irrelevant to comprehending the kinds of processes occurring in present-day Third World countries whose socio-historical and contemporary circumstances are so different.

Yet having said this, it is important to stress that certain of the concepts and generalizations generated by the approach may nonetheless be useful if set within a different analytical framework. I have already indicated that the ideas of structural differentiation and integration are implicit in much empirical research on structural change. They have also been of heuristic value in developing a taxonomy of political systems (see Easton, 1959). But if we wish to develop a comparative or developmental analysis of the type suggested by Smelser then we need to specify much more precisely the types of relationships and institutions to be considered. Smelser's use of ideal-types is clearly inadequate.

There are two major weaknesses in his formulation. The first concerns the question of operationalizing the notion of differentiation when comparing societies. Obviously there exist in all societies both elements of differentiated and undifferentiated relationships and institutions. This is more especially the case if one compares peasant with industrial societies rather than thinking of the contrast between an isolated tribal and a modern industrial situation. Which categories of relationships and roles are therefore to be selected as crucial in one's analysis? This point has been well put by Frank (1967) when he suggests that if one looked at the main centres of economic and political power in the United States one would find just as many undifferentiated relationships and roles as in the same elite groups in an underdeveloped country. Hence it is necessary to identify which institutional contexts and which levels of a structure one is referring to so that the phenomena under investigation are analytically comparable. For example, it would seem more appropriate to compare peasant farming systems in developing countries with family farms in Western Europe, where the patterns of differentiation might be similar, rather than with large-scale Western capitalist farming enterprises which have more in common with agricultural plantations. The impression one gets from Smelser and Hoselitz is that one can somehow arrive at an aggregate assessment of the degree of structural differentiation in the society as a whole. But, given the complexities involved, this seems an unrealistic and theoretically dubious exercise.

Linked to this problem is the difficulty of drawing a sharp contrast between societies that exhibit role systems based more on universalistic-achievement criteria than on particularistic-ascriptive factors. Frank is especially instructive on this issue, arguing that it is necessary to distinguish between role *recruitment* and the *rewards* that follow. He substantiates this point by reference to the study of *The Japanese Factory* by Abegglen (1958). Frank writes:

'role recruitment in Japan is very much based on achievement ... However, the assignment of reward within the role, as Abegglen argues, is highly ascriptive, being based on such factors as age, family obligations, etc. The important distinction between recruitment and reward (rarely made in discussions of achievement or ascription) and obvious differences between Japanese and American practices in this respect would seem to explain a large part of this disagreement on this matter. For example, Bellah and Levy, who emphasize Japan's achievement orientation as a cause of its development, refer to role recruitment. On the other hand, Abegglen, who emphasizes Japan's ascriptive pattern is apparently thinking of reward within roles.' (Frank, 1967. Reprinted in Frank 1969b:26–7)

The same distinction could help to elucidate the problem posed by the use of family labour on commercially-orientated peasant farms in Africa and elsewhere. Hence it could be shown that, whereas ascriptive criteria are important in the recruitment of labour, the rewards are often achievement-based (e.g. by the payment of wages for set tasks or periods of work).

The second major weakness in Smelser's formulation is that, even supposing that a lack of differentiation characterizes an underdeveloped society, can we assume that with economic development this will in fact be replaced by a more differentiated structure and the breakdown of pre-existing or traditional institutions? Here the assumptions seem to be that old traditions are displaced by new ones; also that traditional and modern systems tend to be mutually exclusive and in conflict. From existing empirical data, some of which I have reviewed earlier, these assumptions appear untenable. There is now a growing body of evidence that shows that not only have specific cultural and historical traditions influenced the acceptance, rejection, or fusion of 'modern' forms but that many so-called traditional values and relationships are congruent with development (Bellah, 1957; Epstein, 1968; Salisbury, 1970; Hazelhurst, 1966; Nash, 1958; and Singer, 1968).

The assumptions of displacement and incompatibility are in fact wedded to the kind of linear development implied by the model. Indeed, as Singer (1968) comments, many anthropological studies have also tended to adopt a simple linear view of change. Hence it has often been assumed that urban and industrial development

'must lead to the breakdown of traditional social and cultural forms, or, if in a particular case this breakdown does not occur, then the forces of traditionalism must have been too strong and we should expect a failure of modernization and a persistence of the traditional forms. In reference to Indian modernization these assumptions have usually led to sweeping generalizations about the incompatability between the joint family, the caste system, and Hinduism, on the one hand, and the forces of modern industry, urbanization, science, technology, and education, on the other. The research problem is then posed as one either demonstrating the breakdown of these "traditional" institutions under the influence of the forces of modernization or, if this is not possible, demonstrating that the persistence of the "traditional" institutions is a major obstacle to modernization. Since the "modern" and the "traditional" so often coexist in India, we are led by the application of such reasoning to the conclusion that either India is an anomaly or it is in a state of "transition" from a traditional to a modern society.' (Singer, 1968:431–2)

In Singer's estimation such an approach fails to come to grips with the much more interesting and relevant question of 'how particular groups of people adapt their traditional institutions to changing conditions and how, under such circumstances, they may evolve new institutions' (1968:432). The same criticism applies to modernization theorists when they formulate statements about institutional change at the more global level of the nation.

This leads us to consider briefly the theoretical status of a structural differentiation view of social change. It was originally developed to interpret the effects of industrialization in Western Europe. It presented an evolutionary view of the process by which pre-capitalist, 'traditional' societies changed in the direction of becoming more modern in type. The model was later extended to cover the diffusion of the Western techno-economic system to Third World countries.

Yet, as Smith (1973) and Ocampo and Johnson (1972) have stressed, it is also essentially functionalist in conception. It starts from a functional analysis of a given social system,

'with its functions, structures, and roles, with its input and output, with its values, with its institutional organization. In this context, change refers to the greater differentation of the system, or to the greater degree of secularization that appears within it, or in the autonomy that secondary or sub-systems manage to attain. Evolution in a process of development or modernization is conceived of in relation to system states or stages that grow out of each other and that pass from one to another, owing to determined transformations . . . that operate within the preceding system or to exogenous events. The end result of the evolutionary process is the "modern" society.' (Ocampo and Johnson, 1972:420)

In contrast to the development of Western nations which is regarded as an autochthonous and self-generating process, the main impetus to structural change in the Third World is interpreted as beginning with the disturbance of the traditional equilibrium brought by the impact of external forces, such as colonial rule, commercialization of the economy, urbanization, and industrialization. The modernization theorist is chiefly interested in measuring the magnitude of structural change that results and in describing in general terms the pattern of changes that can regularly be expected to occur. Thus what is analyzed in particular empirical examples is the response of a pre-existing system to a set of given external stimuli. Such an approach shows similarities to the equilibrium model used by some anthropologists in their studies of institutional change (Gluckman, 1968).

The structural differentiation model gives analytical priority then to the effects of exogenous factors in promoting change in the Third World; and uses an ideal-type characterization of 'traditional' societies which over-emphasizes their internal coherence, homogeneity, and stability. Indeed, as Salisbury (1970:2–6) has pointed out, much of the literature on development, it seems, takes this erroneous point of view. These assumptions, he claims, have unfortunately been fostered by many anthropologists who, in their analyses, have placed emphasis on 'the compelling force of "tradition",' on the logical consistency of moral rules, and have ignored the important variations in individual behaviour and normative interpretation. In his opinion, 'no theory of economic development is adequate if it ignores the calculating abilities, the entrepreneurial tendencies, or the range of individual variation found among traditional farmers' (Salisbury, 1970:3–4).[10] These elements of variability and flexibility are of crucial significance when analyzing the ways in which particular categories or groups of individuals respond to changing circumstances. They also enable us to understand how change is mediated through the adaptation of existing structures and relationships, and help to explain why certain innovatory patterns emerge.

The type of institutional analysis advocated by modernization theorists and by exponents of the equilibrium approach merely depicts the overall structural regularities at two or more points in time and isolates the factors initially responsible for disturbing the 'traditional equilibrium'. It cannot show how the social system (or particular parts of it), in adjusting to the new forces operating, itself generates influences which contribute towards determining the outcomes. If, therefore, we wish to develop a theoretically more adequate analysis of structural change we must allow for emergent properties and feedback mechanisms that affect the course of events. The structural differentiation model apparently allows for neither. In addition, of course, we need to examine more closely the ways in which the various external forces are themselves inter-related to one another as part of a wider macro-structure of socio-economic and political relations. Most modernization theorists avoid this problem by taking as 'given' these 'external' processes.

Although Smelser talks about varying *paths* and *sources* of modernization, his model in fact emphasizes the uniformities in the process and offers little analytical guidance to those interested in a detailed study of concomitant variations. Moreover, in common with other modernization approaches, his formulation is beset with various semantic difficulties which arise from his conceptualizing 'modernization' as both a *process* and a *product* or 'end-state'.[11]

The Rural-Urban Conceptualization of Social Change

The traditional–modern dichotomy has also sometimes appeared in the form of a rural-urban or folk-urban conceptualization of social change which has its roots in the early work by Redfield (1941, 1947). The main features of Redfield's concept of the 'folk' society correspond closely to Smelser's view of 'traditional' societies, though the former places more emphasis on cultural than on structural aspects. According to Redfield, the ideal-typical features of a folk society are as follows:

> '[It is] small, isolated, non-literate and homogenous, with a strong sense of group solidarity. The ways of living are conventionalized into the coherent system which we call a "culture". Behaviour is traditional, spontaneous, uncritical and personal; there is no legislation or habit of experiment and reflection for intellectual ends. Kinship, its relationships and institutions, are the type categories of experience and the familial group is the unit of action. The sacred prevails over the secular; the economy is one of status rather than of the market.' (Redfield, 1947:293)

Rephrasing this slightly to eliminate the somewhat naive interpretation of the actor as a passive recipient of his culture and its conventions, then what we have is a relatively undifferentiated society of the kind described by Smelser. Its opposite is what Redfield calls 'urban' society, though he never properly defines it, except negatively as the mirror image of the 'folk' version.

Redfield treats the folk and urban types as representing opposite extremes on a continuum.[12] This continuum cannot simply be regarded as a morphological device facilitating the comparison of different types of social structure. It also implies and depicts the general process whereby folk societies become transformed, through their incorporation into wider structures, into urban-type societies. Redfield first worked out his ideas in his study of *The Folk Culture of the Yucatan* (1941) in Central America. In this study he attempts a comparative analysis of social change in four different types of communities in the same region of Mexico. The communities were chosen to represent points along the rural-urban line of contrast: a village of tribal Indians, a peasant settlement, a small town, and a capital city. Each of these was differently located geographically, and different in its dominant modes of social organization and its history. From this Redfield tried to establish that increased urban influences and modes of behaviour lead to the breakdown of customary ways of life (what he calls 'cultural disorganization'), to more individualistic patterns of behaviour, and to more secularization. The end result of this process approximates very closely to Smelser's characterization of a modern society.

However, Redfield's formulation differs from Smelser's model in that it treats the city as the main source of change, giving only minimal attention to the question of technological change in agriculture and the development of the market economy. Because of this more stress is placed on spatial factors. This point is neatly put by Apthorpe (1970a:17–18) when he writes that,

'The folk-urban continuum is a way of looking at society and social change from the point of view, say, of a migrant moving across a geographical area who, as it were, meets different types of society on his way from his place of birth in the countryside to the urban centre where he hopes to find wage employment. Assuming, as it does, that different "types of society" are the mental constructs that appropriately "classify" social change, it is a typological construct. Like other approaches of this general class, it does not tell us about social change within what it describes as a particular type of society. It is more concerned with the differences between one type and another.'

These differences, which can be described in terms of an order of morphological complexity, tend to coincide with the spatial arrangements of village, town, and city. But they also suggest that 'what is to be found in the more remote communities represents on the whole an earlier condition of the same general custom or institution than what is found in less remote communities' (Redfield, 1941:340). Hence, comparative studies should aim to explore both the structural and developmental implications of this view of change. Redfield's argument is not primarily concerned with an historical analysis but with the functional relations of crucial variables affecting social change. The degree of geographical isolation and of cultural homogeneity are two linked independent variables that can be correlated with the levels of cultural and social disorganization, individualization, and secularization. Thus the peasant village, as compared with the tribal village, is less isolated and more heterogeneous, has a more complex division of labour, is more involved in the money economy, has professional specialists, and greater occupational differentiation. It is also less organized around family and kinship institutions, more dependent on 'impersonally acting institutions of control', less religious in beliefs and practices, and is generally more individualistic to the extent that 'the socially approved behaviour of any of its members does not involve family, clan, neighbourhood, village or any other primary group'. These contrasts hold similarly for the town as compared with the peasant village and become even more marked when comparing the city with the peasant or tribal settlement.

Redfield's scheme has been widely criticized by a number of anthropologists studying peasant communities and by others interested in development issues (Tax, 1941, 1958; Lewis, 1951, 1953, 1965; Hauser, 1965). First it has been argued that the conceptual framework is weak in that the key concepts are insufficiently precise and entail a number of untenable *a priori* assumptions. Thus it has been pointed out that the notions of geographical isolation and homogeneity are merely suggestive of qualitative differences which may or may not prove significant if one were to develop some indices for measuring them. Redfield himself does not offer the means to do this. As has been shown in many anthropological field studies, apparent social homogeneity conceals within it aspects of heterogeneity that may, for example, be shown by variations in demographic or ecological phenomena. However homogeneity in one area of social life does not necessarily entail homogeneity in others. This creates difficulty for analysis unless one clearly isolates the sets of relationships and social contexts one wishes to compare. Similar difficulties arise with the notions of individualization and secularization. Throughout the argument Redfield assumes that rural and urban phenomena are diametrically opposed to one another before he presents any data to support such a view. This skews his analysis towards the discussion of polar opposites, which has many of the shortcomings already noted for modernization theory in general. The sharp distinction he draws between 'organization' and 'disorganization' reflects this predilection, since he associates the latter almost exclusively with urban-type systems and takes no account of the existence of both elements within a single society. In this respect Smelser's view of the discontinuities that may arise due to uneven structural change is a more sophisticated treatment of the same problem. Also Redfield's use of the concept of disorganization directs analysis away from the more important task of analyzing the emergence of new patterns of social organization, rather than describing the erosion of old forms.

Redfield's model has also been criticized for its lack of fit with empirical evidence now available. The folk-urban conceptualization gives too much weight to the city as the major source of change, although the above-mentioned study by Epstein indicates that in certain situations exposure to a wider set of urban-based relations may be crucial. Other research, however, has suggested that changes in technology and the commercialization of agriculture can also bring about a re-structuring of rural social systems. Referring specifically to the Mexican case, Lewis (1951) has argued that considerable inter-societal contact between Indians and non-Indians or *Ladinos* prior to the effects of urbanization and to the construction of modern transport systems had already produced marked changes at the level of the local community. Moreover, when applied to the analysis of rural-urban migration, Redfield's model tends to over-emphasize the factors that attract migrants to cities and does not give sufficient attention to the 'push' elements. It also tends to assume that the volume of migration and/or contact with urban systems varies consistently with distance and size of settlement; whereas recent research shows that this is a complex process which partly depends on the characteristics of the local situation as well as on the employment opportunities and amenities offered by the urban areas (Boswell, 1973). This criticism indicates again that by concentrating on the differences between types of societies, rather than on an analysis of the internal elements and variations contained within any one local system or category, the analyst is likely to undervalue the significance of local patterns or attributes.

Another difficulty concerns the assumption that urbanization produces a weakening of familial organization and the development of a more individualistic ethic. Yet several studies have concluded that certain extended family systems not only survive in a modern economic context but that they often function positively to enable individuals to mobilize capital and other resources essential for modern capitalist enterprises. This has been documented for both rural and urban settings (Berna, 1960; Singer, 1968; Belshaw, 1955). In addition, family and kinship networks are of great importance to sectors of the urban poor as well as to short-term peasant migrants (Lewis, 1952, 1965; Anderson, 1971). This casts doubts on the validity of Redfield's central proposition. It has further been argued that even if extended family organization gives way to a more individualistic mode this does not imply 'cultural disorganization' for the latter notion essentially describes a lack of normative constraints (Apthorpe, 1970a). Clearly this is not the case since people reformulate their norms and values about family and kinship relationships and do not merely give them up.

These criticisms point to the two most serious weaknesses in Redfield's argument. The whole of his analysis rests on the assumption that uniform, simultaneous change occurs in all the institutions of a society as it moves from the folk towards the urban end of the continuum. Thus family institutions change concomitantly with political, economic, and religious ones, and each type is modified in the same direction. Unlike Smelser, he takes no account of the different rates of change between institutional spheres and does not discuss problems of integration except in so far as he regards societies of the urban-type as necessarily less well integrated than those of the folk-type. The second methodological weakness is his claim that it is possible to infer from a study of four contemporaneous communities of different structural complexity the general path of change. This raises the thorny problem of making synchronic observations at one point in time, throwing them into some hypothetical timescale and then talking about a developmental sequence. Although much anthropological work has used this method,[13] such an approach is methodologically unsound when used to construct historical sequences, for we cannot assume that the factors impinging on contemporary communities have remained constant in the past. Thus the evolution of the capital city and small town in the Yucatan were probably conditioned by a different complex of factors from those effecting change in peasant and tribal villages in the contemporary situation. Because of this we cannot arrange them on a single developmental scale: to do so would be to hold absolutely constant all major change variables.

Following Redfield, many rural sociologists have become interested in the notion of a rural-urban continuum. I cannot here review the very extensive literature on this, but, once some of Redfield's crude assumptions are removed, then it would appear that it becomes an attractive conceptual apparatus and one can develop ways of measuring some of the variables involved. The bulk of this work has been oriented towards constructing typologies of communities (rural and urban) based on various criteria suggested by Redfield and others. Such typologies are designed primarily in order to dissect social systems morphologically and do not make assumptions about developmental sequences. For example, Frankenberg (1967) attempts a synthesis of British community studies by arranging them along a typological continuum based on economic organization and technology, though he also revives some of the well-known dichotomies found in sociology (e.g. Tonnies' *Gemeinschaft/Gesellschaft* distinction and Durkheim's mechanical versus organic solidarity) and draws on Marx's view of proletarianization. Thus, as Pahl (1966) comments, there is now more interest in the study of typology rather than process. Also many studies concentrate more on the ideal-types at the extremes of the continuum than on the sorting out of the empirical cases which cluster in the middle. This tends to undermine the main analytical utility of the continuum and leads back to the elaboration of dichotomized concepts that resemble those of the traditional/modern variety.

Yet whether or not one accepts or rejects a rural-urban continuum approach for comparative purposes, this does not detract from the argument that so far it has proved of little value for comprehending the complexities and mechanisms of social change in developing countries. At best it suggests which types of exogenous factors are likely to have the greatest impact on existing rural systems. Hence the implication of Frankenberg's analysis is that the most far-reaching changes result from changes in the economic resource-base and technology, whilst Lerner (1958) attributes the speed of 'modernization' to the development of commerce, to industrialization and to the spread of literacy and mass communications. Furthermore the whole conceptual framework seems to rest on the familiar distinction between so-called 'modern' and 'traditional' systems which I have already shown to be faulty in a number of respects. The mere adding of a spatial component to the modernization argument does not eliminate its theoretical shortcomings. On the contrary it makes it even less palatable, for there is growing evidence that particular patterns of social relationships and cultural orientations do not appear to be tied to specific ecological milieux (Pahl, 1966).

ECONOMIC DUALISM

It is but a short step from Smelser's and Redfield's models of development to certain dualistic theories of economic development. Both models contrast the modern-urban with the folk-traditional system and in doing so they provide a sociological counterpart to economic dualism which depicts the developing economy as divided into two contrasting and largely independent sectors (Lewis, 1954; Higgins, 1956; Meier, 1964:68–71). According to such a view, developing nations contain two separate and radically different sectors: the modern, capitalist, industrial sector which is receptive to change, is market-orientated, and which follows profit-maximizing behaviour; and the traditional, agricultural sector which is stagnant, is subsistence-based with little surplus for marketing, and which displays a high preference for leisure and little interest in profit maximization. Unemployment, though 'disguised', is assumed to be widespread throughout the agricultural sector. Output in the traditional sector is regarded as a simple function of land and labour for there is no significant accumulation of capital: but in the manufacturing or urban sector land drops out of the equation and we have the relation between capital and labour. The only important link between the two sectors is the flow of unemployed labour from agriculture to industry and the export of a small agricultural surplus to feed the growing urban population. Conceptualized in this way, the economy is fundamentally closed and growth occurs through the transfer of labour from agriculture to industry. Eventually all disguised unemployment is eliminated and labour becomes scarce in the rural sector and this triggers off a process of rapid economic modernization which is achieved through the more efficient use of a modern technology and through changed economic attitudes and incentives.

It is clearly not within the scope of this dicussion to outline the numerous variations on this theme: every premise, it seems, has at one time or another been challenged. For example, several economists have disputed that such a thing as 'disguised' unemployment exists; whilst others have tried to demonstrate that within the bounds of available technical knowledge peasant agriculture is highly efficient in the way it allocates factors of production. Its major limitation is the low rate of return from investment, which can only be solved by the provision of a new more profitable set of factors and by the development of a more efficient extension and research service (Schultz, 1964). Despite these differences in emphasis, however, much economic theory rests on the belief that there exist a series of qualitative differences between the 'traditional-rural' and 'modern-urban' sectors of the economy.[14] Hence the economic development of rural areas depends primarily on the transfer of skills and technology from the more modern sector, just as national development requires the diffusion of techniques and expertise from the more advanced industrial nations. It is frequently also assumed that as countries adopt the technology of western nations so they adapt their own social structures to resemble those of the West: hence modernization theory appears compatible with economic dualism both at the international and intra-national levels of analysis.

CHAPTER 3

Social and Cultural Obstacles and Prerequisites to Development

There are two other themes arising out of modernization theory that have commanded considerable attention in the literature. The first is the use made of the notion of social and cultural 'barriers' or 'obstacles' to development when attempting to explain why it is that certain peasant groups resist change and are conservative in their attitudes towards economic development. The other takes up the opposite problem of identifying the social and cultural factors that facilitate economic 'take-off', or that function as structural prerequisites for the emergence of 'modern' socio-economic systems. This chapter explores these themes and assesses their analytical utility in relation to specific empirical materials.

In the first part I discuss the view that peasant cognitive systems and associated institutions constitute major cultural obstacles to change. In the second, I review various studies that analyze the part played by cultural and normative factors in promoting development, and examine the Weberian argument concerning the relationship between economic innovation and religious commitment.

THE IDEA OF THE 'LIMITED GOOD' AS A CULTURAL BARRIER

A major exponent of the cultural obstacles approach to problems of development is Foster (1962, 1965, 1967). He first became interested in this issue during fieldwork in Tzintzuntzan, a peasant village in the north of Mexico, where he found strong evidence that peasants espoused a conservatism and lacked interest in exploiting new social and economic opportunities. From this he generalized his findings to suggest that the peasant's view of the world is strikingly different from that of other categories of person. He writes:

'In Tzintzuntzan, and by extension other peasant communities, I believe that a great deal of behaviour can best be explained if it is viewed as a function of the assumption that almost all good things in life, material and otherwise, exist in limited and unexpandable quantities. If the most valued expressions of goods such as wealth, friendship, love, masculinity and power exist in finite, constant quantities, it logically follows that someone's improvement with respect to any of these forms can only be at the expense of others. This view – that individual improvement can only be at the cost of that of others – seems to me to be the key to understanding why Tzintzuntzeños behave as they do. It also explains why they often seem so conservative in their views, so timid in accepting the opportunities a changing world increasingly offers them.' (Foster, 1967:12)

According to this interpretation, peasants perceive their social world in terms of a competitive game in which one's gains are always at the expense of somebody else;[1] and because of this they will tend to withdraw and not wish to avail themselves of new opportunities for fear that this will lead to increasing socio-economic inequalities and to internal conflict.

Foster's cognitive model forms part of his general characterization of peasant society, which, in many respects, resembles that of Banfield (1958) and others (Rubel and Kupferer, 1968) who write of the 'atomistic' nature of peasant social systems. Since peasant societies of the kind considered by Foster[2] generally do not possess corporate groupings in the form of lineages, extended families, or voluntary associations, individuals are identified instead with local territorially-based units such as the Mexican *pueblo* and its component neighbourhoods. But local and inter-village autonomy is minimal as political control rests largely in the hands of outsiders. This is particularly manifest in the way in which peasant groups form the bottom rung of national religious and political hierarchies. There are no long-standing close ties with other communities in the region and no cooperative mechanisms operating at inter-village level. Institutional roles involving specific rights and obligations show a high degree of choice in the fields of kinship, marriage, and other personal matters. The nuclear family constitutes the basic unit of social organization, but even here, there is considerable flexibility in the performance of family roles and lack of specification concerning the individual's rights and duties. Peasant societies, then, are fundamentally held together by a complex web of dyadic relationships or contracts. These contracts between individuals are informal and implicit. They lack ritual or legal validation; they are not enforceable, and essentially bind pairs of individuals into networks rather than organized groups. The total system constitutes 'an informal structure in which most of the really significant ties within all institutions are achieved (hence selective) rather than ascribed (hence non-selective)'. (Foster, 1967:214).

Foster recognizes two types of contractual ties. The first, called 'colleague contracts', tie people of approximately equal socio-economic position, who exchange roughly equivalent goods and services. Such ties are horizontal and symmetrical, and operate primarily within the community. Though founded upon some expectation of reciprocity, they seldom constitute relationships of perfectly balanced exchange because if all debits and credits were wiped off this would jeopardize the relationship itself. A second type of contractual tie is that of the 'patron-client' contract. Such ties link persons who are significantly different in terms of their socio-economic status or power position and who exchange different types of goods and services. They are vertical and assymetrical, and tend to operate between villagers and outsiders. A significant part of patron-client exchanges are short-term and focus on the question of immediate and specific return for some service. But although these relationships are characterized by a marked imbalance of power or wealth they do not have any immediate effect on the distribution of resources within the village. The patron or superordinate party is generally part of the regional or national system of social relationships and is not involved in the everyday life of the peasant village.[3]

Foster of course notes the existence of more formal contracts for marriage or *compadrazgo* (co-parenthood), or for the buying and selling of property. But these contracts rest upon state and religious laws and have been imposed upon peasant village life to meet certain national legal requirements. Although such contracts may at times be congruent with informal ties, in Foster's view, it is the informal network of highly personalized ties that permeates most aspects of peasant society. Peasant social organization is essentially atomistic, highly particularistic, and competitive in nature; for, despite the existence of a complex web of relationships based upon various types of exchange, there always exists a high degree of distrust between the parties to these relationships (e.g. between neighbours or family members), and a constantly shifting pattern of alignment. It is for this reason that the structure is not conducive to the formation of modern co-operative-type institutions which have often been proposed as a vehicle for village improvement. From early in the 1930s, the Mexican Government tried to encourage Tzintzuntzeños to undertake various community improvement schemes but were unsuccessful.

In an attempt then to resolve the apparent paradox between, on the one hand, a social reality composed of dyadic competitive relations and, on the other hand, a cognitive orientation emphasizing the notion of the 'limited good' and founded upon the ideal of a perfect social equilibrium, Foster develops the following line of argument. If the Tzintzuntzeños see their universe as one in which the good life is limited and unexpandable,

> 'it logically follows that preferred behaviour is that seen by people as maximizing their security, by preserving their relative position in the traditional order of things. Two theoretical avenues of action are open to people who see themselves in threatened circumstances which the image of the limited good implies. They may exhibit cooperation to as pronounced a degree as communism burying personal differences and placing sanctions against individualism, or they may follow the opposite road of unbridled individualism in which everyone is on his own.' (Foster, 1967:133)

The Tzintzuntzeños, like many other peasants, are constrained to choose the second alternative.

Foster admits that the reasons are not altogether clear, but two factors he regards as significant. First, co-operation requires leadership. This may be delegated democratically by the members of the group itself, or may be assumed by a strong man within the group, or it may be imposed from outside. However, peasants see the delegation of democratic authority within the community as a threat to their interests, the more especially as the important economic and political resources are controlled from outside. Second, since more 'good' than already exists in aggregate cannot be produced, cooperation is seen as a fruitless activity. Hence security and safety within the village are best achieved by maintaining the *status quo*, and by permitting no major changes in the traditional allocations of 'good'. Behaviour that is likely to upset these traditional allocations is viewed as threatening to the community at large. It is for this reason that peasants maintain the fiction that they are all equal. Shared poverty characterizes a healthy organism, and individuals or families acquiring more than their share of a good, especially an economic good, are viewed as a threat that requires corrective action.

The idea of the 'limited good' is the most general expression of the peasant's concern for security and for community equilibrium. This, together with other social and cultural mechanisms, helps to redress the imbalance that can arise between individuals and families within the village. Foster identifies several additional mechanisms. There is, first, a code of morality consistent with the image of the 'limited good' which emphasizes that individuals or families should not make public evidence of material or other improvements, lest they arouse envy and criticism from their fellow villagers. And tied to this system of ethics are various informal methods of social control, such as gossip, back-biting, slander, and, as a last resort, witchcraft. It is also regarded as morally reprehensible for families or individuals to allow themselves to fall behind their accustomed place in society for such families are seen as a threat to society at large. Their envy, jealousy, or anger over loss of status can, it is believed, result in overt or hidden aggression toward the more fortunate people of the village.

Mechanisms also exist to neutralize the effects of any economic imbalances which develp within the village community. For example, a person who improves his economic standing is frequently pressured into being a sponsor (*mayordomo*) in a religious fiesta. This obligation involves very heavy expenditure in order to finance the feasting, drinking, and ceremonial activities that take place. Hence, social prestige is offered in exchange for wealth. According to Foster,

'prestige . . . is the only good that is not strictly limited; any number of men achieve it by fulfilling the village ritual obligations, and the only practical limit to the amount will be the number of men who can accept a costly sponsorship. By accepting harmless prestige in return for dangerous wealth a mayordomo is disarmed, shorn of his weapons, and rendered impotent.' (Foster, 1967:141)

Foster argues, following Wolf (1955) and Nash 1958b), that religious fiestas in Central America operate as re-distributive mechanisms and have a levelling function. The system is completely congruent with the image of the 'limited good', for some device must exist whereby any large surpluses of wealth that may develop can be consumed.

In Foster's view, then, it is the existence of these cultural elements and the way they work together which explains the traditionalism and conservatism frequently commented upon for peasant societies. Although such factors as the lack of access to knowledge and information about the contemporary world, and the peasants' involvement in dependency relations with non-village groups are clearly important, Foster's studies in Mexico suggest that it is the cognitive orientation in the form of the 'limited good' which constitutes a central factor inhibiting rapid social and economic change.

Conceptual and Analytical Difficulties

Foster's first published statement on the 'limited good' occasioned immediate comment and criticism (Bennett, 1966; Kennedy, 1966; Kaplan and Sadler, 1966). The criticisms centred upon two main problems: the assumptions of the model, and whether this world view, if it exists, is confined solely to peasant societies.

In the first place it has been suggested that the idea of the 'limited good' is nothing more than an economic truism, for people are always confronted with problems concerning the allocation of scarce means to alternative ends. In economies with little surplus above subsistence needs, for example in peasant or primitive societies or among urban slum dwellers, the limitations are greater but not qualitatively different. A further difficulty arises over the notion of unexpandable resources. This seems based upon the belief that peasants view their communities as essentially unchanging and homogeneous – a highly dubious assumption, since whatever one's criteria for defining a peasant society it is generally agreed that peasants form part of wider national systems that are themselves the products of specific historical processes. The third assumption, that personal advancement must be seen as depriving others or as threatening the community, is a logical outcome of the idea of limited and unexpandable resources. It also implicitly assumes that peasants conceptualize their communities as closed systems. Such an interpretation is unconvincing when one recalls that Foster's own studies of Tzintzuntzan bring out the importance of rural-urban links, discuss the part played by migrants in the mobilization of finance for fiestas, and show how various political controls operate from outside the village.

Another line of criticism has been that the image of the 'limited good' does not adequately distinguish peasant societies from agrarian societies in general. Indeed, Bennett (1966) comments that all agrarian societies have a tendance towards 'zero-sum' game behaviour; for the shortage of capital and credit characteristic of such situations can often lead to cautious, saving behaviour in which present possessions are accepted as adequate and the risks entailed in seeking more considered too great. Agricultural production entails uncertainty over market conditions, over the landlords' demands, and over weather. These conditions pertain whether the society is characterized as of peasant type or not. It is important therefore to distinguish between, what Bennett calls, the objective agrarian situation which produces high uncertainty and risk, and those cultural reinforcements used to validate certain behavioural patterns. These cultural reinforcements may take the form of a cognitive model of the 'limited good' type (though one would have to investigate how far the actors themselves conceptualized problems in this particular way), or they may be associated with a set of institutions, like the Central American fiesta system, aimed at diverting investment away from production and from the risks attached, in order to shore up community relations. Community and neighbourhood ties are important for providing some security against personal calamity and misfortune. In some societies institutions demanding large expenditure of capital may be said to impede development by reducing the stock of capital available for local investment and may prevent the further integration of the community into the wider market economy (Wolf, 1955:158). Yet one should not resort too readily to such economistic arguments, for investment in social relations, with little expectation of immediate return, may later provide the means by which important resources, such as information and labour, are mobilized. The precise relationships between such social, cultural, and economic factors must be investigated empirically case by case.

The analytical difficulties of assuming a one-to-one relationship between the existence of traditionalistic or conservative value patterns and the lack of entrepreneurship in regard to economic matters is aptly illustrated by Bennett's study of the Hutterites of Canada (Bennett, 1967). The Hutterites are a particularly interesting case for they combine a highly traditionalistic family organization, which exhibits many behavioural features congruent with the idea of the 'limited good', with a production system which is technically proficient and economically successful. Indeed, Hutterite agriculture when compared to non-Hutterite farms in the area is shown to be more commercialized, larger in scale, and more productive. Bennett's analysis shows how Hutterites have adapted themselves to take advantage of the economic opportunities of wheat farming by compartmentalizing their social life into two spheres – the production system where modern economic rationality and efficient production techniques are the norm, and the sphere of consumption and family relations, which continue to be structured by a conservative religious ideology. This system works well because the economic returns from farming are controlled by the community and allocated to individual families according to their needs. Strong moral sanctions exist against conspicuous consumption and individual economic advancement. The bulk of profits is re-invested in the production process or is used to buy more land and to help support the founding of new Hutterite communities.

As the preceding comments have indicated, a major difficulty with Foster's formulation is that he tends to give causal priority to cultural phenomena. Although towards the end of his book he lists several different types of obstacles – namely, the type of cognitive orientation, the lack of information and knowledge about the wider world, the problem of peasants being continually exploited by 'unscrupulous city people', and such factors as the ecological and demographic situation of the village – one is left feeling that the weighting is overwhelmingly towards internal cultural elements. The inadequacy of such explanation is best illustrated by reference to Foster's account of a government scheme to persuade potters to adopt more modern techniques of production. Traditional pottery had been produced in Tzintzuntzan for many years, but the government aimed to encourage the use of better glazes and develop better quality products that would command higher prices and would sell farther afield. And to this end they opened a co-operative workshop in the 1940s. In a very short time, however, the project collapsed, due, according to Foster, to the lack of adequate demonstration techniques used by the government agents and to the general unwillingness of peasants to engage in patterns of co-operative work.[4] An alternative strategy was then adopted whereby five of the best local potters were selected and offered special credit facilities so that they might install more adequate kilns. However the equipment did not operate efficiently and they soon found themselves in financial difficulties and unable to pay off their debts. As a result they lost everything and the loans had to be written off. Subsequently they went back to using the traditional method of firing with wood, and to practising pottery as a part-time industry as before. Yet, paradoxically, some years later, the amount of pottery sold in the market had increased five times higher than in 1948 when the government first introduced its scheme. Income from pottery was higher and production was more regular throughout the year.

Although it is possible to argue that the negative reaction to the idea of a co-operative workshop was in part due to socio-cultural factors, and to the prevailing system of social relations which did not encourage the development of enduring groups within the village, the resurgence and further development of pottery production can only be understood in relation to a wider set of factors. A major consideration, according to Ortiz (1970), was the reorganization of market activities which resulted from the industrialization of the neighbouring area. Urban and industrial growth in the region led to an increase in market places with regular consumer demand for everyday cooking wares. It also resulted in a much improved transport system which made marketing trips to the towns of the area more profitable and less time consuming. This, in turn, led to the emergence of many small-scale middlemen, who competed with one another to secure a regular clientele. These developments, then, had an immediate impact on the village production system and stimulated an increase in the output of pottery items. It is particularly interesting to note that the trading arrangements that developed between suppliers and middlemen tended to be based on the same types of personalized contracts described by Foster for the traditional peasant community (e.g. *compadrazgo* ties, and kinship and family connections). Thus, far from impeding development these relationships were turned to good entrepreneurial advantage.

It is difficult in the light of this example to accept the view that peasant culture is a major brake on change. On the contrary, once a viable set of opportunities presented themselves the peasants showed every willingness to increase production and become more involved in the market economy.

Existing cultural norms and social relations provided the raw material for the development of new socio-economic roles. In attempting to explain why in one situation peasants respond positively to new economic opportunities and in another respond negatively, one needs to consider the total complex of both internal and external factors – technical, economic, structural, and cultural. One must also, as Ortiz and others have argued, set this within the context of the types of uncertainties and risks that exist. While it is not possible on the data available to attempt a full explanation of why the initial attempt to improve pottery production failed, it seems significant that pottery continued as a part-time occupation. This suggests that, because of fluctuations in the demand and in the supply of materials, pottery, like other craft industries, is a high-risk occupation which it is better to combine with other economic activities. The phenomenon of multiple enterprises among peasant populations is of course well documented in the literature.

The need to examine in detail the exact nature and extent of economic opportunities open to peasants is further stressed by Acheson (1972), who, on the basis of his own field data, criticizes the work of Foster and others (Belshaw, 1967; Diaz, 1966; and Van Zantwijk, 1967) who carried out research in the Tarascan region. Acheson argues that, although it is true that 'most Tarascan pueblos are poor and have exhibited little capacity either for short term innovation or for long term economic development', there remains a number of notable cases where entrepreneurial capability and rapid economic change have occurred (Acheson, 1972:1153). These communities are located in the same broad socio-cultural zone as Tzintzuntzan and manifest roughly similar cultural and social structural features. The examples cited cover the mechanized production of furniture in Cuanajo (Acheson, 1972), the successful chicken rearing experiment at La Pacanda (Smith,

1966), and the expanding guitar making industry of Paracho (Kaplan, 1960). These developments, he suggests, took place primarily because technical and economic factors were favourable and profitable investments could be made. Although they constitute islands of growth in a generally static economic situation produced by extreme pressure on resources, they nevertheless conclusively demonstrate that 'when new income earning options open up, some individuals are quick to take advantage of them' (Acheson, 1972:1163). Hence Acheson concludes that lack of responsiveness on the part of peasants is basically due to 'limited *goods*' rather than to the constraints imposed on behaviour by adherence to Foster's idea of the 'limited good'. He also argues that in this region socio-economic development at community level is largely a result of individual entrepreneurship rather than of corporate action on behalf of the community or some social group; and that it mostly occurs outside the bounds of government-sponsored programmes.

Another difficulty with Foster's culturological approach is the tendency to treat culture or the cognitive system as a consistent whole shared by all members of the society; whereas in his analysis of dyadic relationships he emphasizes the lack of definition concerning normative expectations and views social relationships in peasant societies as inherently flexible. Thus, as Kaplan and Sadler (1966) have recognized, Foster's image of the 'limited good' is an example of anthropological explanation derived *a priori* which totally excludes non-congruent behaviour.

As the above discussion has indicated, the study of variations in peasant culture and social organization, both within and between societies, is critically important for analyzing how and why peasants respond to changing circumstances. Moreover social flexibility is a crucial element in all social systems enabling the members of the society to adapt themselves to radically different conditions. And another important characteristic is that many cultural items are malleable. It is this that enables certain cultural features to persist in quite different social environments. They are, that is, re-interpreted or modified to take account of new circumstances. If this is the case, then any particular cultural complex is seldom to be seen as an insurmountable obstacle to development. The understanding of any particular development situation requires the close analysis of the interplay of various factors. Furthermore, as Ortiz has put it, 'individuals behave in such a way as to maximize satisfaction within a framework defined by change and opportunities as well as by social norms' and cultural values; and in any case it is 'difficult to prove experimentally that individuals always assign the same value to the same good act' (Ortiz, 1970:156). Hence Foster's conceptual model of reality postulated for the peasant is too simplistic and mechanical. A more complete understanding of peasant responses to socio-economic change requires an analysis of the interaction of both internal and external social, cultural, ideological, and economic factors.

THE FIESTA SYSTEM: THE IDENTIFICATION OF SPECIFIC INSTITUTIONS AS OBSTACLES

Although Foster's analysis is based upon the elucidation of Mexican field material, he attempts to generalize his findings to cover peasant societies in general. Other anthropologists have been less ambitious and confined their analyses to the consideration of how particular institutions function to inhibit economic development at the local level. Two such examples immediately come to mind: the religious fiesta system of Central America, which I have already briefly mentioned, and the Indian joint family.[5] I want now, in concluding this discussion of socio-cultural obstacles, to evaluate the arguments concerning the influence of the fiesta system.

The religious fiesta (or *cargo*) system, sometimes called the civil-religious hierarchy or the ceremonial ladder, is especially characteristic of the Southern Mexico-Guatemala region of Central America but is also found in other parts of Latin America. It consists of a set of religious offices organized hierarchically and occupied on a rotating basis by men of the community. Office-holders serve for a year at a time and must spend substantial amounts of money sponsoring the religious celebrations organized for the saints of the Catholic Church. *Cargos* ('offices') are arranged so that a man may occupy a number of offices in a specified order. In Zinacantan, the Mexican community studied by Cancian (1967), there is a total of forty-six *cargos* organized in terms of four different levels. If a man has had no previous experience then he may serve in any one of the thirty-four offices at the lowest level, whence, after resting a number of years and clearing away his debts, he may pass on to one of twelve offices at the second level. After this there are six offices on the third level and two on the fourth and final level. Almost all men in the community participate at the first level of organization but few pass through the hierarchy to attain the top positions.

Various writers (Nash, 1958b; Wolf, 1955) have emphasized that the degree and the manner of a man's participation in this *cargo* system are major factors in determining his social standing in the community. Nash writes, 'the hierarchy is virtually the entire social structure of the Indian *municipio* (town or district). At the most general level of social integration this structure does for Indians what kinship does for African societies, and what the social class system does for ladino societies' (Nash, 1958b:68). Hence it constitutes a primary organizing structure within the community.

Much of the literature on the *cargo* system emphasizes its integrative functions for the community. It defines the limits of community membership, since participants must be residents and take part in the everyday life of the community. It stresses commitment to community values through the common participation in a religious system focusing upon the adoration of local saints, and thus functions to define the boundaries of the local Indian community as against the wider society. It provides for socially controlled modes of personal display and sets out rules under which a man may enhance his public image. This, it is said, helps to minimize potentially disruptive innovation and competition within the village. Also, since men mobilize much of the capital necessary for financing their duties as *cargo*-holders through a network of kin and family members, it indirectly helps to reinforce existing kinship and family relationships. Economic surplus is then converted into social position, which prevents the accumulation of large surpluses of cash or property and helps to preserve the *status quo*.

Earlier observers drew the conclusion that the *cargo* system tended to homogenize the population with respect to wealth. They argued that the better-off members of the community were expected to spend large amounts of capital on the system and that this had an economically levelling effect. The process was reinforced by the generally low standard of living and poor agricultural technology, by the system of bilateral inheritance which produced a fragmentation of estates, and by the fact that time which could have been spent on production was allocated to the *cargo* system. This interpretation has been challenged by Cancian (1967) who demonstrates that the *cargo* system in Zinacantan reflects the system of social ranking in the community. Performance in the *cargo* system shows that the more expensive *cargos* are open only to the richer farmers. Thus performance in the system is a measure of a man's economic success. Moreover fiesta expenditure does not seem to affect the long-term economic and social standing of individuals and families; for the families that are better-off remain so and tend to marry into families of similar status. Cancian also suggests that greater participation is shown by members of larger families who are able to share the expenses involved. The main thrust of Cancian's argument is that the *cargo* system in fact legitimizes wealth differences and allows for some degree of social stratification. He writes, 'there is in effect sufficient levelling (the result of differential economic contribution to *cargo* service) to satisfy normative prescriptions but not enough to produce an economically homogenous community' (Cancian, 1967:140).

Though different in emphasis both interpretations rest upon a view of peasant society as an unchanging system which manifests community solidarity in the face of external forces. Both imply the persistence of a relatively static economic structure which the *cargo* system reinforces. As Cancian's study shows, cargo systems exhibit a considerable resilience to pressures of population growth and to commercialization of the economy. Demographic change in Zinacantan resulted in an increase in the number of *cargos* available and led to the devising of waiting lists for *cargo*-holders. Similarly the slow development of the market economy of the area led to an increase in the costs involved in participating in the system. But it did not undermine the system.

It is important to point out that interpretations of the *cargo* system have generally been couched in terms of an equilibrium type of analysis and show some of the same inadequacies as Foster's work. The main interest of Cancian is to demonstrate how, despite population growth and increases in wealth, the system maintains itself through the creation of waiting lists and more costly *cargos*. He is primarily concerned, that is, with the problem of structural continuity and gives little attention to analyzing the points of change occurring within the community. The only type of radical change he recognizes is that which is exogenously produced. Thus he documents the ways in which the *cargo* system responds to economic and demographic changes but fails to trace out the logical consequences of this process. For example, the waiting list idea can only be a short-term solution for as population increase continues so applicants can be expected to lose interest in the system and search for other avenues of power and prestige. This point is particularly pertinent since Siverts (1969) mentions that land reform has been taking place in the region near to Zinacantan and has provided a new political arena for leadership. He also describes how peasants of the area have become more integrated into the market system through the development of a main road to the market town of San Cristobal. Indeed from Cancian's own study it would seem that new opportunities of this kind had already opened up and had begun to offer new sources of status that competed with the traditional system of prestige. He mentions, for example, the emergence of specialized clubs whose members contribute relatively small amounts each to the financing of fiestas. This arrangement did not seriously affect their own economic positions and interests but increased their public standing in the *pueblo*. Originally begun in the 1930s as a single small group of young men (*castilleros*) specifically devoted to providing fireworks for the major fiesta, by 1961 this organization had evolved into three large associations which sponsored several fiestas apiece. Another example of the changes taking place is that wealthy men were now tending to by-pass some of the earlier *cargos* to get more quickly into important positions. Such rapid mobility upwards would not have been permissible under the old rules. The data also suggest that there was a growing surplus of economic capacity which could not so readily be absorbed by the *cargo* system (Cancian, 1967:190–91).

Comparative evidence can be adduced to suggest that the *cargo* system in Latin America is far more adaptable to changing circumstances than Cancian implies. Several studies, for example, have shown how the organization of fiestas can become a monopoly of elite groups who use the organizational framework and religious symbolism to advance and legitimate their position (Bunzel, 1952; Long, 1972 and 1973; Roberts, 1974). There is also evidence that as rural-urban relations are intensified through labour migration to the cities and towns and through the development of larger scale peasant marketing of produce and craft goods, so the fiesta organizations, together with other village associations, assume a dominant role in linking rural and urban systems (Buechler, 1970; Long, 1973; Roberts, 1974). Recent studies in Peru, for example, have documented the way in which village fiestas are financed by migrant workers and businessmen, who retain close contact with their home communities for family and economic reasons, and who return to their villages of origin for the fiesta celebrations. Thus, far from impeding the development of the village, these fiestas often serve to consolidate sets of external relationships that are important for the progress of the community or certain sectors of it.

It may of course be argued that the *cargo* system of Central America is a somewhat special case because here the fiesta organization coincides with a civil hierarchy, and therefore cannot easily be compared with other Latin American forms. It is nonetheless true that both types of fiesta systems show remarkable flexibility in the face of change and have been adapted by various groups to serve their different ends. And, if this is the case, then it is difficult to maintain as a general rule that the fiesta *cargo* system acts as an impediment to economic and social change.

STRUCTURAL CONDITIONS AND PREREQUISITES OF DEVELOPMENT

The antithesis to the idea of barriers or obstacles is the view that certain factors act to make it possible for or encourage economic development to take place. These factors have been variously called 'prerequisites', 'preconditions', 'stimulants', or 'facilitating factors'.

A long catalogue of economic and infrastructural factors have been considered necessary conditions for economic growth – e.g., improvements in technology, availability of capital and credit facilities, adequate market structures, etc. – meaning by this that increases in production or *per capita* income must necessarily be accompanied by certain modifications in economic or administrative arrangements or inputs. Whilst no one would seriously deny that capital or credit systems or certain technological changes are necessary for economic development (e.g. commercialized forms

of agriculture or industrialization), the discussion of such conditions frequently becomes intertwined with the more contentious
argument that there are certain social institutional forms that
develop to meet these requirements. This is illustrated by Wilbert
Moore's discussion of industrialization (W. E. Moore, 1963:93–7).

Moore attempts to outline briefly the basic structural conditions
for industrial development. He first emphasizes that values are
important because they provide the rationale for particular norms
or rules of organization and conduct. Thus 'the value of economic
growth requires, for example, a fairly high degree of individual
mobility and a placement system grounded on merit in performance'. Such a value orientation is likely to come into conflict with
strongly held values of a more traditional kind based on kinship
status and obligation. 'In this sense extensive value changes are the
most fundamental conditions for economic transformation' (W. E.
Moore, 1963:93). Another value of importance is that of nationalism, which has frequently provided the ideological framework for
the integration of various traditional structures.

In discussing the institutional conditions for industrialization,
Moore focuses predominantly on political and administrative
aspects. He argues that it is necessary to have property institutions
which make rights over land, raw materials, semi-finished products, and financial capital easily transferable, and which restrain
property transfers that impede or prevent such mobilization.
Labour too must be mobile, and its recruitment based primarily on
qualifications and experience, without regard to social position. An
industrial order also entails the existence of a commercialized and
monetized system of exchange; and national integration must be
matched by the development of political codes and procedures
designed to promote political stability.

Another important condition is what Moore calls 'the institutionalization of rationality'. He writes,

'The important point is that some leading sectors of the
population must be committed not only to the idea of economic
growth but also to its practical implementation in terms of
programmes and plans, the identification of necessary techniques
to be borrowed or adapted or even invented for unusual
applications. A problem solving orientation and dedication to

deliberate change . . . among governors and administrators is a condition for even getting started.' (W. E. Moore, 1963:95)

The latter qualities are most likely to be found among entre-preneurs, though for co-ordinated national development to take place it is necessary that these attitudes permeate government planning agencies as well.

In addition there are certain organizational requirements of industrialization. The technology of factory production must be tied to a viable pattern of work organization. This generally means that some approximation to the model of a specialized and hierarchically structured bureaucracy or administrative organi-zation is essential. Also an appropriate fiscal organization of the state, at least as banker and tax collector, is necessary.

From the motivational point of view, Moore believes that some degree of 'achievement orientation' or ambition for personal betterment and for the acquisition of education and skills must exist in some social sectors. These attitudes will later be diffused more widely in society and help to sustain growth.

These, according to Moore, are the major social requirements for industrializing an economy, to which he would add 'the more strictly economic conditions concerning capital formation, in-vestment ratios in the various sectors of the economy, or the character of foreign assistance and foreign trade' (W. E. Moore, 1963:97).

A similar discussion on agricultural development leads Mosher (1966) to identify five 'essentials': (1) transportation, (2) markets for products, (3) new farm technology, (4) availability of purchaseable inputs, and (5) incentives. He also isolates five 'accelerators', i.e. those factors that, while not absolutely essential for agricultural growth, can make a contribution to the speeding up of develop-ment once the essentials have been met. The five accelerators are: (1) education, (2) production credit, (3) farmer associations, (4) an improving or expanding land base, and (5) planning.

Although Mosher is less interested in detailing the types of social institutional conditions his list of essentials and accelerators clearly has sociological implications. For example, the notion of incentives can be extended to include something wider than simply mere price, and could be related to the problem of the existence of appropriate value orientations and motivations. The stress on technical skills and on the availability of banking and planning systems reflects an emphasis similar to Moore and implies the development of a politico-administrative infrastructure.

Other discussions of the social conditions of economic development suggest that one can identify certain normative and institutional changes that precede economic growth and that may prepare the ground for it. These constitute what some sociologists have called social and cultural prerequisites. Geertz, for example, writing of Indonesia, argues that,

'The years since 1945, and in fact since about 1920, have seen the beginnings of a fundamental transformation in social values and institutions towards patterns we generally associate with a developed economy, even though actual progress towards the creation of such an economy has been slight and sporadic at best. Alterations in the system of social stratification, in world view and ethos, in political and economic organization, in education, and even in family structure have occurred over a wide section of society. Many of the changes – the commercialization of agriculture, the formation of non-familial business concerns, the heightened prestige of technical skills *vis-à-vis* religious and aesthetic ones – which more or less immediately preceded take-off in the west have begun to appear, and industrialization, in quite explicit terms, has become one of the primary political goals of the nation as a whole.

Yet that all these changes will finally add up to take-off is far from certain. It is clearly possible for development to misfire at any stage, even the initial one.' (Geertz, 1963:3)

Thus while Geertz recognizes that there may be many false starts and even breakdowns in the process of modernization, he considers it analytically legitimate to pose the question: 'What sorts of social and cultural transformations are underway during the pre-take-off period which may later facilitate development?'

One type of answer to this question in the modernization literature is the notion that the existence of certain 'modern' attitudes is a precondition to development (Hoselitz, 1960; McClelland, 1961; Hagen, 1962). This school of thought believes that attitudinal and value changes or re-interpretations of ideology are essential prerequisites to creating a modern society and economy. The intellectual origins for this argument can be traced to the work of Max Weber, who both in his writings on *The Protestant Ethic and the Spirit of Capitalism* and his comparative studies on religion emphasizes the role of ideology in social development.[6]

Religious Asceticism and Rationality as Prerequisites

Weber was particularly fascinated by the process of rationalization taking place in Western Europe; and drew the distinction between traditional and rational social values when characterizing the contrast between feudalism and capitalism. Traditionalism in economic behaviour for Weber meant 'fixation on an immutable standard of concrete preferences' with established ways of attaining them, whereas rationality entailed a continual weighing of preferences in terms of relative cost of attaining each and according to the criteria of technical efficiency.

'The point Weber made, and in which Marx concurred, was that the canons of rationality not less than the dicta of traditionalism were arbitrary in the sense that both were concrete sets of values, guiding action that took historically variable forms . . . The application of the canon of rationality unloosed an intrinsically dynamic force in economic behaviour. A given producer was no longer obliged to confine his activities to a limited sphere, if he could maximize gain in another one. The effects of this continuous calculation of means-ends relationships were experienced in all other aspects of capitalist society as well: rationality, so destructive of precedent, could hardly be confined to economic life. It gave a decisive cast to the entire modern cultural ethos.' (Birnbaum, 1953:4)

In his studies of European capitalism, Weber attempted to trace the origins of this new economic rationality to the religious ethics practised by certain ascetic Protestant sects. Nevaskar (1971:3–4, 5–6) writes:

'Weber was interested in the combination of circumstances responsible for the cultural uniqueness of Western civilization. He thought this uniqueness was related to the process of rationalization in the West. He theorized that the religious ethic of the Puritan middle-class man was a major factor in the rise of modern industrial capitalism. To test his theories, Weber undertook comparative studies of India and China where, in spite of many favourable factors, industrial capitalism failed to develop. In the East, the process of rationalization was largely wanting, as were various other phenomena often associated with it . . .'

'Capitalism rests on the inclination of men to adopt certain types of practical rational conduct. Since the magical and religious notions, as well as the ethical ideas of duty based upon them, have influenced the conduct of all men in the past, Weber reasoned that religious ideas may also have influenced the development of the present Western economic system . . . because rationalization played a central role in Western capitalism, Weber proposed to investigate the influence of religion on its development.'

Following Weber's lead, several studies have been conducted in non-Western countries to identify whether or not there exist similar sorts of incentives deriving from religious beliefs. There is, for example, an impressive body of literature that documents the significance of various ascetic religious sects and their role in economic development both in Islam and Hinduism. In his account of the religious doctrine of Sikhism, Pieris (1969:155) suggests that, like Puritanism, it had a direct effect on Sikh daily life. It broke free from Hindu caste restrictions, and enabled Sikhs to engage in every kind of occupation, excepting only that of begging. And it stressed the values of hard work combined with an austere style of living. The lives of Sikhs illustrated the confluence of worldliness and other-worldliness, which expressed itself most strikingly in their positive attitude towards entrepreneurship and their willingness to move into new types of occupation. Sikhs became concentrated in the small industrial enterprises of the Punjab and gradually moved out of the agricultural sector into various transport and mechanical occupations in the large cities. Yet Sikhism never managed to embrace the majority of the population; the latter remained tied to the economic restrictions of Hindu caste society.

Other pockets of so-called rational economic activity like that of the Sikhs were found among the Parsis. The life of J. N. Tata, the pioneer industrialist of that community, abounds with pictures of the Puritan businessman: he was renowned for his honesty and determination, and was never regarded as an avaricious money-monger. He was esteemed by his associates and friends as being both noble and prudent. As a Zoroastrian he was free from the constraints of Hindu asceticism, yet advocated temperance and was puritanical over the wasting of time or money. His son was compelled each day to give a full account of his use of time, well aware that any attempt at deception was punishable by the cane. His main preoccupation, it seems, was to inculcate in his followers the idea that time is money. It was for this reason, too, that he sought to teach the workmen in his textile mills the value of regular labour.

Kennedy's study of the Parsis (Kennedy, 1962) isolates five values to be found in Zoroastrianism which appear to have guided their conduct: the two acquisitive rationalities, representing the desire to maximize one's material prosperity; financial rationality, expressed in rational accounting procedures; the rationality of work which involves the belief that material work is intrinsically good; and lastly, scientific rationality, which assumes an underlying order in nature and the belief in a sensate standard of verification. Kennedy then produces evidence to demonstrate the effect of these values on Parsi economic and social activity. He notes that as early as 1761 various European writers had commented on their early shipbuilding ventures and later, in the 1880s, on their part in the construction of railways. Moreover, according to Dursobay, writing in 1858, 'the largest number and more than one half of the whole of Parsi population follow their advocation of merchants, bankers or brokers which fact furnishes a proof of the commercial bent of the Parsi mind'. By the census of 1920–22 the Parsi population (which constitutes only 0.03 per cent of the total population of India) had obtained 6.8 per cent of engineering degrees, 4.7 per cent of medical and 1.7 per cent of science degrees, and 1.4 per cent of all Western degrees in India. These data lead Kennedy to suggest that there was a positive association between the acceptance of commercial and technological values and the appearance of commercial and technological behaviour.

Further evidence of this kind of association is provided by Nevaskar's comparison of the Jains of India with the Quakers of America (Nevaskar, 1971). His investigation starts from a passage in Weber's *Religion in India* which draws attention to the fact that there might be some parallels between Jain and Quaker religious beliefs that could be correlated with their everyday economic behaviour. Jainism, like Buddhism, arose as a reaction against Hinduism. Originally a heterodox Hindu sect, it evolved as a means of perfecting basic Hindu ideals. The founder, Mahavira, organized his followers into a religious community composed of both monks and laymen. The Jain monks took five major vows: (1) never to destroy any living thing, (2) the denial of untruthfulness, (3) never to steal, (4) chastity, and (5) complete detachment from any thing or person. The Jain laymen, in turn, were exhorted to develop some 21 different qualities ranging from personal cleanliness to honesty in business.

Nevaskar's work identifies several important similarities between Jain and Quaker religious ethics which relate to their everyday life. These are: pacificism, asceticism, and a code of honesty and fair dealing. Hence both groups avoid certain types of occupations: for example, political and military careers as well as certain types of agricultural and industrial pursuits. Yet they favour urban and commercial pursuits, particularly those associated with the retail trade, which appear consistent with their religious attitudes. In both cases strict religious prohibitions exist with respect to the expenditure of wealth on display and other forms of self-indulgence. Wealth should be used for reinvestment in business and for acts of charity, and not for conspicuous consumption. Commenting on Nevaskar's analysis, Martindale argues that,

'In the case of neither is it necessary to assume that their religiosity was exclusively caused by their economic practices or their economic practices exclusively caused by their religiosity. However, that these two components of their life styles were linked stands beyond any question. This linkage appears to have developed in a spiral of mutual reinforcement over time, increasing the solidarity and effectiveness of the respective sub groups within the context of their wider societies.' (Martindale, 1971:xx)

The Jains came to occupy an important position in the trading network of eighteenth century India and were one of the main trading communities in North East India around the Ganges River. Then, in the nineteenth century, large numbers of Marwari Jains migrated to the Calcutta region and occupied key entrepreneurial positions, especially in trade and finance. Later, in the 1920s they began opening manufacturing plants; and since then they have risen to become one of the foremost of Indian business communities (Nafziger, 1971).

These examples of ascetic religious sects in India suggest that, even though India may be generally described as somewhat conservative in its religious beliefs, with a caste system that inhibits social mobility, nonetheless there exist pockets of religiously motivated entrepreneurs practising ethics that closely parallel those of Protestant Christian groups. Thus, according to one line of argument, the response of such groups to the new economic opportunities brought by colonial rule and the penetration of capitalist forms of production was essentially based on a set of incentives deriving from the religious sphere. These groups were distinct from others in India because they already possessed the necessary ideological prerequisites to take advantage of the newly developing system.

Another example outside the Christian tradition of the association of asceticism with entrepreneurship is that analysed by Geertz (1963) in his study of traders in Modjokuto, Java. Geertz is interested in documenting the change from a 'bazaar economy' characterized by fragmented and disconnected person-to-person transactions, towards a 'firm economy' in which trade and industry take place within a framework of impersonally defined corporate institutions which organize production and distribution. A major finding of his study is the predominant part played by a group of reformist Moslems who practise an ascetic religious ethic similar to that of the Christian Protestants in Europe.

Islamic reformism, which spread through the urban trading classes in Java between 1912 and 1920, emphasized the purification of Indonesian Islam of Hinduist and animist elements, and focused on questions of dogma and morality. It also stressed the importance of pilgrimages to Mecca: 'A shift in increased concern with things Islamic as opposed to things more generally Javanese led to a greater interest in the teaching of a more purely Islamic tradition and the provision of content for such teaching naturally depended upon increased contact with the centre of the Moslem world' (Geertz, 1956:145). This necessitated the accumulation of capital in order to finance the trip to Mecca and led to emphasis on the value of *gemi* (obsessive thrift). For the reformists it was a source of pride to work hard, to dress and eat simply, and to avoid large ceremonial expenditures; and strong value was placed upon individual effort. According to Geertz, the ethic had 'in abundance the classic free enterprise virtue of the rational pursuit of self-interest' (Geertz, 1963:126).

Geertz documents the involvement of these religious reformists in the developing commercial and manufacturing life of Modjokuto. Of the seven well-established non-Chinese stores in the town in the late 1950s some six were run by reformists, and of the two dozen or more small factories all but three or four were in their hands too. Economic development in Modjokuto appeared to be taking the classic form of 'an at least in part religiously motivated, generally disesteemed group of small shopkeepers and petty manufacturers . . . rising out of a traditionalized trading class' (Geertz, 1963:50).

Like the other examples, this case would seem to point to the importance of religiously derived attitudes and incentives for entrepreneurship in the Third World. Yet although Geertz conceptualizes development in terms of the neo-Weberian model of increasing rationalization of economic activities, his study in fact shows how difficult it is to isolate particular facilitating ideological factors from the totality of factors operating. His analysis of economic development in Modjokuto is complemented by a similar study in Tabanan, another rural town in Indonesia, where the social composition and value orientation of the entrepreneurial class is quite different. In contrast to Modjokuto, the entrepreneurial group is made up of local aristocrats who are not concerned with the reorganizing of a bazaar economy but with readjusting an agrarian one. The entrepreneurs are Hindus of aristocratic status who capitalize on their political ties with the peasantry and their control over the collective resources of the region so that they might mobilize labour and other resources for the establishment of modern economic enterprises. And in this way they are able to bring together hundreds of villagers and subjects as stockholders in new industrial ventures. However, unlike the reformist Moslems who constitute a deviation from the main religious traditions of the area, they represent religious conformity and are seen as the cultural exemplars of Hindu custom and practice. The town of Tabanan itself was a palace town with an aristocratic descent line spanning some five centuries. This nobility was transformed into a class of civil administrators by the Dutch but still retained its economic ascendancy and privileges of caste. Later, when new economic opportunities arose in trade and industry, this religiously conservative economic and political elite was able to enlist the help of the bulk of the population in securing the necessary capital and resources for the formation of large-scale corporate enterprise.

Geertz's study, then, emphasizes the difficulty of isolating particular variables and treating them as prerequisites. It also warns against assuming a one-to-one relationship between a particular form of religious ideology and the propensity to engage in entrepreneurial activity.

Similar conclusions emerge from an analysis of the relationship between socio-economic innovation and religious commitment among peasant farmers and small-scale businessmen in rural Zambia (Long, 1968). This study demonstrates a close association between membership of a congregation of Jehovah's Witnesses and involvement in new types of economic activity, but stresses the importance of viewing religious affiliation in terms of the organizational and interpersonal resources entailed rather than merely the ideological dimension.[7] It also illustrates how a religious ethic is used situationally, when appropriate, to legitimize new patterns of socio-economic behaviour or to repudiate traditional ones.

A CRITIQUE OF THE WEBER THESIS AS APPLIED TO THE THIRD WORLD

Clearly a wide range of socio-cultural factors, including religious disposition, may facilitate development in specific contexts, but one should not preempt analysis by assuming that certain value orientations constitute necessary preconditions. Thus, as Gerschenkron (1962) argues, we should guard against converting historical facts (e.g. the role of Calvinism) into the status of logical prerequisites since this implies the untenable notion of historical necessity. Gerschenkron also suggests that we should acknowledge the possibility of the same functions being performed by different institutions. For example, credit generated by banks or a public tax system may substitute for the use of accumulated wealth by individuals, or the state may invest when private entrepreneurs do not. Moreover values that we might be inclined to describe as traditional may in fact hasten development, depending on the social context and the use to which these values are put. Many different value systems exist in modernizing societies and there is no reason to expect that one type is more effective than any other. Hence, as Weiner (1966) notes, Catholicism, which is frequently characterized as being a conservative social force, did not apparently impede the high rate of growth in certain Latin American countries (e.g. Mexico, Brazil, and Peru) during the 1950s and early 1960s. Nor does an analysis of religious beliefs throw any light on why overseas Indians and Chinese have been so much more entrepreneurial and productive outside their home societies than within.

Another important point is that the seeking for value incentives of the kind associated with Puritan groups during the rise of capitalism in Western Europe may be quite misplaced in the context of Third World development. Indeed, according to Wertheim (1971:162), the experience of Japan may be much more pertinent than the form that capitalist development took in Western Europe. Bellah's study of *Tokugawa Religion* (1957) argues that whereas industrialization in the West was the product of a slow process of accumulation, industrialization in the East was government-controlled and sponsored because only government was able to marshall the necessary capital; and because of this he finds that religious values in Japan were not so positively correlated with the growth of private capitalism as to justify an interpretation of Japanese economic history in neo-Weberian terms. His analysis of Tokugawa religion shows that it contained various elements that were conducive to an ideology which, during the Meiji period, reinforced the government's efforts to initiate planned economic change. However it was the *samurai* (warrior) class of aristocratic officials not the merchants who were the spearhead of this new economic ethos. Hence, in Bellah's view, we find a correlation between religion and bureaucracy in Japanese history; and this questions the universal validity of the view that a Protestant-ethic type of value change is necessary for the development of modern industrial capitalism.

Geertz makes a similar point in his Indonesian study when he contrasts what he calls (following Hirschman) the 'ego-focused' approach to change exhibited by the Moslem reformists, with the 'group-focused' image found among Hindu aristocrats of Tabanan.

Whereas in Modjokuto the pattern is of the *homo economicus* type which tends to give legitimacy to attitudes supportive of democratic liberalism and encourages an individualistic, free-enterprise economy, in Tabanan the pattern is *homo politicus* which is characterized by the way in which political motivation stimulates economic innovation and the entrepreneurial and political elites become indistinguishable. The latter model he regards as more relevant and functional to rapid economic expansion in underdeveloped countries (Geertz, 1963:131-2).

A basic methodological problem with the neo-Weberian approach to understanding facilitating factors, then, is that like other modernization approaches it tends to assume a common end-state (i.e. a capitalist, liberal-democratic system). If, however, one adopts a more eclectic standpoint and recognizes that there are many varied outcomes to economic growth and different modes of organizing the pattern of development, then it would seem that a wide range of contrasting value commitments can serve as facilitating cultural ideologies. This is aptly illustrated by the important role played by nationalist and socialist ideologies in countries like Tanzania (see Nyerere, 1967; Feldman, 1969) and China (Schurmann, 1966; Gray, 1974); or by the collectivist approach to religion and economics among the Hutterites of Canada.

Yet having argued this, it is equally important to recognize that in certain micro-contexts, religious asceticism does appear to be associated with entrepreneurship and indirectly functions, along with other factors, to stimulate economic endeavour. The reasons for this are complex and will vary somewhat from situation to situation, depending on the interplay of socio-cultural factors and on the types of resources available to, and the life-experiences encountered by, the members of the religious group. To explain this phenomenon primarily by reference to ideological components and to make assumptions concerning necessary value incentives, is to shy away from the interesting complexities presented by each case. A key analytical problem posed is why members of such a group are apparently more strategically placed than others for mobilizing resources and making a success of new economic opportunities. This question cannot adequately be answered by recourse to an analysis of moral and religious precepts, since it raises problems concerning social organization and resource management (see Long, 1970a). Another dimension concerns the degree of flexibility of interpretation tolerated by the belief system and by the religious authorities, as this will affect the adaptability of the ethic in the face of changing circumstances. This latter problem will need to be investigated carefully, for evidence suggests that ascetic forms of religion frequently become obsessed with the minutiae of everyday life and are rather doctrinaire in approach. This, together with the closed and incapsulated nature of the social group, leads, I suggest, to decreasing competitiveness in the field of economics and possibly in other spheres as well. Hence, an ideology, which during the earlier phases of development actively encourages capital accumulation and investment in profitable enterprise, may later discourage the re-organization of businesses along lines that would improve performance and lead to further growth. If this process can be documented, which I believe it can, then the search for value incentives which persist and remain constant over time is on difficult theoretical ground.

Similar difficulties arise when we turn to consider other kinds of facilitating factors (e.g. certain land tenure systems, family structures, and patterns of stratification). It becomes extremely difficult to specify which of the many varied factors constitute preconditions for rapid economic growth.[8] Furthermore, having selected a particular syndrome of factors, it is fairly easy to encounter contrary cases to refute one's interpretation. It has sometimes been argued, for example, that land reform, involving changes in ownership and control of land and leading to increased personal freedom for the peasantry, is a prerequisite for growth in the agricultural sector since peasants will now be more inclined to invest and work harder in order to increase productivity and rural incomes. Whilst in some cases land reform has had this effect, in others this has clearly not happened and certainly is not likely to occur without supportive reforms in marketing, pricing, and infrastructure generally. Other examples indicate, of course, that growth can be initiated without re-structuring existing socio-legal and land tenure systems. Similar debates concern the question of whether or not the emergence of a nuclear family system is necessary for the evolution of petty capitalist production; and whether or not Western criteria for social status provide essential motivation for the pursuit of economic advancement. These and other such arguments concerning prerequisites are difficult to solve so long as one aims at broad generalization, for one will always face the problem of explaining the apparent exceptions. The fundamental errors involved in this type of approach remain those of positing a linear, Western-biased model of development and of abstracting specific factors from a complex socio-historical process and assuming them to be crucial.

CHAPTER 4

Structural Dependency and the Analysis of Modes of Production

A major challenge to modernization theory has emerged in recent years among various branches of social science (Baran, 1957; Stavenhagen, 1965, 1969; Frank, 1967, 1969a; Cardoso and Faletto, 1970). It takes as its central premise that it is impossible to comprehend the processes and problems of development in the Third World without treating this within the wider socio-historical context of the expansion of Western European mercantile and industrial capitalism and the colonization of the Third World by these advanced economies. Thus Griffin writes:

> 'underdeveloped countries as we observe them today are a product of historical forces, especially those released by European expansion and world ascendency . . . Europe did not "discover" the underdeveloped countries; on the contrary, she created them.' (Griffin, 1968:38)

Viewed in this way, underdeveloped countries are and have for some time been dominated economically, as well as politically, by external centres of power and hence function as their satellites. Moreover, just as these societies are linked by dependency relationships to the outside and are unable to exert much influence on the operation of world markets or in the sphere of international politics,[1] so within a nation there exist mechanisms of internal domination and striking inequalities between different sectors of the economy, and in the social structure generally. Hence, it has been said that the rural-agricultural sector is dependent economically, politically, and culturally, on the urban-industrial complex and that 'the country appears divided between a minority who monopolize the power and economic resources, and a majority who are principally peasants' (Matos Mar *et al.*, 1969:14, my translation).

Writing of the 'development of underdevelopment' in Chile,

Frank argues that,

> 'this same structure [of dependence] extends from the macro-
> metropolitan center of the world capitalist system "down" to the
> most supposedly isolated agricultural workers, who, through this
> chain of interlinked metropolitan-satellite relationships, are tied
> to the central world metropolis and thereby incorporated into the
> world capitalist system as a whole. The nature and degree of
> these ties differ in time and place; and these differences produce
> important differences in the economic and political consequences
> to which they give rise. Such differences must ultimately be
> studied case by case. But these differences among relationships
> and their consequences do not obviate their essential similarity
> in that all of them, to one degree or another, rest on the
> exploitation of the satellite by the metropolis or on the
> tendency of the metropolis to expropriate and appropriate the
> economic surplus of the satellite. (Frank, 1969a:16–17)

Given such an interpretation, then sociological investigations
consist in isolating the specific modes and relationships of
domination and dependency that exist at various points in the
socio-historical process and of showing how these operate to limit
economic growth or to perpetuate patterns of underdevelopment.
This approach does not assume a uniformity among non-capitalist,
so-called 'traditional' societies, and allows for the incorporation of
dissimilar social structures (e.g. of a tribal, feudal, or peasant type).
Rather, it maintains that the penetration of the capitalist market
tends to produce changes in the existing system such that features
that are incompatible with the newly evolving structure are
eventually eliminated. Hence, the impact of western industrial
nations has destroyed many of the characteristics of the traditional
economics of Third World countries (e.g. it has in some cases
eliminated craft production and certain trading patterns) and
thereby has effected changes in social structure too. In many
instances this has not been associated with economic growth but
has led to the impoverishment of rural peoples (see Griffin,
1968:38–41, for evidence on Indonesia and India). Moreover, in its
more sophisticated versions, such a view claims to explain why and
how certain traditional patterns and modes of production are
maintained in the face of major economic change.

Such an approach substitutes for the largely atheoretical

discussion of social and cultural obstacles to development, an analysis of the social consequences of capitalist development and imperialist expansion, and of the ways in which new exploitative structures are established, which themselves act to impede economic growth. Thus economic development signifies for these countries the setting up of metropolitan-satellite relationships at different levels in the structure and the emergence of marked inequalities, based on the differential control of economic and political resources, between regions, sectors of the economy, and different social groups. It is the task of the anthropologist or sociologist interested in these matters to analyze the social mechanisms by which these relationships and structural imbalances are maintained.

Two main analytical approaches to this problem can be distinguished. The first defines the characteristics of satellite status and analyzes the causes and consequences of 'internal colonialism' in the Third World. The second explores more specifically the ways in which the capitalist mode of production articulates with various non-capitalist modes and how structures of underdevelopment are perpetuated. Obviously these themes are closely connected, but for purposes of exposition and criticism it is convenient to discuss them separately. They also represent different stages in the debate concerning dependency.

STRUCTURAL DEPENDENCY AND METROPOLITAN-SATELLITE RELATIONS

As the above quotation suggests, Andre Gunder Frank is an important figure in neo-Marxist writings on underdevelopment. His mentor was Paul Baran, who argued that the advanced industrial nations of the West are fundamentally opposed to the industrialization of the underdeveloped countries since the latter provides them with raw materials and investment outlets (Baran, 1957). Hence, Baran attributed the economic backwardness of the Third World to its dependent status in an international market system that favours the industrialized countries who control the capital, technology, and markets essential for economic growth.

Frank set out to explore the implications of this for understanding the problems of structural underdevelopment at national and local level. He starts with the view that underdevelopment is a logical outcome of the expansion of the capitalist system to colonial areas; but rejects the dualistic interpretation which argues that the pattern of external domination produces a structure of dualism in underdeveloped countries, such that there exists on the one hand, a modern, partly industrialized urban sector and, on the other hand, a traditionalized and economically backward peasant sector. These two opposing sectors are said to be poorly articulated and it is this lack of integration that constitutes a major obstacle to socio-economic development. In opposition to this view, Frank maintains that the sectors of an underdeveloped economy are in fact well integrated in terms of a structure of metropolitan-satellite relationships which results from the penetration of capitalism into even the remotest corners of the Third World.

As an alternative model, he suggests that we visualize 'a whole chain of metropolises and satellites, which runs from the world metropolis down to the hacienda or rural merchant who are satellites of the local commercial metropolitan center but who in their turn have peasants as their satellites' (Frank, 1969a:146–47). Hence, we find that close economic, political, social, and cultural ties bind the satellites to each metropolis, which expropriates their economic surplus (or a large part of it) to use for its own economic development, whilst the satellites themselves tend to become progressively more dependent. Ties of economic dependence are matched by a concentration of political power and social resources in metropolitan centres. This manifests itself most strikingly in the way that the members of a relatively small urban-based elite control the economic and political life of the masses. According to Frank, this tendency towards centralization is an essential element of the capitalist system.

From this he deduces a number of hypotheses about the nature of metropolitan-satellite relations. First, national metropolises, since they function as satellites of the advanced industrial countries, cannot achieve a pattern of self-sustained and autonomous development. Their growth is contingent upon the actions of other more powerful nations, and a similar process operates for lower-level satellites tied to national or regional centres. Second, where a weakening of relations of dependence occurs then we expect development to take an 'involuted' form. This can produce one of two outcomes. It can lead to what Frank calls 'passive capitalist involution', which denotes the move towards the re-establishment of a subsistence-based economy characterized by extreme poverty and underdevelopment, as happened in the North and Northeast of Brazil with the collapse of the sugar industry in the late seventeenth century as a result of the opening of the plantations in the West Indies. Or, alternatively, it can lead to 'active capitalist involution', which allows for some degree of autonomous development by the satellite but of a limited kind. The latter process is illustrated by the drive towards industrialization that took place in Brazil, Mexico, Argentina, and India during the Great Depression and the Second World War, when Western Europe was preoccupied by economic and political crisis and when the terms of trade for these underdeveloped countries improved considerably. Such growth, however, was short-lived and was finally stunted by the restoration of strong metropolitan-satellite relations once the war ended and 'normal' commercial ties were again established. The economic development of satellites, therefore, is never able to lead to long-term growth and independent status.

Frank also suggests that the economic and socio-political connections between satellite and metropolis generate increasing interdependence of their bourgeoisie who develop a mutual interest in maintaining the system. This growing interconnection also produces increasing polarization between the two ends of the chain of metropolitan-satellite relationships:

'A symptom of this polarization is the growing international inequality of incomes and the absolute decline of the real income of the lower income recipients ... [And it is also shown by the] acute polarization at the lower end of the chain, between the national and/or local metropolises and their poorest rural and urban satellites whose absolute real income is steadily declining.' (Frank, 1969:150)

In later works, Frank and others (see Cockcroft, Frank, and Johnson, 1972) have discussed the class basis of metropolitan-satellite relations. For example, it is argued that,

'the key point about Latin America's class structure is its polarization into those classes with jobs, income, status and participation in society as against those classes either without employment or in jobs of high exploitation. Among the classes that together form a "marginal mass" are most Indians, peasants, unemployed or under-employed workers, and highly exploited service workers. On the other end of the scale are the best paid of the stable working class, the entrenched middle class, and the dominant bourgeoisie of urban elites and landholders.' (Cockcroft, Frank, and Johnson, 1972:xvi)

While most marked in Latin America, this polarization, they would claim, is also an emergent feature of the newer nations of Africa and Asia (see also Saul and Arrighi, 1973).

They argue further that there is an interlocking of economic and political interests between rural and urban elites who make up the ruling class, and that the national bourgeoisie is dependent, to one degree or another, on the actions of a foreign bourgeoisie that controls world markets and capital for investment. At the other end of the spectrum we find what the authors call the 'marginal underclasses' or urban poor and the 'internal colonies' or rural satellites that are predominately composed of poor peasants and workers.

Internal colonies can be conceptualized economically as those populations that are primarily involved in producing commodities for sale in markets in the metropolitan centres and that supply labour for the enterprises controlled by these centres. In addition they constitute a market for the products and services emanating from these centres:

'Institutionally, the appropriation of wealth generated in the satellite takes place directly through capital transfers by land-owners (often absentee) or mine-owners to metropolitan centres (national or international) or directly through the terms of trade between products of the satellite and products of the metropolis and through metropolitan control of the commercial and financial sectors. There is little opportunity for capital accumulation by indigenous, non-oligarchic entrepreneurs.' (Cockcroft, Frank, and Johnson, 1972:278)

The pattern of rural economic exploitation and dependency in Third World countries is associated, therefore, with a sharply differentiated class structure which separates the owners of the means of primary production, together with a merchant and moneylending class, from the mass of poor peasants, craftsmen, and rural workers. The dominant class of a colony is well integrated into the national elite and participates actively in various national institutions, whilst the rest of the population is discriminated against generally in the fields of economics, politics, and culture. The rural masses are limited in their access to external institutions and frequently are tied to the landowning and merchant class through a set of personal ties of dependence which are often legitimized by reference to certain paternalistic ideologies. They are also subject to the political and administrative control of the dominant class and accorded inferior ethnic or cultural status (see Stavenhagen, 1965, on Mexico; and Cotler, 1967–8, on Peru).

According to Frank, eventually this 'polarization sharpens political tension ... until the initiative and generation of the transformation of the system passes from the metropolitan pole, where it has been for centuries, to the satellite pole' (Frank, 1969:150). It is at this point in the historical process that revolutionary action is called for: it is Frank's conviction that radical structural change and self-perpetuating economic growth will only come to Latin America and other similar underdeveloped areas once the national and regional bourgeoisie is overthrown and the links in the chain of dependency relationships broken.

Frank's thesis, then, is both an attempt to develop a new analytical framework for the study of economic development and social change in the Third World, and also a piece of political writing. I am concerned here only with the analytical usefulness of his scheme, not with its implications for political action.

Recent Attempts at Empirical Application

The notions of structural dependency and internal domination, which Frank conceptualizes in terms of a structure of metropolises and satellites, have recently been used by some anthropologists and sociologists in their studies of rural populations. Hence, before presenting a critique of Frank's argument, I intend to outline briefly some empirical applications of this type of theoretical approach.

One recent attempt to apply these concepts to problems of rural development and change is that by Matos Mar and others (Matos Mar *et al.*, 1969). This study opens with an account by Jose Matos Mar of the general socio-historical processes of Peruvian development, in which he argues that the pattern of external domination established by Spanish colonization and continued by advanced industrial countries is repeated in a multiplicity of ways at the level of the nation and its differentiated social sectors. Thus, analysis requires an explanation of the mechanisms by which this structure of internal dependency relations is maintained. Like Frank, Matos rejects the commonplace dualistic interpretation of the problems of underdevelopment. He argues that the rural agricultural and urban-industrial sectors cannot be regarded as separate, opposed structures or social systems, for they are mutually related to one another in a complex web of relationships. He proposes instead to use the concept of 'plural' society.[2] This concept he believes emphasizes both the 'singularity' of Peruvian society, its unique history and persisting cultures, while also giving attention to the patterns of inequality and dependence that have emerged as a result of its incorporation into a wider system of international relations of an economic and political nature.

A similar position is maintained by Fuenzalida and Alberti in a later chapter when they state that, 'In contrast to the concept of a dualistic society which is defined by reference to its internal disarticulation, a plural society is defined in terms of a specific, mode of articulation whose fundamental character is imprinted by the persistence of feudal types of domination' (Matos Mar *et al.*, 1969:284, my translation). This formulation differs somewhat from the Frankian thesis in that it allows for the continuation of forms of domination other than that specifically created by the capitalist system. However, the phenomenon of domination remains central to their analysis and provides the unifying element of what they call a pluralist system of the 'aborescent type'. Similar to Frank's notion of metropolitan-satellite relations, this metaphor is employed to describe a structure where

'the units of each subordinate level are connected to one another only by means of a superior instance. It depicts a form of articulation that is highly centralized and in which the different instances of power assume gradually more capacity for decision, control a larger amount of wealth, and have access to a wider range of information as one approaches the summit.' (Matos Mar *et al.*, 1969:289–90, my translation).

At the base of such a structure there is a variety of different types of rural social systems, represented in Peru by the so-called 'traditional' haciendas of the southern highlands, the modernized haciendas of the coastal region, the indigenous communities, and the settlements of smallholder farmers. These systems, however, are interrelated within specific micro-regional contexts and tied into the overall pattern of domination at national level. Hence the concepts 'domination', 'pluralism', and 'micro-region' are analytically interdependent.

As a general statement of the kind of theoretical orientation required to analyze problems of rural development in Peru, such a formulation represents a considerable advance on previous conceptual frameworks which by and large took a modernization view of change. However, certain difficulties emerge when the various authors try to elaborate their interpretation in the context of specific field data on the Chancay Valley of coastal Peru. For example, although there is a discussion of the micro-region and pluralism, much of the analysis is taken up with a specification of the different types of social organization represented by the haciendas in the lowland zone of the valley, by the peasant communities of the higher altitudes, and by the settlements of smallholders. Relatively little attention is given to how these systems are interrelated economically and/or politically and of the ways in which the region is tied into the wider politico-economic structure. Hence, more emphasis is in fact given to pluralism than to regional structure; and the discussion of domination and dependency relations tends to be restricted to the analysis of the internal organization of settlements.

In this same work, Cotler (Matos Mar *et al.,* 1969:60–79) develops two models for application at local level which he claims enable us to gain a better understanding of the patterns of domination and of the kinds of changes occurring in regions like the Chancay Valley.[3] He calls these the 'triangle *without* a base' and the 'triangle *with* a base'. His discussion centres around the comparison of two contrasting situations: one characterized by being 'typically traditional' such as can be observed in the Peruvian highlands, and the other an area where more marked economic change and development is taking place. (By 'highland Peru' Cotler means the southern regions of Puno, Cuzco, Apurimac, Ayacucho, and Huancavelica, and Ancash in the central region.)

Cotler first identifies the general structural conditions associated with the 'traditional' hacienda system. These are: (a) low level of urbanization; (b) low socio-economic differentiation; (c) primitive technology and low productivity; (d) absence of effective communications; and (e) high incidence of illiteracy. Although not necessary, these conditions are sufficient for the emergence and persistence of 'traditional' relations of dominance.

In such a structural context the Indian peasants of the highlands have few alternatives open to them and are forced to submit to whoever has control over the key resources of the area (i.e. land and education). These dominant figures (normally non-Indians or *mestizos*) link the local structure with the outside and have access to important institutions of national significance. The peasants may be permanent or temporary workers who provide labour and other services to the *hacendado* (i.e. the landowner and patron) but 'between mestizos and Indians there is established an exchange of services whereby the former control the type and quality of reciprocity' (Matos Mar *et al.*, 1969:64). The stability of the system is maintained by a normative system which functions as a rationalization of the *status quo*: the *mestizo* is perceived by the peasants as the most powerful source of potential benefits and the only person who can improve their condition. Because of this they lack group solidarity and compete with one another for the favours and protection of the *hacendado*.

The combination of structural conditions and the form of existing social relations and values severely limits the possibility of changes being generated internally. The peasantry is atomized and subordinated. Diagrammatically the structure of social relations can be depicted in the following manner:

where P = patron, and s[1] etc. = subordinates:

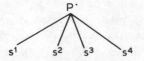

The model isolates two basic elements:
    (a) the complete atomization of the subordinates, and (b) the funnelling of relations through the patron who controls access to external persons and institutions.

Using this model as a baseline, Cotler then goes on to outline the means by which the structure can be transformed. Change is produced by the following processes:

(a) The creation of new economic opportunities through, for example, the intervention of the state in the construction of roads and other types of infrastructure that open up new sources of work. This enables peasants to find work outside the hacienda. Another example is the appearance of traders or intermediaries who compete with the *hacendados* for the marketing of agricultural produce. In certain circumstances this can substantially undermine the authority and social position of *hacendados* and lead to a mobilization of peasants (e.g. the peasant movement that occurred in the Valley of Convención where coffee was developed as an important export crop, see Craig, 1968).

(b) The development of mass communications, which may broaden cultural horizons and bring about a reorientation in the normative structure.

(c) The falling away of institutional support at state level given to the *mestizos* and *hacendados,* and the appearance of political parties, trade unions, and student organizations which mobilize the peasantry. Also powerful bodies like the church and army may sever their close ties with local elites.

The final outcome of such processes can be depicted as the closing of the base of the triangle as the peasants develop more solidarity among themselves and as new kinds of apex emerge.

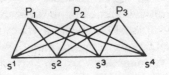

In this way the *hacendado's* monopoly over material and other resources is broken and the taking of decisions becomes based more on the mutual adaptation of distinct groups and social categories that have the power to negotiate over the content and form of exchanges. These changes are characteristic of the transformation of the traditional pattern of domination into one based more on consent and bargaining, though patron-client relations may not be totally eliminated, and power imbalances may still be present. The main feature of the new structure is the existence of several apexes representing dominant groups operating in varying fields of action. Hence a simple metropolitan-satellite structure is replaced by a more complex one.

Cotler's two models have been used by Fuenzalida and Alberti (in Matos Mar *et al.*, 1969:285–325) to analyze the differences between haciendas, 'traditional' Indian communities, and smallholder settlements in the Chancay Valley.[4] The authors suggest that one can treat these two models as representing opposite ends of a morphological continuum and that the settlements in the valley can be placed on this continuum according to how far they approximate to either of these ideal-types. Several different dimensions are considered: the question of administrative functions and structures; the control of economic resources; the availability and use of information; and the type and intensity of external contacts.

Fuenzalida and Alberti examine data on six settlements: two haciendas, two Indian communities, and two smallholder settlements. Their results show that the commercial haciendas of the region approximate most closely to the pattern of traditional domination described by Cotler, whilst the Indian communities, where land and resources are still largely held under communal ownership, fall towards the other end of the continuum, with the smallholder settlements coming at some midway point between these two extremes.

The haciendas exhibit a pattern of centralization whereby the hacienda administration controls most of the organizational, economic, and natural resources of the settlement. This severely limits the possibility of workers forming effective bodies such as trade unions and associations to protect their own interests, though they do show some willingness to participate in national elections. The peasant workers are further disadvantaged by their generally low level of education and by their lack of other useful skills.

In contrast, the Indian communities show a greater propensity to engage in co-operative modes of organization: the bulk of their pastoral land remains firmly in the control of the community, and the District Council, composed of local residents, collaborates with community leaders in the running of local government and services. Clubs and political parties abound and are active in representing the interests of their members in local and national affairs. Although there is evidence of growing economic differentiation between larger and smaller scale farmers and a small commercial sector consisting of shopkeepers and traders, there is no clearly defined economic or political elite. Indian communities, therefore, show a greater degree of egalitarianism and social solidarity than do either of the other two types of settlement. But despite this, they are still tied into the wider politico-economic structure through their export of crops and labour to the urban markets controlled by other more powerful interest groups; and are largely dependent on government for the provision of the capital and expertise necessary for the development of their agriculture. It is perhaps for this reason they show a high level of participation in national elections.

The smallholder settlements are characterized chiefly by the existence of major social divisions which affect both the running of local government and the relations between different social strata. Indeed, in one of these settlements there are two District Councils in competition for control over local government affairs. Political parties and clubs are poorly organized and internally divided. The most important criterion of social status is one's economic standing and it is also this that tends to affect the degree to which farmers are in regular contact with urban areas. Land is gradually becoming more unequally distributed as a relatively small group of better-off farmers acquire access to larger extensions and control the water supplies necessary for irrigation. In comparison with the Indian communities, the average level of education of smallholders is low, though some have achieved post-secondary education and specialist training.

Each of these types of local organization is embedded in a regional and national structure which places restrictions on the kinds of changes that can occur. For example, Fuenzalida and Alberti point out that marked changes have occurred in the haciendas in recent years due to the increase in external contacts and the growth of the regional capital of Huaral. This led to the development of trade unions and to a deterioration in administrative control at some of the haciendas, which at the same time felt the impact of economic crisis resulting from fluctuating prices for export crops in the world market. But these developments did not result in the workers gaining substantially more control over the management of the haciendas. Changes in ownership and control had to await the intervention of the state, which under its new land reform policy, has now expropriated them and transformed them into production co-operatives.[5]

Another problem concerns the lack of social integration in the smallholder settlements. Fuenzalida and Alberti stress that the heterogeneity of their populations, which have been drawn from different social and economic sectors of the rural population of the valley – from the Indian communities and from the haciendas – has been an important factor contributing towards a high level of social conflict and has led to the reinforcement of existing patterns of economic differentiation. One positive effect is that there is not much likelihood of a structure of domination emerging similar to that found on the haciendas. But, on the other hand, it tends to encourage the development of a 'yeoman' class of commercial farmers who have already begun to gain control over large tracts of land and who monopolize the scarce water supplies. This suggests that what we now find in some of the settlements in the Chancay Valley is the emergence of dependency relations based not on the traditional type of patronage system described by Cotler for highland haciendas, but on differential control of the means of capitalist production, the *hacendado* being replaced by the rural merchant and agricultural entrepreneur.

Fuenzalida and Alberti also draw attention to the different responses to economic change shown by the two Indian communities. While one has been able to mobilize resources and organize for commercial production within the existing structure of communal-type relations, the other has experienced a gradual decline in the importance of these institutions and is now fraught with serious internal conflicts. The reasons for this are complex and would require a detailed socio-historical account of the interplay of various internal and external factors in the history of the two communities. A key factor was that one of the communities had the initial advantage of possessing much better communal land resources that were well suited to the cultivation of fruit on a cash-crop basis; it also lost fewer of its able men through labour migration; and managed to retain close contact with its better educated members working in town who helped with the financing of community-organized enterprise (see Fuenzalida *et al.*, 1968, and Degregori and Golte, 1973 for details on the development of the two communities).

Theoretical and Methodological Problems

As the foregoing discussion indicates, the theory of structural dependency has built into it propositions that can be tested either historically or functionally. A large part of Frank's argument relates to the genesis of underdevelopment and can therefore be explored empirically through a detailed account of the history and consequences of colonization and the intrusion of the capitalist market economy. It is this type of analysis that Frank and others, like Furtado and Cardoso, have attempted for specific countries of Latin America. The other approach is to study the contemporary situation of Third World countries either at the level of the national economy and social structure or for particular sectors or regions. In so doing one aims to examine how far it is possible to interpret the problems of development and change in terms of regional or sectoral imbalances and/or a structure of dependency relations between social groups. The studies by Matos Mar *et al.* (1969) focus on the latter problem. Similar types of analysis have been developed by Stavenhagen (1965) in his study of the differential access to economic and political resources exercised by Indians and *ladinos* in Mexico and Guatemala; by Burgos (1970) for the Riobamba region of Ecuador; and by Castillo (1970) and Preston (1972) who present data on the pattern of domination found in the Andes between urban-based *mestizo* groups and the peasant Indian population.

I now examine, in the light of the above empirical data, the analytical utility of the structural dependency approach. The main burden of my discussion will be to show that Frank's formulation is too simplistic to provide a satisfactory framework for understanding the complexities and variations in metropolitan-satellite relations, and that it contains a number of assumptions which seem unwarranted. I shall also offer some criticism of Cotler's argument.

In the first place, Frank's analysis assumes that the intrusion of capitalism leads to the elimination of non-capitalist forms of organization. This is evident from his assertion that Latin America has been capitalist from the time that it was incorporated into the world market during the colonial period. He rejects social and economic dualism, and at the same time refuses to allow for the persistence of certain feudal-type relations or other non-capitalist modes. Yet, as Laclau (1971) has argued, this is to confound two quite separate issues. To claim that feudal-type relations survive into the modern capitalist era, albeit somewhat modified in form, is not the same as adhering to a dualistic interpretation. Criticisms of the dualistic model emphasize that the less developed and more traditionalized sectors are in fact tied into the national system through a complex pattern of economic, political, and socio-cultural relations. Hence, one can argue 'that the modernity of one sector is a function of the backwardness of the other', showing, for example, how 'the maintenance of feudal backwardness at one extreme and the apparent progress of a bourgeois dynamism' at the other, are actually functional for the persistence of underdeveloped forms of capitalism (Laclau, 1971:31). Indeed, as Peruvian and other studies have demonstrated, both capitalist and non-capitalist modes of production frequently co-exist within the same empirical context, involving the same or neighbouring peasants in qualitatively different types of production relations.

According to Laclau, this weakness in Frank's argument arises fundamentally from his failure to define at all precisely what he means by capitalism. In common with certain other writers, he tends to deal with the problem from the point of view of commodity exchanges rather than production relations. It is because of this that he can argue that the enlargement of the world market during the sixteenth century, which led to the colonization of the Third World, was thoroughly capitalist in nature, and that it brought about the destruction of feudalism in these areas. Drawing on Marx, Laclau stresses the necessity of distinguishing between *capital* and *capitalism*. He writes:

'Did the structural conditions of capitalism exist in 16th century Europe when, according to Frank, the process of capital domination started in Latin America? Could we consider free labour to be the rule then? By no means. Feudal dependence and urban handicrafts remained the basic forms of productive activity. The existence of a powerful commercial class which greatly enlarged its stock of capital through overseas trade did not in the least modify the decisive fact that this capital was accumulated by the absorption of an economic surplus produced through labour relationships very different from those of free labour.' (Laclau, 1971:27)

The same point can be made for contemporary rural areas where labour for export crops may be recruited through a patron-client system like that found on haciendas, or where commercially-oriented peasants use non-wage labour from the extended family. This suggests the importance of analyzing problems of development from the point of view of how different modes of production are articulated rather than from just an exchange point of view. This aspect will be discussed later when I examine the contributions made by French Marxist anthropologists.

Frank's analysis, then, is primarily concerned with demonstrating how the establishment of a market economy, now based on the demands of capitalist production in advanced industrial countries and in national metropolitan centres, leads to the setting up of metropolitan-satellite relations which operate to maintain a structure of unequal exchange between the groups involved. This does not only function in economic terms but has its social, political, and cultural components. The studies by Cotler and Fuenzalida and Alberti explore the variations in this pattern as it exists in one region of Peru. The main limitation of their work, however, is that it does not focus explicitly enough on the points of contact between the various local and regional systems. If Frank is right in emphasizing the importance of documenting the types of exchanges that occur at regional, national, and international levels, then sociologists and anthropologists should be studying the groups and individuals involved in these processes. It is for this reason that studies of entrepreneurship, of trading and market organization, and of political and cultural brokers, many of which have been undertaken from quite a different intellectual standpoint, become pertinent to the Frankian thesis.[6]

A further difficulty arises over the use of the concept of 'dependence'. According to Dos Santos (1969),

'dependence is a conditioning situation in which the economies of one group of countries are conditioned by the development and expansion of others. A relationship of interdependence between two or more economies or between such economies and the world trading system becomes a dependent relationship when some countries expand through self-impulsion while others, being in a dependent position, can only expand as a reflection of the expansion of the dominant countries, which may have positive or negative effects on their immediate development. In either case, the basic situation of dependence causes these countries to be both backward and exploited.

Dominant countries are endowed with technological, commercial, capital and socio-political predominance over dependent countries ... and can therefore exploit them, and extract part of the locally produced surplus. Dependence, then, is based upon an international division of labour which allows industrial development to take place in some countries while restricting it in others, whose growth is conditioned by and subjected to the power centres of the world.' (Dos Santos, in Bernstein, 1973:76–7)

Whilst this may characterize in general terms the types of relationships that exist between advanced industrial and under-developed economies and may be extended to cover similar patterns at national and regional levels, it necessarily avoids specifying the other elements in the relations between nations or groups within a nation which may not so easily be categorized in terms of dependence. While I do not deny the importance of satellite status for understanding the problems of underdevelopment, a fuller analysis of the complexities involved would be better achieved, I believe, if the study of exploitative relationships were matched by studying the patterns of co-operation and colla-boration that may also exist. Indeed, the existence of dependency relations normally entails the maintenance of co-operative ele-ments based on some degree of mutual interest in order that the former might be perpetuated; and there are also important types of horizontal exchanges that occur between the satellites them-selves, as is shown, for example, in the Chancay Valley where peasants from smallholder settlements work as temporary . labourers on the haciendas.

The point I am making is well illustrated by Gluckman's analysis of the situation in the Republic of South Africa where a policy of apartheid enforces an extreme type of domination by whites over blacks in economic, political, social, and cultural matters. According to Gluckman, there exist in South Africa both elements of domination and co-operation in that, despite the inequalities, certain blacks and whites tacitly collaborate in the pursuit of common political or economic goals (Gluckman, 1955: Chapter VI). Thus any analysis of problems of structural depen-dency must, in addition, examine the bases for co-operation and for coalition within and between opposing interest groups. Though protagonists of dependency theory would not dispute the importance of such elements – there is, for example, much discusion concerning the overlapping interests of national and foreign bourgeoisie – most studies tend in fact to give little attention to them. Hence, Cotler assumes that horizontal relationships among peasant workers on the traditional haciendas of southern Peru were unimportant, and that the relationship between patron and peasants was one of extreme, unmitigated domination. Yet evidence to refute both these assertions can easily be adduced. Other hacienda studies document a considerable exchange of services and produce among peasant workers. This functions to counteract temporary food and labour shortages which individual households sometimes suffer and it helps to build up some degree of trust between particular households that may later become important for the contracting of marriages and for organizing religious fiestas (Miller, 1967; Johnson, 1971). Indirectly, of course, these relationships contribute towards the maintenance of the hacienda system and the *status quo*. In addition, recent evidence (Martinez-Alier, 1973) questions the assumption that haciendas in highland Peru severely exploited their workers and suggests that frequently independent smallholder peasants and wage labourers were much worse off than those peasants tied to so-called 'feudal lords'.

It would seem, therefore, that in order to develop the Frankian type of analysis we need to be much more precise in defining what is implied by the concept of dependence as it relates to different structural contexts. Dos Santos and others have clarified the matter in relation to economic and political dependence at international level, and some attempts also have been made to define it in terms of sectoral or inter-regional inequalities that exist within nations. However, a major difficulty with micro-studies is that they seldom provide a satisfactory characterization of dependency as it pertains to specific types of interpersonal relationships. Moreover, if they do, then the analysis tends to be framed almost entirely in terms of a discussion of institutional roles as Cotler (1970) and Castillo (1970) have done.

A basic conceptual problem is that participation in any kind of relationship involves some degree of dependence on the part of the parties concerned since having a relationship with someone implies the exclusion of other possible alternatives. It is important therefore to try to specify the conditions under which different types and degrees of structural dependency or domination exist.

Even Cotler's attempt to set out the structural conditions associated with the pattern of domination found on haciendas basically fails because it does not distinguish the hacienda situation from that of other types: all of the conditions he lists could in fact apply equally to other situations of a peasant or indeed tribal nature.

It is in this context that Blau's discussion of power imbalances deriving from unilateral exchange becomes relevant (Blau, 1964: 118–25). Blau attempts to isolate the conditions under which persons or groups having scarce resources at their disposal can use the resources to make an undeniable claim to power over others, and this enables him to specify the nature and degree of dependency present. Such an analysis, in my view, provides a sounder conceptual basis for the discussion of imbalances in power that exist between different social categories and groups and of the mechanisms by which certain structures are maintained. Hence, it could offer additional insights into the study of structural dependency at a micro level of interpretation.

Another weakness in Frank's formulation is that he assumes that metropolitan-satellite relations are arranged in a simple hierarchical ordering. He writes of the chain of metropolises and satellites stretching from the world metropolitan centres to national, regional, and local satellites, down to the lowest level in the structure which involves the most isolated peasant farmer or agricultural worker. In essence this model has much in common with 'central place' theory developed by geographers for characterizing the socio-spatial arrangement of villages, towns, and cities that can be differentiated in terms of increasing size and specialization of socio-economic function (Berry, 1967). But whereas geographers are mainly interested in ecological formations, Frank focuses on the problem of superordinate-subordinate relationships, suggesting that the smallest rural satellite is linked to the national metropolis through a hierarchy of sub-regional and regional centres which successively expropriate the economic surpluses of their immediate satellites. While it is possible to show that this pattern pertains for certain cases (Skinner, 1964), it is clearly inadequate for understanding other situations where more direct links with national centres exist. For example, recent research in the central region of highland Peru has shown that many villages in the Mantaro Valley operate a whole series of economic and social transactions directly with Lima the capital (some 250 miles away) and have minimal contact with the local regional city of Huancayo (Long, 1972; and Roberts, 1973). In order to explain this, one would need to take account of various factors: the development of communications between the capital city and its hinterland, the rate and types of labour migration from the villages to the mines and cities of the coast, and the development of certain patterns of social organization (e.g. migrant clubs, and fiesta and political associations) which provide the means by which close relations with the capital city are maintained.

The notion of metropolitan-satellite relations also assumes that changes in the development and organization of satellites are largely dependent on forces emanating from the metropolitan centres. While this may be substantially true if we are identifying the initial sources of major structural change, later in the process the satellites themselves may come to play a determining role in the allocation of national and regional resources. This is documented for both Latin America and Africa where certain provincially-based political parties and interest groups have succeeded in obtaining more favourable terms for their areas of origin. Frank's argument directs attention away from the analysis of such matters and suggests that instead we view the actions of such groups from the point of view of how their protagonists come to be absorbed into the national bourgeoisie and thus no longer represent the 'real' interests of their provincial compatriots. Hence the elite members of a satellite acquire metropolitan status *vis-à-vis* their followers, and the system remains unimpaired. Such an interpretation espouses an essentially static view of development and underestimates the part played by internal factors in promoting economic or social change or in contributing towards the maintenance of inequalities between sectors of the economy and society. It also, as Roberts (1974) has argued, overlooks 'the significance of provincial developments in shaping the character of urban organization' and 'runs the danger of giving an overdetermined view of the evolution of provincial society'.

This tendency to see structural change from the point of view of the impact of exogenous factors is characteristic of Cotler's analysis as well. He interprets changes in hacienda organization as a response to changes in the external environment. Hence, he stresses the importance of the emergence of new employment opportunities, the development of national political parties, and changes in the relations between national and regional elites. Clearly one would not wish to reject such an interpretation but the mere listing of types of environmental changes cannot explain the differential impact that these forces have had on different haciendas. To explain this one needs to examine much more closely the types of internal differences that exist between haciendas (e.g. in the types of relationships that exist among tenants and between them and their *hacendado*). It might also be important to examine the cumulative effect of demographic change leading to changes in the distribution of resources as holdings become more fragmented or when peasants slowly encroach upon the land of the *hacendado* (see Altamirano, 1971).

Given these qualifications, however, the study of structural dependency and internal domination is obviously important if we wish to understand more fully the impediments to economic growth and social change among rural people of the Third World. As I have suggested earlier, such an approach does not necessarily make assumptions about the nature of traditional or 'pre-modern' societies, nor does it assume that traditional patterns are eliminated by more modern forms. It sees the outcome in terms of the evolution of a more capitalistically-oriented society but it does not assume that this will closely parallel that of Western Europe. Indeed, it emphasizes that because the socio-historical conditions are so different for these countries, their paths of change will be markedly different. Hence, studies of rural situations should examine both the modes of incorporation consequent upon greater involvement in the capitalist system and also the variations that are found in different ecological, economic, and socio-cultural zones. As yet, analysis of these problems is in its infancy: the research by Frank has pointed the way but it is weak in that it tends to overstress the uniformities in the pattern and does not address itself adequately to the variations that arise, except insofar as it treats these as the result of the concatenation of highly specific historical circumstances.

THE ANALYSIS OF MODES OF PRODUCTION

The next type of approach offers some way out of the conceptual and analytical difficulties posed by the metropolitan-satellite or dependency model. It attempts to do this by focusing more explicitly on the problem of the interconnections between different modes of production.

The discussion of modes of production in the Third World has recently concerned itself with the ways in which the capitalist mode articulates with, and eventually comes to have a controlling influence over, traditional or non-capitalist modes. The criticism of Frank's thesis by Laclau (1971), the work by the French Marxist anthropologists, such as Terray (1969), and Dupré and Rey (1973), and the critique of Myrdal's writings by Ulyanovsky and Pavlov (1973), represent an attempt to come to grips with the multi-structural character of economic systems in the Third World through an analysis of production systems. Through this it is hoped to gain insight into the mechanisms by which particular types of production relations are maintained and how they are connected with other modes existing within the same macro socio-economic framework. When applied to the analysis of underdevelopment, this approach aims to explain how and why certain non-capitalist forms of production persist despite their involvement in modern marketing systems based on commodity exchange.

While Frank is right in emphasizing the importance of exchange processes it is equally important to attempt to relate patterns of circulation and distribution to production. Hence, Meillassoux (1972) argues that exchange elements (whether they be located within a predominantly capitalist or non-capitalist system) must be examined in relation to the part they play in reproducing the material conditions of existence. For example, in the lineage-based subsistence societies he studied in West Africa where labour is the crucial condition of production, the circulation of women through marriage, which is controlled by the lineage elders, is critical for the reproduction of the productive unit itself thereby allowing the producers to benefit in the future from their past labour. He also shows that the movement of children between classificatory fathers and the adoption of strangers into the system enables adjustments to take place in order that certain lineages, which, because of differential fecundity and accidents of birth and death, are low on labour, may be replenished. Indeed he extends his argument to suggest that many of the customs concerning gift-giving, reci-procity, and dowry arrangements can be interpreted in terms of this notion of reproducing or maintaining the basic conditions of subsistence production. Similar functions are performed in capitalist societies by various economic and politico-legal institutions and processes which encourage capital accumulation for investment in production, and which reproduce the basic social relations of production (see Balibar 1970:254–308).

Dupré and Rey have developed this type of analysis to provide some account of the ways in which the capitalist mode impinges upon non-capitalist modes at different stages in the development of Third World economies. Their argument shows that in certain contexts a capitalist mode of production can indirectly contribute to the persistence of non-capitalist forms. During the early trading period the capitalist mode supplied important goods and even injected money into the subsistence system but these items were absorbed into the system and did not undermine the traditional production process. Hence, in West Africa there was a flow of trade goods into the interior in return for slaves and other products. In other cases (e.g. the Bemba of Zambia) the supply of important items like guns and gunpowder led to significant changes in political organization, but it did not affect agricultural production much (A. Roberts, 1966:107–114). Later with colonial rule the capitalist mode came to have a dominant influence over non-capitalist modes as commercial and industrial capital was invested in production itself. This resulted in the development of small-scale commercial agriculture, plantation systems, mining, and limited industrialization. Yet, despite these changes, some rural areas continue to be primarily concerned with satisfying subsistence needs and keep almost intact their traditional modes of production. This is well illustrated by Watson's study of the Mambwe of Zambia. Watson (1958) argues that although the Mambwe are well integrated into the urban-industrial economy through the export of labour to the mines, their system of subsistence production is unchanged and will remain so providing the ratio of women to men left in the rural area is kept at approximately 2:1, and there is no pressure on existing land resources.

A recent important contribution to this discussion is that by Wolpe (1972, 1975), who argues that the presence of a non-capitalist agricultural mode of production in the African areas of South Africa results directly from the requirements of the dominant capitalist sector which needs a low-wage labour force for its mining, manufacturing, and agricultural industries. 'The capitalist sector benefits from the means of subsistence produced in the noncapitalist mode of production to the extent that it is relieved of paying a portion of the necessary means of subsistence by way of indirect wages' (Wolpe, 1975:248). But in order to ensure the flow of labour-power and at the same time sustain the non-capitalist sector so that Africans can continue to rely partly on traditional forms of subsistence, the state has implemented a whole series of politico-legal measures and sanctions (i.e. pass laws, policing, and the creation of Bantustans and apartheid regulations) aimed at controlling the mobility of labour and preventing the growth of a fully-stabilized urban proletariat. This strategy, however, has only been partly successful since it creates its own internal contradictions due to such factors as overgrazing and the pressure of population on resources in the African areas.

These examples emphasize that the study of different modes of production and how they are articulated requires an analysis of the types of exchanges that occur between them. It is for this reason that I believe that the findings of what some Marxists have called the 'bourgeois or liberal' tradition of economic anthropology are relevant (Meillassoux, 1972). Much anthropological work has concerned itself with the taxonomy and analysis of different systems of economic and social exchange in tribal, peasant, and 'more developed' societies and it has studied the effects of the introduction of new marketing structures. These studies are important for they enable us to determine the extent to which certain exchanges originate and/or terminate within a specific region or institutional structure. Also, the analysis of systems of distribution entails some consideration of the control over the means of production exercised by various social groups. Thus, the study of markets and distribution connects up with the study of modes of production and enables us to assess the role played by exchange in reproducing or modifying the conditions of production and in articulating different modes of production.

Of particular interest here is the recent work by Forman and Riegelhaupt (1970) who analyze changes in the marketing system of North East Brazil and who suggest 'that there is a point at which capitalization in the distributive sector of a rural economy requires like commitments of capital in the production sector, leading to the displacement or transformation of the peasantry'

(1970:207). Their analysis shows that the reorganization of the marketing system from one based on a traditional pattern of regional markets with small-scale middlemen to one catering for the increased demand for food produce from urban consumer markets, led to increased investment in these local markets by wholesale merchants, who also later themselves purchased or rented land for production. The overall effect on agricultural production was that it became more capital-intensive, with more concentrated land holdings and a larger landless class.

Modes of Production in Highland Peru

I want now to show how one might begin to develop such an analysis of different modes of production and their interconnections. I illustrate my argument by reference to highland Peru. Before proceeding, it is necessary to clarify certain basic concepts. By 'mode of production' we mean that complex made up of the forces of production (i.e. technical rules, resources, and instruments of labour and labour-power) and the social relations of production. Production is the process by which men with their labour-power and instruments of labour transform the object of labour (in this case, land) in order to reap some material or economic return. The object of labour and the instruments used constitute what we call the means of production, but the process itself requires the participation of men who are brought together in terms of a specific set of social relations. These social relations are principally defined in terms of the ownership and control of the means of production and of the social product. [7] Thus, in theoretical terms, a mode of production equals the combination of social relations of production and the level of development of the productive forces: comparing, for example, the capitalist with the feudal mode, we find that both systems exhibit qualitatively different relations and forces of production. Certain difficulties arise, however, when we attempt to apply this formal definition to particular empirical material. Montoya (1970) argues, for example, that although it is possible to show that various types of production systems found in highland Peru have roughly similar levels of productive forces, they, in fact, represent a wide variety of systems based on different types of social relations. It would seem better therefore to differentiate between them by describing the different patterns of ownership and control that exist.

Taking social relations of production as the main criterion, Montoya identifies four main non-capitalist modes in rural Peru: the traditional hacienda, the smallholder property type, the sharecropping type (of which there are several variants), and the indigenous or peasant community type. Since most regions of Peru are fairly heterogeneous in terms of production systems, an analysis of the economic structure of any one area would normally involve consideration of each of these modes and of how they interconnect. Here it is important to recognize that although there is a tendency for a particular mode of production to be associated with a certain type of settlement and land tenure system, several modes (both capitalist and non-capitalist) will normally be found to co-exist within the same agricultural zone.

This point is well illustrated by studies of highland haciendas (Palacio, 1957; Matos Mar, 1967). The hacienda mode of production can be characterized in the following way:

1) It consists basically of two classes of persons: the landowners (or persons who rent the land from the state) called *hacendados* or *terratenientes*; and the tenant-workers called *colonos*. In between these two classes is a small group of administrators or foremen, sometimes recruited from the *colonos*, employed by the hacienda.

2) The *hacendado* has legal control of the land, but *colonos* have effective possession of their plots for usufructuary purposes. In addition there is land which is set aside for the *hacendado* himself. The proportion of land controlled by the *hacendado* and by the *colonos* varied considerably. In one (possibly rather exceptional) case the *colonos* possessed 65 per cent of cultivable land and 30 per cent of pasture (Martinez-Alier, 1973:15–16).

3) The contract between the *hacendado* and *colono* is general and often of a verbal kind. It gives land to the *colono* for his personal use and in return secures his services for various duties. Hence, the 'rent' is paid for in labour.

4) Labour service generally takes three forms:
   (a) Agricultural work by the *colono* on the lands of the *hacendado*. This is normally fixed in terms of a set number of days per week, month, or year. The normal requirement is about two or three days per week or 100 to 150 production days in the year. The rest of the *colono*'s time, when he is

not involved in helping the *hacendado* in other ways, can be spent cultivating his own plot. This arrangement enables him to satisfy his basic subsistence requirements and market a small surplus, though how successful he is will, of course, be affected by his household demands and by the size and quality of the plot.

(b) Domestic work for the *hacendado*. Depending on the number of *colonos* available, each one must complete a work quota as servant in the house of the *hacendado* either on the hacienda or in the town house where he lives. The wife, too, must periodically assist in domestic chores and the children are normally expected to look after the *hacendado*'s children and small animals.

(c) Periodic work on the clearing of roads and water channels and repairing the *hacendado*'s house and outbuildings. Frequently the *colono* must also assist in carrying the *hacendado*'s produce to the town markets for sale.

At some haciendas additional forms of service include the lending of oxen (if the *colono* possesses them) to the *hacendado* when the latter needs them for ploughing or the drying of potatoes which are stored for sale later in the season.

5) In addition to providing a small plot of land to the *colono*, the *hacendado*'s obligations consist of:

(a) The giving of small gifts of money for work done on the hacienda. This is normally only a token amount and is not regarded as a full salary.

(b) The provision of alcohol and cigarettes for workers when engaged in collective work parties (*faenas*).

(c) The offer of pasturage for the tenant's animals and of firewood for cooking purposes.

(d) The provision of food for servant workers and persons involved in *faenas*.

This dominant pattern of production relations is frequently combined with other types. In addition to the *colonos*, there is also often a class of '*sub-colonos*'. These are usually younger men who have not yet been allocated their own plots for cultivation. In return for food they will substitute for a *colono* when he is called for work parties. Also in some cases there is sub-letting of plots. Under this system the sub-tenant is obliged to work for the original tenant for a specified number of days in the week just as the *colono* does for the *hacendado*. Hence, within the hacienda we may find similar patterns of patronage operating at lower levels in the structure.

Another variation is that sometimes there is differentiation among the *colonos* themselves whereby some are granted more land than others, and may be required to do more labour service (see Cotler's discussion of the difference between *manay* and *yana pacu* tenants in Paucartambo, Southern Peru, Cotler, 1970:543–44). There are also *colonos-comuneros*. These are peasants living outside the hacienda who have insufficient land of their own to satisfy their needs and who seek work on the hacienda. Whilst some of them may be recruited temporarily for a fixed payment in money or kind, others are able to acquire plots and provide labour for the *hacendado* in the same way as do resident *colonos*. But, unlike the resident *colonos*, these *colonos-comuneros* continue to live in their peasant communities and retain an interest in cultivating their own smallholdings there too.

A similar type of contract exists between the *hacendado* and *colono* on livestock haciendas. The *colono* is required to herd the flocks of sheep and graze the llamas of the *hacendado* and in return is allowed to retain a proportion of the new-born each year, normally in order of one in ten new animals. In addition he must send all the animals down to the *hacendado*'s land to provide manure when requested, must sell his own animals through the *hacendado,* and undertake whatever other duties the *hacendado* demands.

The hacienda mode of production binds the tenant-worker closely to the *hacendado* who owns and, in the last analysis, also controls the use of the means of production.[8] But the *colono* is generally tied to the *hacendado* not only by economic ties[9] but also by other types of relationships based on *compadrazgo* (co-parenthood) and on membership of a common religious congregation (Miller, 1967). An understanding of the system requires a detailed analysis of how these other types of relationships reinforce and maintain the social relations of production.

It is important to emphasize that the hacienda mode of production is not geared to subsistence production, for the *hacendado* is primarily interested in exporting produce to local or external markets. Hence, the city and the market feature as central points of orientation and the *hacendado* frequently has a part to play in the commerce and administration of the region (Montoya, 1970:19).

The hacienda mode of production is linked to other modes: there is a peasant family, sharecropping system within the hacienda which operates through the exchange of labour between kinsmen and neighbours, and the hacienda draws in other types of labour (of a wage and non-wage form) from nearby communities and settlements and employs its own cadre of administrators. In some areas of Peru haciendas are linked to nearby mining centres through the provision of food and labour for the mines and occasionally the *hacendado* is himself a mine owner (e.g. the livestock haciendas that were owned by the American Cerro de Pasco Mining Corporation). Also on the coast we find a tenant system combined with a capitalist mode of production: some cotton and sugar haciendas have both tenant-workers and an agricultural proletariat (Klaren, 1973:63–4; Miller, 1967:193). The latter work regularly for the hacienda on certain parts of the production process and run the factories where the product is processed. Each hacienda, then, represents a combination of social relations based on different modes of production.

If we were to extend this analysis to cover the other non-capitalist modes we would find a similarly complex pattern of relations, both with other modes and with various capitalist forms. For example, in peasant communities we normally encounter not only a mode of production based on the exploitation of communally-owned land but also a smallholder-private property system combined with different sharecropping arrangements, and a small but significant capitalist sector based on private ownership of the means of production, wage labour, and commercial agriculture. Furthermore, a careful study of production units would reveal that various types of exchanges occur between these systems (e.g. labour, capital, and technology transfers), and that, like the hacienda system, these relationships are further consolidated by various types of non-economic exchanges (e.g. participation in religious fiestas, political activities, and family and kinship relations).

The complexities involved in developing such an analysis can best be illustrated by considering the participation of particular household units in different modes of production. Thus, a peasant family owning a small plot of land might from time to time also supply labour to nearby haciendas or commercial farms; or, if it has the resources to do so, it might rent or sharecrop land owned by a neighbouring family. In addition, this same family might be linked to the mining sector through the labour of one of its members, or it might engage in some handicraft production of pottery or ponchos which it will sell or exchange in the local market. Hence, the existence of other modes of production (both capitalist and non-capitalist) affords the peasant family operating predominantly under a smallholder system the means by which it can acquire supplementary income or additional resources to cover various production and non-production expenditure. On the other hand, the *hacendado* or capitalist farmer also benefits from this arrangement for the continuance of a smallholder mode ensures that he can obtain a supply of temporary peasant labour when he needs it.

This suggests that the reproduction of the social relations of production for one mode (in this case a smallholder peasant system) is dependent on the continuity of other social relations of production found in other modes (i.e. the hacienda or capitalist systems). In the same way, smallholder family production found among tenants on the hacienda caters for the material means of peasant subsistence, whilst at the same time enabling the *hacendado* to extract surplus labour. Also the provision of a subsistence plot and other perquisite serves the important function of keeping the hacienda financially solvent and its system intact during periods when the market undergoes severe decline. Since the labour force is able to meet a substantial part of its own consumption requirements within the framework of the hacienda, it can maintain itself in a state of 'suspended animation until market trends are reversed' (Wolf and Mintz, 1957:390). A similar interpretation can be applied to the existence of commercial farms, based on a capitalist or semi-capitalist mode of production, alongside smallholder peasant agriculture. Peasants can supplement their income by becoming temporary wage labourers for the landowners of the district and may sometimes become bound to them through debt relations (i.e. they borrow money or acquire seeds, fertilizers, or equipment on credit). In addition to receiving money for their work, they frequently look towards these landowners for other favours (e.g. they may act as brokers for them in negotiations with government or help in the financing and organization of local fiestas). In return, the commercial farmer has a ready supply of labour when he needs it and a potential political following too.

Exchanges of this kind, which involve categories of individuals who depend primarily on different modes of production, seem especially characteristic and are more likely to persist in zones where agricultural production involves relatively low levels of capitalization combined with high production risks, as is the case with much of the Third World.

A consideration of modes of production also leads to an analysis of the ways in which different production systems are articulated with different types of local and regional markets. Here we need to distinguish between markets of the more traditional type (e.g. *ferias* of highland Peru), which predominantly cater for exchanges among peasant producers who bring their products to the market to sell or barter for other goods, and the distribution markets which buy up local produce for sale in the major urban centres. In other situations, certain types of produce are exported directly from the farms to the cities by middlemen and wholesale merchants, like those described by Forman and Riegelhaupt (1970) for North East Brazil. As yet, no detailed work has been done on regional marketing systems in Peru: the Chancay Valley study makes little mention of this and Castillo's study of Pisac in the southern highlands concentrates almost exclusively on the peasant marketing sector and says little about the activities of the large-scale merchants in the area (Castillo, 1970). However the work by Burgos (1970) on Ecuador, which includes a detailed discussion of marketing in one provincial area, is suggestive of the way in which market studies could be married to an analysis of different modes of production. He shows that there are differences in the control over market resources held by different participants and suggests that pricing mechanisms operate to perpetuate a pattern of structural dependency between peasant producers and market middlemen.

CONCLUSION

This chapter has dealt with two related approaches to the study of linkages between local rural structures and the wider socio-economic framework of Third World countries. A substantial part of the argument was devoted to a critical appraisal of the structural dependency models formulated by Frank and Cotler. Frank's approach was criticized for a number of reasons. It concentrates upon the penetration of the capitalist market economy and gives little attention to the ways in which different types of production systems, capitalist and non-capitalist, co-exist at local, regional, and national levels. It describes underdevelopment in terms of a pattern of metropolitan-satellite or vertical relations and neglects the importance of horizontal ties for sustaining dependency structures. The stress on colonialist or imperialist forces as the main sources for change tends to overlook the significance of internal social and cultural factors that interact with these to produce historically specific outcomes.

Although Cotler takes cognizance of forms of domination other than those associated with capitalism, he, too, emphasizes vertical relations and fails to comprehend the interconnections between different production systems. This is most strikingly demonstrated by Cotler's failure to take account of the ways in which tenant-workers on traditional haciendas develop relationships among themselves and with other non-resident peasant families for economic, social, and religious purposes. He also, of course, takes no note of the fact that haciendas normally draw upon other forms of labour from outside as well. The attempt to apply Cotler's two models to other settlement types in the Chancay Valley likewise falls down because it tends to treat these as separate organizational entities, when from the point of view of a mode of production analysis they are clearly interconnected. Each type contains a smallholder mode of production and this is variously linked to other modes through transfers of labour, capital, and technology. It is this set of relationships that characterizes the main features of the regional socio-economic structure. Cotler also stresses exogenous factors in his interpretation of structural change.

A somewhat different perspective is provided by the group of French Marxists who have re-kindled interest in the analysis of the articulation of different modes of production and of the processes by which specific types of production relations are reproduced. This approach is particularly valuable for comprehending the multi-structural nature of Third World economies, for non-capitalist modes often persist in the face of economic change and can be expected to do so in the foreseeable future. The usefulness of this type of analysis was briefly explored through an examination of the hacienda mode of production and its connections with other modes in highland Peru. I also indicated how one might apply a similar analysis to non-hacienda zones where there exist a multiplicity of modes based on capitalist, semi-capitalist, and non-capitalist production relations.

A third type of analysis, which could usefully be combined with a structural study of modes of production, is that represented by anthropological studies of rural entrepreneurs and economic brokers. The main focus of this research is to identify the social characteristics of, and strategies adopted by, individuals and social categories who play a major part in interconnecting local production systems with the wider socio-economic structure, and who control the crucial sets of relationships involved. Whilst a mode of production analysis explains how certain social relations of production function for the extraction of economic surplus, the study of brokers analyzes how particular individuals acquire positions of economic power and attempt to maintain their pre-eminence. It also shows how sets of relations deriving from different modes of production and from different institutional contexts can be combined for entrepreneurial profit. These, and other themes relating to the study of entrepreneurship, are taken up in the following chapter.

CHAPTER 5

Differential Responses to Change: The Analysis of Entrepreneurship

Sociological studies of entrepreneurship[1] tend to focus upon two related themes. The first concerns the attempt to isolate those values and attitudes which act as incentives for entrepreneurial behaviour. This approach, as I have already shown, draws extensively upon Webber's discussion of the relationship between ideological commitment and economic innovation.[2] The second theme examines the question of social recruitment. Here the emphasis is on the analysis of the social background of entrepreneurs in an attempt to locate them in some definable stratum of society. Hence, some writers have argued that entrepreneurs come from social strata that are in some sense 'marginal' to the established order of society and that they attempt to compensate for the disabilities they suffer in various social contexts by applying themselves more vigorously and systematically to economic matters.[3]

Yet, despite the enormous amount of literature devoted to these themes, analysis has not led to the formulation of sound propositions of a general nature. All grand theoretical syntheses, it seems, have failed, as counter evidence can always be adduced (Gerschenkron, 1962). In order then to get out of this impasse we need to move the analysis to a different level. We must ask why it is that, in particular development situations, persons possessing certain social and ideological characteristics are apparently more strategically placed for successfully engaging in new forms of economic activity. We need to define more precisely the types of entrepreneurship we are dealing with, and we need a model that attempts to look closely at the mobilization and organization of resources. Such an approach should enable us to explore the relationship between social attributes (e.g. minority group or ethnic status, or age and sex etc.) and ideological commitment (e.g. membership of ascetic religious sects or of a political elite) and ask how these give differential advantage in the organization and development of enterprises.

Two recent attempts to develop such an analytical perspective are the transactional approach developed by Barth (1963; 1967), which concentrates upon identifying the types of exchanges that occur between the entrepreneur and his social environment; and the decision-making approach (see Ortiz, 1973; Moerman, 1968; Long 1970a), which analyzes the process by which entrepreneurs and others make, or are constrained to make, certain decisions relating, for example, to the mobilization of resources and to questions concerning investment and market strategy. The overall analytical objectives of both these approaches is to show how various restrictions and incentives, both instrumental and moral, operate to affect economic behaviour and performance and to show why it is that particular individuals or social categories may come to monopolize entrepreneurial positions.

However before discussing these models and their empirical applications, I wish to look briefly at the contribution made by economists to the study of entrepreneurship and to enquire how far their formulations are helpful in understanding the social factors involved.

ECONOMIC AND BEHAVIOURAL THEORIES OF THE FIRM

Work by economists falls into two categories. First, there are macro-economic studies, which provide important data concerning the economic parameters within which certain types of entrepreneurs operate. Some economists, for example, have attempted to isolate the variables in the economic structure that shape the demand for entrepreneurial activity and have also examined a variety of factors (economic and non-economic) that affect the supply of entrepreneurs. Thus it has been suggested that differences in per capita income levels and expectational variations regarding growth rates are all functionally related to the supply of entrepreneurship. Others have specified the economic conditions conducive to the emergence of new forms of entrepreneurship and have examined the economic effects of technological change, the emergence of potential external markets, and the feedback effect which expansion of the external sector has on domestic markets. Macro-economic data of these kind are important for determining the opportunity structure under which entrepreneurs operate.

A second contribution is that of micro-economic analysis; and an important area of research in this field is the economic theory of the firm. This, in effect, is a theory of entrepreneurial behaviour with respect to prices and quantities that is concerned more with the operation of the market than with the actual decision-making of the entrepreneurs themselves. Hence, it is a theory of markets explaining at a general level the way in which resources are allocated by a price system; it does not deal or claim to deal with the internal allocation of resources, with the mobilization process, or with decision-making as such. A great deal of criticism has been made of this theory, but, as Cyert and March (1963) point out, the controversy is based upon a misunderstanding of the types of questions the conventional theory was meant to answer.

A more useful approach is that of the 'behavioural theory of the firm' which was developed explicitly for understanding the organizational decision-making of enterprises (Cyert and March, 1963). It is particularly interesting in that it makes a number of assumptions which connect up with the sorts that sociologists and anthropologists might make. It assumes, first, that a firm consti- tutes a coalition of individuals whose interests from time to time conflict. The goals of the enterprise are established by a bargaining process and will change over time and consist of multiple rather than single objectives. Thus, unlike the traditional theory of the firm, it does not assume that profit maximization or some such objective is the primary goal. The model deals with the various major goals of the firm, such as production, inventory, sales, market share, and profit; and could be extended to cover social and political ends as well. The second assumption is that the selection of a satisfactory alternative in a decision-making context in- volves a number of components, the most central of which is the search for information that arises in response to a particular problem. Search activity occurs when existing decisions are no longer considered satisfactory and when information is needed to define a new range of possibilities. A corollary of this is that alternatives are examined sequentially and that the first available satisfactory solution is adopted. A third assumption is that the business firm is an adaptive organism which essentially reacts to, rather than forecasts, changing circumstances. It attempts to avoid uncertainties rather than to predict them. It does this in two ways. It tries to reach agreements with market competitors and negotiates within the internal organization with the different participants in order to establish routine procedures and general policy commitments. The final assumption is that rules of thumb and standard ways of organizing things are evolved to ensure the smooth operation of the business. These practices will change over time but will be relied upon in decision-making situations involving short-run problems.

Although the behavioural theory of the firm was developed for the study of large-scale modern business enterprises, it raises questions of general relevance for the understanding of entrepreneurial activity at whatever scale. Its emphasis on bargaining, on information, on standard operating procedures, and on the need to develop policy commitments all seem directly pertinent to the analysis of entrepreneurial decision-making, whether this be among peasant entrepreneurs, small industrialists, or large-scale business magnates.

The work of Cyert and March suggests that in order to analyze entrepreneurial activity we need to develop four kinds of models:

(i) A model that identifies the types of transactions that occur between the entrepreneur and his social environment, but that relates this to the structure of socio-economic opportunities and existing systems of exchange.

(ii) A model that depicts the types of information sources used by entrepreneurs for gathering information essential for the running of their enterprises and that characterizes the types of feedback necessary to maintain relevant contact.

(iii) A model that focuses upon entrepreneurial decision-making as it relates to specific types of decisions (e.g. concerning the mobilization of resources, investment, and market strategies). Cyert and March argue that modern business firms seek to avoid uncertainty in decisions not by forecasting the environment but by concentrating on solving pressing problems on a short-term basis and by negotiating with both their competitors and employees in order to establish recognized conventions and forms of behaviour. In the same way it would be possible to explore the ways in which small-scale entrepreneurs also try to avoid uncertainty and how this affects their decision-making behaviour.

(iv) A model that characterizes the internal organization of enterprises in terms of the types of social relations and bargaining processes that occur among members and that predicts the structural consequences of different modes of organization.

Though focusing on different dimensions, taken together, these models represent parts of an analysis seeking to explain variations in the behaviour and success of entrepreneurs. The rest of this chapter concentrates upon exploring these various dimensions in relation to anthropological studies of rural entrepreneurs.

The Transactional Approach

This approach starts by mapping out the structure of socio-economic opportunities and systems of exchange and then aims to identify the types of transactions associated with entrepreneurs as compared with the rest of the population. The study of exchange processes is, of course, not a new concern in social anthropology, but goes back to the work of Malinowski (1922) and others (Mauss, 1925; Polanyi, Arensberg, and Pearson, 1957; Belshaw, 1965) who were interested in analyzing the ways in which different goods and valuables are exchanged in both primitive and peasant societies.

Whilst recognizing the dispute between theorists who give a different analytical weighting to the exchange and production elements of an economy (for details, see Godelier, 1972; and Prattis, 1973; and Cook, 1975), we must nonetheless acknowledge the important work done on describing the different spheres of exchange that operate. For example, Bohannan (1955) found in his study of the Tiv economy that some valuables circulated in one sphere and others in another. Sanctions operated against the exchange of valuables belonging to the different spheres except through special institutional means. He used the term 'conveyance' for exchange taking place within one sphere and 'conversion' for exchange of goods belonging to different spheres. Hence, the channels of conversion indicate the points at which spheres meet. Utilizing this concept of economic spheres, Bohannan distinguishes between 'multicentric' systems, where there exist several distinct barriers to the conversion of goods between spheres, and 'unicentric' systems, where there are very few such barriers. While the traditional Tiv economy and most non-monetary systems are clearly multicentric in character, our own economy, a money economy, is unicentric. A multicentric economy is, according to him, one in which society's exchangeable goods fall into two or more mutually exclusive spheres each marked by different institutionalization and different moral values (Bohannan, 1959). We usually find a distinction between the subsistence and the prestige spheres. These spheres are separated and there exist barriers of value which prevent the exchange of goods from one sphere into the other except in times of extremity. Closer examination of the Tiv traditional system shows that there were in fact three spheres: the subsistence sphere where the exchange of gifts and of agricultural and craft products was characterized by a fair degree of bargaining and haggling; the prestige sphere, which was in no way associated with markets, consisted of the exchange of slaves, cattle, houses, ritual offices, white cloth, medicine or magic, and prestigious brass rods, but where there were no prices, only rough equivalences; and the third sphere which was made up of exchangeable values concerned with rights in human beings other than slaves, especially dependent children and women. Bohannan shows how exchanges within these spheres operated independently and only under exceptional circumstances was there any transfer from one to the other.

The analysis of spheres of exchange has been further developed by Barth, who relates it to the study of the commercialization of local economies. He argues that

'a separation of spheres based on the criterion of exchangeability alone gives an unnecessarily inadequate representation of the structure of the economy. The concept of spheres has much greater analytic utility if it relates to all forms of circulation and transformation of value, whether by exchange, production, inheritance, or other means.' (Barth, 1967:157)

By transformation of value he means both conveyance and conversion of material goods as well as activities or whatever people consider of value. The analysis of the flow of value in an economy requires a description of all possible strategies an actor may adopt when he wants to gain something out of his assets, whether these are of material or non-material kind. Barth illustrates this point by reference to economic spheres among Fur-speaking hoe agriculturalists in south-western Sudan. His analysis depicts all the standard choices of alternative allocation of resources open to the units of management in this particular economy, and delimits the types of spheres that exist with respect to the total circulation and flow of value. As he sees it, the units of management (which in this case constitute individual adults) are faced with the basic problem of transforming their efforts into a range of items that satisfy their consumption needs. Yet, unlike Bohannan who stresses barriers between spheres, Barth focuses on the possibilities for breakthrough. This, he claims, is crucial for understanding entrepreneurial activity for it is the entrepreneur who discovers new channels for conversion and who breaks through between spheres. Hence, the entrepreneur is someone who recognizes the discrepancies of evaluation that exist in a situation and who constructs 'bridging transactions' so that he might exploit them.

The analytical points Barth is making become clearer if we look at the example given. The Fur economy contains within it three basic circles of flow which can produce, what he calls, spirals of growth. The first takes the form of converting labour into cash crops which provide capital for the acquisition of more wives who in return bring with them into the marriage yet more labour (Labour-Cash-crops-Cash-Wives-Labour). The transactions, however, provide no opportunities for cumulative increases in assets.

In the first place, the total process is controlled by the availability of marriageable women, by their acceptance of the marriage offer, and ultimately by the Koranic limit of being allowed only four wives. Second, the labour obtained from the wife is not of the same kind as that needed for cash cropping, since she can provide female services only and is herself an independent cultivator growing cash crops. Only infrequently, therefore, do spouses help one another in cash-crop production, and only then on a strictly reciprocal basis. Plural marriages also deplete a man's savings, for they incur an increase in cash expenditure without providing any immediate additional labour for cash-crop production.

The second circle consists of converting cash into cattle and then later selling them for cash again (Cash-Cattle-Cash). Providing there is sufficient juvenile labour for herding, this is a genuine circle for investment. The main limitation is the supply of cattle by the Baggara Arabs who live in the plains. The Fur buy the cattle when they are young heifers and rear them for resale. But the trading of cattle by the Arabs is somewhat erratic and the markets unreliable.

The third and best circle is that which involves the use of labour for the production of millet, which is then brewed into beer and used to recruit labour for millet production (Labour-Millet-Beer-Labour). A central problem with this type of arrangement is the tendency for the large work parties to degenerate into huge beer drinking sessions. Nevertheless, it does offer some possibilities for a spiral of growth to develop, although this is clearly limited by the amount of millet that can be consumed. Furthermore, social convention normally rules out the use of labour obtained in this way for work on cash-crop production.

On the basis of this analysis, Barth distinguishes four main spheres of exchange. First, we have the sphere involved with the production of millet for subsistence; second, the sphere associated with the circulation of cash and cash goods; and third, that concerned with items of rank and prestige which in fact have no direct feedback into the economic system. It is into this latter sphere that one can place the pilgrimages undertaken to Mecca to acquire Hadji status. The fourth and last sphere is that concerned with the circulation of wives. This allows for conversions into the sphere of kinship and affinal relations, though, as we suggested, it has very limited feedback on the labour side of the economy. The total system is characterized by the existence of barriers to ready transformation between these separate spheres. Thus, for example, cash can be converted into a ticket to Mecca but this of course can never be reconverted into cash. The barriers that prevent or restrict flow between spheres are made up of a variety of factors, only some of which are of a morally or socially sanctioned nature. From the point of view of the individual member of the society, the main management problem he faces is that of allocating labour wisely between the two main production spheres – the subsistence and cash crop.

The barriers that separate the different spheres and limit the amount of flow between them allow for considerable discrepancies of evaluation to persist as between items in different spheres. These discrepancies are exposed once the barriers break down and new patterns of circulation made possible. This forces people into revising their former evaluations. Barth illustrates how discrepancies occur by taking the case of the difference between the subsistence and the cash spheres. By constructing a common denominator, namely the market price for millet, he shows how there is a basic discrepancy between the values placed on beer plus labour and those placed on money. Calculating the amount of millet used to brew for the organizing of a work party, he shows that when working for beer, one man-day is equivalent roughly to twopence worth of millet, whereas working for a wage for the Forestry Department is equivalent to a rate of twelve times as much. Yet despite this major difference in value the Forestry Department, in fact, found it difficult to recruit labour.[4]

According to Barth, the discrepancy that exists between these two spheres has in recent years provided an opportunity for entrepreneurs to initiate new and profitable transactions. He gives the example of an Arab merchant, well acquainted with the mountain zone, who decided to spend the wet season in a village and who obtained a plot of land to cultivate tomatoes. He then purchased millet in the lowlands at a low price and transported it to the village where his wife made it into beer. The beer was used to recruit work parties for tomato production, rather than for millet as is customary. The tomatoes were dried and sold in a lowland market at the end of the rainy season. Barth calculated that for an initial investment of £5 worth of millet the merchant received a return of more than £100. This man had broken through an established barrier to conversion and now had additional capital for investment, which he could of course re-invest in the same fashion in the ensuing years. This strategy was copied by several merchants and local villagers in the succeeding years, with results that were, according to Barth, 'nearly as spectacular' (Barth, 1967; 172).[5]

Barth's analysis of the Darfur economy and flow system is essentially a descriptive model which maps out the choices available in a particular economic and cultural terrain. The lines joining the different features of the landscape represent established or customary paths or modes of acquiring goods and services by exchange or production. Hence, it depicts the general framework of socio-economic opportunities and does not focus upon an analysis of the decision-making of specific individuals or categories of individual. One should not be misled, therefore, into thinking that the model really has anything much to say about how individual allocative decisions are made, and their consequences. It is by and large a descriptive account of the overall socio-cultural constraints operating on exchange processes. As such, it is important for locating the points of possible entrepreneurship, for it suggests where new channels of conversion are likely to occur and isolates the process by which capital accumulation and expansion takes place. However, it tends to see the basic framework as largely one determined by social and cultural rules. It does not, for example, consider other constraints such as the structure of interpersonal relationships (or networks) in which the entrepreneur or potential entrepreneur is embedded. Nor does it take account of the effect of antecedent decisions on current decision-making, or the question of the levels of information available concerning alternatives and outcomes.

Nevertheless, despite the shortcomings of the model, it is useful for exploring the flow systems associated with different social and cultural arrangements, and for identifying the potentialities of growth for different types of structures. It can also be used to examine the differential responses to economic change shown by different social categories or sub-groups. Thus, by comparing the flow systems of sub-groups in a population, we may comprehend what it is that gives opportunities for entrepreneurship and growth; and we may enquire why it is that certain categories of individuals are able to effect transactions which others cannot or will not make. It is to this problem that Klausen (1968) addresses himself in his book on Kerala fishermen of South India.

Spheres of Exchange in South India

Klausen documents the different reactions to a development project organized under an agreement between the Indian and Norwegian Governments. This project followed the Community Development approach characteristic of Indian planning in the 1950s by attempting to initiate simultaneous change in the fields of economic activity, health and sanitation, and community services. In the first place, fishing techniques and productivity were to be improved by the introduction of new mechanically operated boats and new types of nets, and the building of an ice factory was planned for cold storage of fish together with new methods of fish processing and distribution. Capital was provided in the form of subsidies and loans, and training courses were to be established for the teaching of new skills such as the operation of motor boats. Technological improvement was accompanied by the introduction of new forms of organization. For example, attempts were made to re-structure the existing village co-operatives in order to develop

new marketing co-operatives to replace the many private merchants and middlemen in the area. On the health side, the plan was
to build more latrines, improve water-supplies, build new clinics
and to give more attention to infant care and hygiene, and generally
to improve the medical treatment in the region. The building
programme involved the establishment of an ice plant, a new
boat building yard, a factory for the production of water pipes,
and the construction of health centres and administrative offices.
An important side-effect of the project was an increase in
employment opportunities both on the project itself and as
servants for project personnel.

Like most programmes of this kind, the initial assumption was
that the benefits would be equally available to all members of the
population. However, from an early stage it was noticed that there
was in fact a marked difference in response between two fishing
communities in the zone – the Latin Catholics, who were
descended from the original converts to Christianity made by
Vasco da Gama in the fifteenth century, and the Arayas, a Hindu
group of low caste. Whilst in relation to such matters as health,
construction, and administrative activity their reactions were more
or less equivalent, there was a noticeable difference when it came
to new fishing techniques. The Catholics responded fairly enthu-
siastically to the fishing technology but inadequately to the new
system of distribution, whereas the Arayas showed little interest in
either.

Klausen attempts to explain this difference using Barth's model
of value transformation. Analysis of the Catholic flow system
shows its potential for growth, even before the arrival of the
Norwegian experts and the development project. The system has
no clear cut barriers; there are several strategies producing capital
accumulation, and also possibilities of social mobility both inside
and outside the local community. On the other hand, the Araya
system contains one very strong barrier to conversion (i.e. the line
of pollution) which makes it impossible to convert money or other
assets into higher rank or status within the caste system itself. This
basic difference correlates with other differences. The Catholics
constitute a minority in the society and have developed a
relatively high degree of self-sufficiency with regard to social and
occupational roles. They do not accept the ranking system of
Hindus and have developed their own, based on such criteria as

wealth and education, that allows for some upward mobility. They possess more initial capital for investment, have higher educational levels, and maintain social networks that are geographically more widespread and open. Their local political organizations are more effective and, as fishermen, they practise an occupation which is not stigmatized as in the Hindu system. And finally, the geographical location of their villages is more favourable for the exploitation of fishing grounds.

There are two important contrasts. First, the Catholic system is one where money is highly convertible, and can be invested in numerous ways. It can be used for the purchase of new equipment and for acquiring labour for production, or for gaining access to land or other resources. It can be used for educational purposes, for the provision of a dowry for marriage, for investment in gold and jewellery, for political ends, for financing of religious festivals, and also as a way of moving out of fish production into marketing. The system is unicentric with few barriers to conversion. Some kinds of prestige items may not have immediate effects on growth, in that one may not be able to convert them immediately back into productive resources, but it may be possible to convert them into other kinds of prestige which can later be turned to good entrepreneurial advantage. For example, through education or marriage into a higher status family or through demonstrating one's willingness in sponsoring religious ceremonies, one might acquire increased social esteem. This in turn may give strategic control over resources useful for development, or increase one's chances of acquiring government loans.

The Araya system, on the other hand, is essentially multicentric in that the channels for conversion are fewer and major barriers exist. There is no opportunity of improving one's position within the ranking system through greater occupational activity. Money may be converted into education but this generally leads to a movement out of the local caste structure. Also investments in gold and jewellery for marriage purposes do not increase social status, since marriage is prohibited outside the caste group; and investment in religious ceremonies likewise has little effect upon one's status position. While sanskritization of the caste as a group remains a possibility, the literature suggests that only among middle-ranking castes is this successful (Srinivas, 1969).

The second aspect of importance is the existence of institutional mechanisms for accumulating capital. The Catholic group is remarkable for having a number of savings clubs that operate to mobilize cash when needed. These are of two types: the ordinary *chittie*, whereby a number of persons agree to save a fixed amount each month and draw lots to decide who in turn is to dispose of the monthly sum. This provides a way of securing a large loan free of interest. The second type is the 'auction' *chittie*. The agreement here is that there should be a monthly stake for a fixed period. The *chittie* is administered by a chairman, who himself receives a percentage of the takings and who must be in a position to stand bail for any of the guarantees, either in cash or land. Participants do not draw lots for the monthly capital but let it go for auction to the highest bidder. This may mean that a man pays in more than he draws out, but it has the advantage of his being able to draw upon future savings. In addition to these *chitties*, people can secure loans through private fishmongers or well-to-do people, but in this case the interest is high (around 25 per cent). The existence of these savings clubs among the Latin Catholics places them in a good position to mobilize capital for investment in the new technology. And this gives them an edge over the Arayas who do not possess such institutions.

Differences in the systems of value transformation and institutions for mobilizing capital explain the different reactions of the Catholics and Arayas to the new methods of fishing. The introduction of new boats and nets requires greater working capital for oil, petrol, spare parts, and repairs. These new demands are met along already established lines of conversion among the Catholics, whereas for the Arayas the possibilities are much more limited.

The generally negative response shown by both groups to changes in the distribution sector, however, has to take account of other factors. An important economic conversion for Catholics is that associated with the change from being a fisherman to becoming a fish merchant; and even those who remain as fishermen regard the merchant as a valuable source of credit. The establishment of a marketing co-operative, therefore, was perceived as a threat to their economic positions and mobility, and seemed unlikely in the short run to replace the important credit role played by the fish merchants themselves. It was for this reason that little enthusiasm for the idea was evinced by the Catholics. On the other hand, the Arayas who might have been expected to take active control of the co-operative, did not do so. This, it seems, was due to their lack of organizational and administrative experience and because of their strong commitment to their traditional type of occupation. Furthermore, if the Arayas had controlled the co-operative, then this would have further exacerbated the social divisions existing in the area, something which the development agents themselves were keen on eliminating.

The theoretical inadequacies of the model. Klausen (1968:28–30) traces his theoretical pedigree back to Barth (1967) and Homans (1961) who see society as made up of a complex set of exchange processes and who concentrate on maximization and .choice-making as central dimensions of social behaviour. Yet Klausen's final formulation hardly draws upon these ideas and turns out to be little more than a statement of the types of social exchanges sanctioned by Latin Catholics as against the Arayas. Hence, like Barth's paper on the Darfur, it presents an exposition of the value and institutional frameworks for the two groups. The analysis suggests that the Catholic framework has built into it more possibilities for increasing one's own productive resources and for social mobility. It is for this reason that the Latin Catholics are in a more favourable position for exploiting the new economic opportunities.

Klausen's analysis, however, fails to substantiate the quantitative differences between the two groups. He writes of more capital and land being avaliable to Catholics and of the greater opportunities that they have for wage employment because of their higher educational levels, but he nowhere provides a detailed breakdown to indicate the extent of these differences.[6] In addition, he documents the types of conversions that are used by both groups but gives no indication of the frequency with which the different types are used, nor of the specific problems they are designed to solve. The end result is a description in very general terms of the differential advantages of Catholics as against Hindus.

The major theoretical limitation of the study is that there appears to be no necessary connection between his transactional model and the assumptions concerning maximization and choice making associated with exchange theory to which he refers. A further difficulty is that Klausen does not explore how these value transformations and institutional structures actually affect the process by which individuals or entrepreneurs invest and make economically viable decisions. His analysis, in fact, does not enable us to understand the process by which particular enterprises are initiated and developed. Yet it is only through an analysis of this kind that one can appreciate how certain types of relationships and values become relevant to specific forms of economic activity, and to different phases in the development of a business or household. For example, capital, which may be crucial in the initial stages of an enterprise may, at another point in time, be less significant than, for example, the need to develop dependable external relationships based on political or religious connections. Indeed, it may be necessary for certain types of entrepreneurs to forego their immediate economic interests in order to consolidate a set of social and political relationships. Klausen may talk of strategies and make use of the maximization principle but such discussion is empty unless these concepts can be related to the analysis of specific types of decisions. While Barth gives some clue as to how one might develop such an analysis through isolating the points at which entrepreneurs discover new channels for conversion, Klausen merely uses the idea of a flow diagram to depict the general institutional pattern of exchanges. He is not interested in analyzing particular sets of transactions seen in relation to different categories of individuals or different social contexts. Hence, his analysis inevitably takes a somewhat static view of the situation and, at times, seems little more than a cultural obstacles theory of change.

Transactions, Networks, and Brokers

The foregoing discussion illustrates how the study of exchange systems might contribute to an understanding of entrepreneurship. However, as I have already argued, such analysis falls short if it does not document the specific types of transactions and relationships developed by entrepreneurs as compared with other social categories. This problem requires the adoption of an interactionist or actor-oriented perspective.[7]

The interactionist approach views social relationships primarily as the outcome of face-to-face interaction between particular individuals who are engaged in a series of transactions that evolve over time. It contrasts with the view that behaviour is basically rule-governed and the result of various internalized social conventions, norms, and values. While the interactionist may take account of institutional frameworks, his main concern is with the transactional content of interpersonal relationships and with analyzing the process by which the parties involved negotiate the 'terms of trade' and attempt to maximize their interests. As Blau (1968: 454) puts it,

> 'Typically, social exchange relations evolve in a slow process starting with minor transactions in which little trust is required because little risk is involved and in which both partners can prove their trustworthiness, enabling them to expand their relation and engage in major transactions.'

Barth's *Models of Social Organization* (1966) provides an example of interactional analysis. In it, he tries to develop a model that focuses upon the consequences of reciprocal prestations between individuals occupying a set of related status positions. The transactions are viewed as taking place within a framework of established rights and obligations which the participants gradually redefine in significant ways. He illustrates his analysis by reference to the crew of a Norwegian herring boat where the maritime convention prohibiting crew members from occupying the bridge is relaxed by the skipper. The main line of argument examines the goals of the captain and how these affected his exercise of authority. Barth shows that the skipper was primarily concerned to maximize the catch of fish but that this could only be achieved by efficient co-operation on the part of the crew. A poor performance by any one of them in his job could cost the whole crew and the captain a good catch. However, the crewmen were increasingly unprepared to accept the customary status and power differential between themselves and the captain, and so the skipper, not wishing to jeopardize the returns on fishing, entered into a series of transactions which led eventually to a redefinition of their relative statuses and expectations. Thus the crew were allowed privileges that, in fact, violated the maritime code, in return for their efficient performance of necessary tasks.

This short example emphasizes the need to examine leadership from the point of view of the management of interpersonal relationships. It also suggests that one should consider the total configuration of personal ties impinging upon the leader or entrepreneur, since personal networks of this kind affect decision-making and possibly the viability of the enterprise itself. The study of transactions and exchange relationships leads, then, into an analysis of the structure and content of social networks (Kapferer, 1972; Boissevain, 1974).

Network studies concentrate on characterizing the linkages existing between a specified set of individuals, and the resultant network is described in terms of various morphological properties and interactional criteria.[8] As yet, there has been little systematic application of network analysis to the study of entrepreneurship, though several studies have indicated the importance of network factors. Geertz (1963), for instance, in his study of Indonesian entrepreneurs, draws attention to the functional significance of extra-local networks for both Moslem reformists and Hindu aristocrats; and the same point has been made by Cohen (1969) in his study of Hausa entrepreneurs, by Mines (1972) for Moslem merchants in South India, and by Long (1968) for Jehovah's Witness farmers and shopkeepers in Zambia.

It would seem important, therefore, to move beyond the Barthian description of channels of conversion and of institutionalized spirals of growth to consider the various sets of interpersonal relationships utilized by the entrepreneur in the running of his enterprise. This requires looking at both the transactions that occur within the internal organizational framework of the business (i.e. at the evolving patterns of authority, division of labour, and use of resources) and also at the relationships that the entrepreneur operates in the wider arena for obtaining information and for maintaining ties with market traders, business associates, or political allies. This should enable us to understand more fully the ways in which involvement in certain types of social networks influences entrepreneurial decision-making and performance. It would also be useful to compare the networks of entrepreneurs occupying different occupational niches (e.g. in commerce, industry, and agriculture).

A related issue concerns whether or not particular entrepreneurial roles are combined with brokerage functions. The study of economic brokers aims to identify the groups and individuals that control the crucial sets of relationships linking the local economy with the wider regional and national structure. Through this we may gain insight into the mechanisms by which economic surplus is extracted and invested in production and non-production activities, and some indication as to whether it is invested locally or elsewhere. It also enables us to describe the social characteristics of economic brokers. For example, whether they are 'local' or 'cosmopolitan' entrepreneurs (Paine, 1963; Long, 1972), whether they run multiple enterprises and invest in agricultural production, the extent of their urban experience and contacts, and whether they hold local or extra-local political office. A further aspect concerns the networks of social relationships used by them to consolidate their positions. Studies by Wolf (1956), Geertz (1963), Long (1968), Cohen (1969), Parkin (1972), and others, have shown, for example, how in differing contexts relationships based on kinship, tribal affiliation, common religious bonds, *compadrazgo* (co-parenthood), and patron–client relations are utilized to secure entrepreneurial advantage. While most of this research is concerned with processes at the local-community level, some anthropologists have begun studying brokers at the national and international levels. For example, Gonzalez (1972) has produced a fascinating account of the transactions which occurred between members of an industrial elite in the Dominican Republic and USAID officials over the provision of development aid.

A main task for analysis, then, is to isolate the networks of relationships used by entrepreneurs and brokers in the operation of their businesses. It is also necessary to relate this to the social and economic characteristics of the local and external situations within which they function, and to the range and types of resources available to them. But the study of such aspects is complex because it often requires an appreciation of how particular individuals operate in several and often geographically distant localities. It also requires close attention to the ways in which brokers may control important communication channels and access to centres of power and influence.[9]

Some examples from Highland Peru. These themes can be illustrated by reference to recent studies of marketing and transportation entrepreneurs in Highland Peru (Long, 1972, 1973). A major finding of this research is that network structure (i.e. geographical and social span) and content (i.e. the types of transactions effected between members) vary according to occupational requirements and are also affected by the type and level of resources available to the entrepreneurs in question.

In the remoter regions of Peru where the *hacienda* system predominates, we find a pattern of centralization whereby the major landowners control marketing and transportation, play an important role in the commerce of the region, and often hold major administrative and political offices. Only with major structural change, like the implementation of land reform or the emergence of cash-cropping among smallholder peasants, do we find a shift in this pattern of control. Hence, the development of coffee production among hacienda tenants in La Convención Valley led to the appearance of a multiplicity of middlemen who competed effectively with the *hacendados* for control of the marketing system (Craig, 1968).

Because of their control over land and various socio-political institutions *hacendados* are normally well placed for the extraction of labour and products from the peasantry and frequently derive substantial profits from it. They are linked to production through landownership and patronage and, at the same time, form part of a regional elite that is interconnected through a web of ties based on kinship, affinity, and common economic and political interests. Thus the *hacendado*-trader will utilize his various ties to the peasantry and bring together sets of relations deriving from the different systems of production characteristic of the area: in this way he will satisfy his own labour needs and also build up a clientele for marketing. In addition, he is favourably placed for negotiating with town merchants and probably already has close personal ties with them.

There will of course be variations in the degree of success achieved by particular *hacendados* and this may be explained in terms of the availability and utilization of material and social resources. The *hacendado*'s involvement in local production systems works to his advantage in that this keeps him in touch with, and enables him to understand the complexities of, various cropping systems and his contacts in town provide him with up-to-date information on price fluctuations for particular crops in the regional and national markets. In contrast, peasant producers who market their own produce directly to local markets are disadvantaged by their poor control over Spanish (the language of commerce) and by their lack of information on market conditions.

In other areas where there is a more developed economy and few haciendas, the pattern appears to be much more complex. Here we often find a multiplicity of economic brokers specializing in the marketing and transportation of different products and operating at different economic scales. In this context it becomes important to distinguish between different brokerage roles, between, for example, the large-scale agricultural middlemen, the livestock trader, the timber merchant, the middlemen dealing in craft goods, and the transporter. Each of these occupational types will require slightly different kinds of local and external networks for the operation of their businesses. There will also be differences in the extent to which they are involved and invest in local production systems. In some situations, like the Chancay Valley on the coast (Matos Mar *et al.*, 1969), we find a group of agricultural entrepreneurs who control reasonably large tracts of land and produce crops. These individuals are frequently closely connected to the local peasant population through kinship, affinity, and friendship ties, and they often use these relationships in the running of their enterprises. The main problem confronting them is that of weighing up the various rewards and costs associated with the utilization of these interpersonal ties so that they might achieve a satisfactory level of economic return. Naturally some entrepreneurs are more skilled in manipulating these ties than others. My own work in the central highlands of Peru has shown (Long, 1972, 1973), for example, how some of them use kinship relationships to recruit workers and clients, but have adopted various devices for re-defining these relationships so that some of the uncertainties and inherent difficulties associated with the bilateral kinship system might be avoided. Thus, whilst paying lip service to kinship sentiments and obligations, they may re-cast them by reference to notions of *compadrazgo* or patronage and in this way are able to exploit them more effectively. Indeed, if we look closely at this type of entrepreneur we find that he presents a striking contrast to the stereotype of the capitalist entrepreneur, for, like the *hacendado*, he is able to combine different types of social relations deriving from various modes of production and various institutional contexts. This enables him to build up a widespread network of ties which become functional for mobilizing labour and other resources for production and for the buying and selling of produce. It is this bringing together of diverse elements which sets him apart from the more capitalistically orientated entrepreneur. How successful he is in doing so depends partly, of course, on the level of resources available to him and how much competition there is.

Some of these entrepreneurs have to devote a considerable amount of time to building up contacts in external markets and this can sometimes cut into the time available for their other commitments. This may account for the fact that there is a tendency in these situations for intermediaries to specialize in the marketing of particular products and in the use of certain markets. Several studies suggest that a common mechanism used by middlemen for establishing external ties is to invite persons to become godparents to their children: this establishes a *compadrazgo* (co-parenthood) relationship between the parties concerned and is said to generate a higher degree of trust (*confianza*). On the other hand, the rurally-based entrepreneur may be fortunate in that some of the town merchants or traders may come from the same village or district as himself and thus are his *paisanos* (fellow villagers). An example of this occurred in the village of Matahuasi of central Peru (Long, 1972). This village has, since the opening of the Cerro de Pasco mines, been a major exporter of labour and produce to mining centres and to Lima the capital. As a result of migration, there now exist in several highland and coastal towns and cities groups of migrants from the village who retain contact with their home community and who have organized clubs in the urban areas to bring together persons of the same rural origin (Long, 1973; Mangin, 1959; and Doughty, 1970 for details on the functions and composition of such associations). Several of these Matahuasinos occupy important positions in city commerce, own shops, or work in the wholesale markets as traders. Others are professionals working for mine administration or for government departments. The presence of such persons has had a feedback effect on the development of commerce in the home community and agricultural entrepreneurs and market traders from the village have been able to use these relationships to set up contacts in the urban markets. A frequent pattern is for initial ties to be established by investing in kinship and friendship networks in the village and then to use these to generate connections with more distant kin (genealogically and geographically speaking). This provides a good example of a group of rurally-based traders who avoid some of the difficulties of operating through 'strangers' in the urban markets and competing with other traders from other regions: they do this by seeking out their compatriots so that the latter might develop a regular set of contacts and trustworthy business partners. Such an arrangement is of mutual advantage to both parties involved for several of the urban-based entrepreneurs have an interest in maintaining their links back at home and will from time to time use their trading partners to determine where they might best invest some of their profits.

In contrast to agricultural middlemen, timber merchants have direct contact with officials at the mines where they sell the eucalyptus timber which they have cut for use as pit props. In the Matahuasi case we find that several of these merchants had spent a number of years previously working at the mining centres and have close *compadrazgo* relationships with key officials in the administration. These officials are of crucial importance for negotiating contracts for the supply and transportation of timber and they are invited to attend fiestas in Matahuasi when the occasion arises. At the rural end, the timber merchants generally maintain a broadly-based clientele made up of both large-scale commercial farmers and smallholder peasants. Since most agricultural holdings grow eucalyptus trees around the gardens (however small they may be), timber operators must try as far as possible to extend their relationships and contacts to cover a wide spectrum of the farming population so that they might learn when and where trees are available for sale. This seems to require the working of a large geographical zone and regular visiting of farms in the area. In addition, since many peasants decide to sell their trees only when confronted with a sudden financial crisis, perhaps occasioned by sickness or a death, timber merchants need also to be well plugged into a network of gossip about family affairs. It is probably for this reason that they spend a lot of time in the bars and shops of the zone.

The types of economic brokers so far mentioned are all closely connected with agricultural production and normally own land themselves. However, there is another type that specializes in the transportation, rather than the buying and selling, of produce. Truckers (*transportistas* or *fleteros*) are a common phenomenon throughout Peru. They are primarily concerned with the movement of produce from the rural areas to the urban wholesale and consumer markets, though they also bring consumer goods from the cities to the countryside. These individuals own lorries and, according to my data, seldom invest in land (possibly because of the tremendous geographical mobility necessitated by their occupation which makes it difficult to manage a farm at the same time). They undertake contracts from middlemen and distribution agents for the transportation of goods and produce. Because of this they tend to evolve close links with market entrepreneurs both in the villages and the towns and are continually trying to build up new relationships. While they may live in a rural location and have similar networks of kinship and affinal relationships to other economic brokers, they apparently do not place premiums on developing close links with the peasant farming population at large. Instead they extend and consolidate their commercial ties. They also tend to form themselves into associations which have the implicit if not explicit aim of protecting their economic interests. These associations serve first, to develop a system of mutual assistance among truckers for obtaining help on the road when they breakdown, and second, as a way of protecting themselves from competitors with whom they compete for contracts.

The Matahuasi example is particularly interesting from this point of view as there exists a group of truckers who constitute the bulk of membership of a fiesta club which is organized to run the annual patron saint fiesta of San Sebastian. These truckers are inter-related through a network of kinship, affinal, and *compadrazgo* ties and co-operate each year in the financing and running of the fiesta; they also maintain close bonds of friendship during the rest of the year and are often seen together at the weekends drinking in the local bars, exchanging gossip and information about the people they have worked for during the week and about the places they have visited. At the time of the fiesta, which lasts for nearly a week and during which various religious and secular activities take place, the club invites prominent businessmen from the towns and other notables of the village to take a major part in the proceedings, and they are suitably dined and wined. This serves to reinforce existing relationships and to develop new contacts that may prove useful in the coming year's business activities. Many migrant Matahuasinos return to the village for the celebrations during their holidays; later these same individuals may be important for securing contracts and doing business.

The above examples suggest that we need to examine the ways in which particular entrepreneurial roles necessitate the development of certain types of local and external networks, and of how these networks are maintained or extended. The data also suggest that persons from certain family backgrounds and with certain patterns of work experience (e.g. employment in the mines or as petty traders in an urban situation) may be more advantageously placed for pursuing particular entrepreneurial occupations. Thus, the analysis of the sets of relationships involved in the operation of particular types of enterprise must be complemented by a study of the patterns of recruitment and the life careers of the entrepreneurs concerned. These dimensions have yet to be fully investigated for the Peruvian material, and there is little systematic treatment of this problem in the rest of the literature.[10]

The Decision-Making Approach

The entrepreneurial career typically involves the bringing together of resources (both material and non-material) in new and profitable combinations. This process entails high risks and a willingness to experiment with relationships and strategies. Moreover, having established a particular branch of economic activity and developed a distinctive pattern of organization, the entrepreneur will be faced with a constant stream of decisions concerning the operation of his enterprise. Entrepreneurship, then, constitutes a complex process of decision-making aimed ultimately at economic expansion. It seems eminently suitable, therefore, for treatment in terms of a decision-making model.

Briefly stated, a decision-making approach to social behaviour attempts to comprehend social action from the point of view of how individuals or categories of individuals attempt to maximize certain preferred values by making decisions about the use of rules, resources, and relationships in their environment (Moerman, 1968:28). The approach is essentially actor-oriented and assumes that actors are confronted by a series of possible alternative modes of behaviour or courses of action with probable outcomes; and that they will select whichever alternative they consider to offer maximal return or value.

It is important to emphasize, as do Howard and Ortiz (1971:216), that not all kinds of behaviour can be subjected to this type of analysis: 'conditioned behaviour and behaviour that forms an integral part of a continuous stream such as friendly encounters between intimates cannot really be cast into a decision framework'.

The approach, it seems, is more appropriate to instances where behavioural alternatives are relatively clear-cut and discrete, although there is probably a large body of intermediate forms of behaviour not typically regarded as made up of decisions which could also be viewed in this way. For example, Howard and Ortiz mention social events that entail sequences, such as religious ceremonies, political meetings, and economic cycles, which might be conceptualized in terms of a series of contingent decisions that result from antecedent situations and which affect subsequent outcomes.[11]

The decision-making model [12] assumes that individuals confronted with problematic situations will seek out relevant information, process it, evaluate the outcomes, and make a decision. Hence, the main analytical challenge to the investigator is to decipher the 'programme' by which this is done to specify the conditions under which it operates.

Underlying the model are a series of assumptions concerning actor-rationality. In the first place, individuals are assumed to be free to act or choose between alternatives. This means that a decision-making approach is not very applicable to analyzing situations where coercive force has been used. Second, in order to talk about decisions, there must be more than one possibility open to, and perceived by, the actor in question. Moreover, he must be able to conceptualize not only the possibilities open to him but also the probable outcomes of each. He must, that is, have some subjective appreciation of the likely consequences, although it is not necessary to assume that these can be expressed in quantitative terms. This presupposes then that he will have access to information concerning the results of previous decisions based upon his own experience and that of others. Another assumption is that the choices perceived must be seen as mutually exclusive and comparable, otherwise it is difficult to talk about having made a choice between alternatives. Last, we must be able in some way to rank or differentiate between outcomes according to some notion of preferences. That is, we need to know the rules used by the actor for determining his preferences and the factors that define the sets of opportunities to be evaluated. The concept of preferences, of course, is different from the notion of expectations, for what a man prefers may not be what he expects. Hence, in talking about rational decisions we imply an awareness on the part of the actor of the conditions affecting his choices, and in order to analyze the strategies of decision-making we have to focus upon the actor's goals, whether they be maximization of profit, some idea of satisfactory returns,[13] or various non-economic objectives of short-term or long-term significance. We also have to consider the information available, the actor's perceptions of alternatives and outcomes, the effects of various resource inputs (e.g. when discussing peasant farming we must consider cash, labour, land, technology, and organizational aspects), and we must identify the uncertainties (e.g. market conditions, climate, or social factors such as interpersonal ties) that may affect decisions and outcomes.

Decision-making among peasants in Colombia. An interest in decision-making models raises complex methodological and theoretical issues which can best be exemplified through the examination of specific applications. The discussion is introduced by reference to Ortiz's study of the economic behaviour of Páez peasants in Colombia (Ortiz, 1973).

Ortiz is mainly interested in analyzing production strategies and in showing how decisions can be interpreted as rational responses to particular socio-economic milieux. She emphasizes that,

'the [Páez] population of peasant producers is characterized by its heterogeneity, the small population, the relative independence of each producer, and the limited output of each farmer. It is heterogeneous in the sense that not all producers share the same aspirations, the same knowledge, the same responsibilities or hold the same amount of capital assets; each unit of production is different from the next. The productive units consist of only one family, their technological knowledge is limited and the amount of land they control can yield only a small surplus for sale. Furthermore, although they participate in the national economy they form a specific sector within it, which, owing to its geographical isolation has only limited contact with the market conditions.' (Ortiz, 1973:1–2)

Within this situation of social heterogeneity and generally low productivity, Ortiz distinguishes between two different patterns of decision-making, which tend to be associated with differences in economic status and orientation. The first type involves 'programmed decisions' or planning well ahead of time, and the other the deferring of decisions until a course of action has already been initiated.[14] She illustrates her point by reference to the ways in which decisions occur in the cash-crop and subsistence sectors of the economy.

The main cash-crop for the area is coffee. Its production requires an initial investment of at least fifteen years and must take account of expected future needs and demands. It commits the individual to maintaining the plantation under production for a long period of time, with the expectation of receiving good economic returns when the crop matures. Involvement in coffee production, therefore, requires considerable forward planning in order that the relevant factors of production can be brought together in a profitable arrangement. According to Ortiz, the planting and cultivation of coffee is characterized by a series of planned decisions that involve the careful evaluation of expected outcomes (i.e. yield and price) against the inputs of land and labour in order to maximize return on investment. Although the farmer may inadequately predict the outcomes in terms of yield and price, at the time of planting he will aim, on the information available, to take account of as many relevant factors as possible.

In contrast to cash-crop production, the basic objective of subsistence agriculture is to satisfy the dietary and social needs of the farmer and his family; not to maximize economic returns. Hence, decisions in this sector tend to be made in the course of action and not well ahead of time. Instead of evaluating assets and planning one's activities, the subsistence farmer will make his decisions as he is confronted with particular tasks and demands, and thus will react to problems as and when they arise. Ortiz argues that this leads to:

'the evaluation of consumer needs for the immediate future against personal wishes. Factors of production are considered when they are made available or are easily accessible. Careful calculations of yields and costs are not possible because this particular strategy does not allow for the mental recording of amounts planted, the labour required, and the cost of seeds and response to different goals. Maximization is irrelevant, satisfaction and security are the main concern.' (Ortiz, 1973:269)

While the behaviour of most farmers exhibits both types of decisions, the implication is that certain farmers are more prone towards programmed decision-making. These are what Ortiz describes as the 'progressive' as against the 'traditional' Indians (Ortiz, 1973:177f). The former show greater interest in the maximization of their cash resources, with which they purchase manufactured goods for productive or luxury use. However, they avoid selling their own labour or expanding the cultivation of food crops beyond their subsistence requirements; instead, they invest in coffee production or extend their pasture lands for cattle rearing. Additional labour is hired rather than recruited through work parties; and they generally refuse to become sponsors or major participants in religious fiestas, preferring instead to make direct money contributions to the church. A proportion of their income is spent on clothing, rice, and processed foodstuffs, and the rest is earmarked to improve their housing and to invest in agriculture.

The 'traditional' Indians, on the other hand, show as much interest in the cultivation of manioc and maize, as in coffee production, even if they have planted a reasonable acreage of coffee. They aim not merely to produce enough food for subsistence and labour purposes throughout the year (as is the case with the 'progressives') but to have extra produce available for gift-giving and for contributing to fiestas. It is because of their interest in providing hospitality to friends and kin that they grow sugar cane, which is fermented as an alcoholic drink. Among this group of farmers there is strong commitment to reciprocate and to assist one another when short of produce. Furthermore, the sale of food crops in the market is disapproved of, and so there is no good reason for expanding one's manioc or plantain fields much beyond the needs of one's family and network of friends. Help for agricultural work is provided through a system of labour exchanges and work parties, and wage labour is seldom used.

These two categories of farmers can also be differentiated in terms of their degree of articulateness in discussing economic planning. The 'traditional' Indians were less interested in conceptualizing the future decisions they might make about farming in terms of abstract measures, and apparently less au fait with agricultural techniques and the associated folklore. When asked how much they would plant in the following season, they replied that 'they would plant as much as they would need, no more no less'. Also they had no conception of the number of plants growing in their fields. On the other hand, the 'progressives' could converse extensively about farming matters and took an interest in calculating yields and costs. They also displayed concern about production targets and willingly discussed various management problems.

(Ortiz (1973:179) emphasizes that 'this difference in approach to management cannot simply be explained by lack of foresight or ability on the part of the "traditional" Indians. "Progressive" and "traditional" Indians could, with individual differences, plan ahead if necessary'. The difference, it seems, results from the way in which farmers' aspirations and expectations are shaped by existing socio-economic opportunities. According to Ortiz, each type is basically orientated to increasing productivity, improving living standards, and achieving prestige within the ranks of its own reference group. However, whereas the 'progressives' attempt to maximize their cash resources at the expense of traditional obligations, the 'traditional' Indians try to maintain a balance between the acquisition of cash and subsistence agriculture in order that a basic level of security is assured. The 'progressives', whose capital assets are often considerable (e.g. they possess cattle and have large coffee plantations which bring in a good income), are less concerned with problems of security, since they can always in a crisis raise cash by selling off some of their assets. Hence, wealthier farmers are more likely to evaluate future prospects and engage in longer term planning. It is the poor farmer with limited land who will defer decisions and react only to pressing problems. Consequently, he will tend to be more conservative, will avoid the uncertainties and risks involved in innovation, and will concentrate upon meeting his immediate family and community obligations.

The specific ways in which these factors combine to affect the socio-economic situation and farming strategy of particular individuals will, of course, vary from case to case (Ortiz, 1973:275 for examples). Ortiz is primarily interested in delineating the overall patterns; and in depicting the factors that determine the timing of decisions and how this influences the evaluation of factors considered by the decision-maker. She also attempts to generalize about the different types of economic and social goals and expectations found among Páez farmers. She argues that the two types of farmers differ in their production and consumption objectives, have varying views about social status, and are differently involved in local networks.

The importance of actor perceptions. Although Ortiz emphasizes that decisions are shaped by the availability of economic and social resources, she also argues that 'it is the individual who confronts himself with opportunities by recognizing their existence' (Ortiz, 1973:17). This means that close attention should be given to the question of how individuals or particular categories of individual perceive and evaluate alternative courses of action and assess their probable outcomes. Leaving aside the psychological dimensions, such an investigation requires that we understand folk categorizations and socio-cultural preferences, for these will influence the ways in which particular choices are viewed. Ortiz's comparison of the 'progressive' and the 'traditional' Indians[15] deals briefly with this problem.

A fuller statement is contained in Moerman's study of *Agricultural Change and Peasant Choice in a Thai Village* (Moerman, 1968: 27–9) where he argues that farming techniques and strategies make sense,

> 'in that the village farmer categorizes and compares, demands a close fit between what he observes and what he talks about, makes judicious use of previously successful means, anticipates the alterations that his actions will produce, plans possible alternative courses of action, is concerned with timing, finds ways to increase the predictable features of his situation, decides his correctness in terms of rules of procedure, is aware of and actually exercises choice, and works to increase the scientific corpus of information he uses for making and explaining his farming decisions and their rewards.'

Moerman goes on to document the distribution of choices made by the Thai farming population for various farm matters. These patterns are then explained by reference to what he calls 'the grammar' of farming, which includes such aspects as the level of information available, the culturally perceived alternatives and outcomes, and the social and technical rules which serve to guide farming behaviour.

A similar point is made by Salisbury (1970) in his study of the Tolai of New Britain. Like Ortiz and Moerman, he stresses the importance of focusing upon subjective expectations rather than simply presenting a so-called objective evaluation of alternatives. The latter, in fact, he regards as the outsider's, inevitably European, view of things. Its major shortcoming is that it 'omits almost all mention of development by self-help, of local people selectively utilizing knowledge made available to them and incorporating it into their own economic planning' (Salisbury, 1970:8). Salisbury attempts to correct this outsider bias by examining, in relation to specific fields of activity, the economic concepts used by local people in their allocational choices. Thus his study is essentially an exposition of indigenous concepts and modes of organization.

Decision-Making and Entrepreneurship

We are now in a position to assess the relevance of a decision-making approach for the study of entrepreneurship. Since decision-making recognizes the existence of alternative courses of action, it highlights the variability within a structure or situation. Even in a relatively homogeneous social context, the interest in decisions leads on to a discussion of the flexibility of the social structure; and to an appreciation of the ways in which actors weigh up the pros and cons of particular courses of action and attempt to legitimize their decisions by reference to normative or pragmatic values. A more differentiated structure reveals similar processes, but, here the distribution of choices is likely to show several distinct peaks representing the decisions made by different sectors of the population. This is particularly the case when, as a result of the impact of new types of factors (e.g. a new technology or changes in the economic or political structure), the range of possible choices is suddenly widened.

Here problems of decision-making link up with the analysis of differential responses to change. Indeed, as I have suggested earlier, an understanding of why certain social categories or groups respond more readily to new opportunities requires an exploration of why it is they are apparently more strategically placed for doing so. This necessitates mapping out their access to, and control over, resources of various kinds (e.g. land, labour, capital, informational networks, political connections, etc.); and documenting the ways in which they utilize these resources in new and possibly novel combinations. One method of doing this is to focus upon problematic situations that present a range of possible solutions. Attention is then given to analyzing why it is that certain individuals or social categories pursue particular courses of action; and to assessing the economic, organizational, and other outcomes (intended and unintended) of such decisions.

However, this type of analysis raises a number of complex issues, not least of which is the question of dealing with actors' perceptions. Most decision-making analysis presents a kind of aggregated view of social choice which describes the distribution of choices made by the members of a society at a particular moment in time and in relation to a specific set of problems. The overall pattern and the variations within it are then explained *post facto* by reference to certain folk concepts and rationalities that are imputed to have influenced the actors' decisions. The best example of this type of argument is Moerman's analysis of Thai farmers' decisions concerning the use of various types of fields (distant or close to the village, and irrigated or non-irrigated), and of ox-plough or tractor cultivation. He shows that, although all farmers recognize that some fields and techniques offer better returns for certain productive inputs than others, the inputs are evaluated differently depending on the age, wealth, and household size of the farmer in question. He also examines at length native modes of conceptualizing yields and costs of production; and describes certain social attitudes towards labour organization that affect their decisions. The main emphasis of Moerman's analysis, then, is to elucidate the way farmers view their activities and to identify the basic goals and criteria by which they make their decisions (Moerman, 1968:187).

Despite the obvious methodological shortcomings of this kind of explanation, it does have the merit of elaborating the important ideological and conceptual frameworks used by actors in evaluating various choices or, at least, in rationalizing decisions they have already made. The charting of such frameworks must of course be complemented by an assessment of the other types of constraints (e.g. ecological, economic, political) operating. Here it must be emphasized that a sociological approach to decision-making is fundamentally interested in explaining the distribution of choices, in respect to certain decisions, in terms of relevant social, economic, cultural, and ideological factors, and not in analyzing the psychological process by which a person defines and reaches a decision. Nor are we interested in individual behaviour *per se* (i.e. the personality or idiosyncratic features), only in identifying the various sociological components that interact situationally to produce specific types of response.

In order to illustrate how one might utilize a decision-making

model for the analysis of entrepreneurial behaviour, I draw upon
my own study of socio-economic change in rural Zambia.

In my initial account I included a chapter (Long, 1968: Chapter
III) on the strategies of small-scale commercial farming, the final
section of which was devoted to an analysis of differences in the
mobilization and organization of labour. Later I re-worked this
material in terms of a decision-making model (Long, 1970a), and
showed that there existed two distinct categories of agricultural
entrepreneurs who opted for different solutions to the same basic
problem.

One major finding of the Zambian study was the central role
played by Jehovah's Witnesses in the socio-economic development
of the region:

'Although somewhat younger and with less urban experience
than their economic rivals, Jehovah's Witnesses were dispro-
portionately represented in the commercial farmer and shop-
keeper categories. They also tended to live outside the traditional
matrilineal village in their own independent settlements, and in
their spare time practised such trades as bricklaying, carpentry or
tailoring from which they earned extra cash. Not all economic
innovators, however, were members of this religious sect, for
approximately half of all commercial farmers and shopkeepers
were in fact non-Christians.' (Long 1970a:146)

The discussion of labour organization was aimed at exploring more
fully the choices made by these two types of entrepreneur.

The analysis outlines the range of alternatives empirically
available for recruiting regular, extra-household labour and traces
out their probable organizational consequences. This shows that
there are four modes of labour recruitment: (1) the use of
permanently resident kinsmen-workers; (2) the acquisition of a
second wife and the use of an additional affinal pool of labour; (3)
the operating of a jointly-owned farm with a kinsman and family;
and (4) the exchange of labour with neighbouring farmers. It
emerges that of these, the latter two are less likely to generate
conflicts over status and reward which can seriously disrupt the
running of the farm. The main reason for this is that they are based
on a series of largely balanced exchanges between status equals. On
the other hand, the former two modes of recruitment exhibit major
organizational imbalances. The use of kinsmen-workers, who do

not share in the ownership of the farm or its equipment, is likely over time to lead to difficult farmer/worker relations which centre around the problem of reconciling the rights and obligations of matrilineal kinsmen with their role as workers on the farm. In some cases, underlying tensions had exploded in accusations of sorcery being made against the farmer, or amongst the kin themselves. The other arrangement, involving the marrying of a second wife, is also unstable in that the functioning of the farm is frequently affected by disputes between the wives. These might start out as domestic issues but will quickly feed into the work context. There is also the possibility that difficulties will arise between the two sets of affines, who compete for the farmer's favours or quarrel with him over labour deployment and the rewards for work. (For more details on the structural outcomes of these various arrangements, see Long, 1970a:148–51.)

Having described the alternatives and their probable outcomes, the analysis looks at the actual distribution of choices made by the eighteen farmers in the sample. This shows that they are equally divided between alternatives 1 and 2, and 3 and 4, and that, with almost no exceptions, it is the Jehovah's Witness farmers who select the latter two types of labour organization. How then, does one explain this?

The first analytical hurdle concerns whether or not one can assume that the same conditions of choice exist for both groups. Is it valid, that is, to presuppose that all farmers possess full information about the empirical alternatives and understand their organizational consequences? Can we also assume that they can effectively choose between them, and that the alternatives are simultaneously available? And last, can we take it for granted that the farmers possess similar economic goals and aspirations? In answering these questions we come to comprehend more precisely why there is this sharp difference in strategy between the Jehovah's Witness and non-Jehovah's Witness farmer.

Although all farmers are aware of the existence of the different patterns of labour recruitment and may themselves have experimented with or have experienced more than one of them, they will, it seems, evaluate them somewhat differently. Whereas Jehovah's Witnesses tend to shun involvement in matrilineal kinship networks unless the members are co-religionists and thus share similar ethical and social attitudes, the other farmers positively value matrilineal kinship bonds and, initially, at least, are not worried about establishing close ties with a body of kinsmen-workers. Indeed several of them view the presence of a group of dependent kinsmen as a move towards acquiring increased status within the framework of traditional notions of prestige. The Jehovah's Witnesses, on the other hand, have little interest in traditional status criteria and espouse an ethic which emphasizes the spiritual and moral dangers of associating too freely with non-believers, even if kin, and of adhering to 'Satan-influenced custom' or 'the Old World system of things'.

These differences suggest that the strategies adopted by the two groups are in part determined by their contrasting perceptions of the alternatives and by their evaluations of the pay-offs entailed. Thus one could argue that Jehovah's Witnesses are constrained by their ideology and by their membership of the local congregation to value more highly certain types of social relationships. Moreover, for a zealous Jehovah's Witness, the possibility of acquiring a second wife is unrealistic since it goes against basic doctrine and therefore should not be included within his decision matrix. In a strict sense, then, what we have for Jehovah's Witnesses is a somewhat narrower range of alternatives, such that the original assessment of empirically available choices requires modification to take account of ideological limitations on decision-making.

The question of why Jehovah's Witnesses and not others apparently choose to enter into arrangements based on joint ownership or reciprocity between neighbouring farmers must also be dealt with in relation to ideology. Common church membership generates a higher degree of trust among status equals than is normally the case in the traditional kin-based system and seems to be crucial in transforming the nature of bonds between brothers. Whereas in the traditional tribal system uterine brothers are in competition for control over their sisters and female matrikin, under the new ideological order, uterine brothers are brought closer together through bonds of religious brotherhood. This, I believe, is a critical factor in explaining why it is that Jehovah's Witnesses are more willing to enter into financial partnerships than others (two out of three jointly-owned farms are owned by Jehovah's Witness brothers) and to form mutual aid groups for agricultural purposes (five out of six are between Jehovah's Witnesses). (For details on interpersonal co-operation and conflict see Long,

1970a:154–5.)

The assumption concerning common economic objectives raises fewer problems since there is little evidence that the two categories of farmers differ significantly in their economic goals: each is basically concerned with increasing economic returns on the crops grown and in improving living standards, though there are differing attitudes towards consumption and investment (Long, 1968:38, 215–7). The recruitment of a labour force is primarily motivated by the desire to meet production requirements and to select an organizational form which would best achieve this. Analysis of the observed outcomes of the strategies shows, however, that from the point of view of organizational stability, the Jehovah's Witnesses have opted for solutions which are structurally more viable and less likely to generate major conflicts between the participants. Thus a main conclusion of the study is that Jehovah's Witness enterprise is more soundly based in terms of the organization of labour, which, providing that other factors do not intervene to affect performance, seems likely to lead to better economic returns as well. The study emphasizes, too, that differences in farming strategies can be related to differences in the rationalities of decision-making and to the interplay of various social and material constraints and incentives.[16] It remains to be seen how far the same sorts of factors affect the decision-making of farmers and commercial entrepreneurs in other contexts; for example, in relation to investment or market strategies or in pursuit of socio-political goals. A broad aim of the analysis was to isolate the factors that might account for the different and apparently more successful organizational forms established by Jehovah's Witness cash-crop farmers. This problem, which was examined using a decision-making approach, forms part of the much larger issue of explaining why it was that Jehovah's Witnesses occupied a prominent part in the changing social and economic organization of the area (see Long, 1968, for details).

This type of analysis I believe could be extended to cover other forms of entrepreneurship and could focus more explicitly on such problems as the alternative sources of information available concerning market prices and conditions, or on an analysis of strategic decisions involving investment and the development of particular branches of economic activity. The latter problem is complex since it entails adopting a diachronic view of the development of enterprises and thus necessitates relating economic decisions to the changing pattern of economic opportunities and to the life careers of particular categories of entrepreneur.[17]

The understanding of such aspects using decision-making models connects up, of course, with transactional analysis, since the former assesses the significance and development of particular types of social relationships and networks seen in relation to existing opportunities for the utilization and conversion of resources. As Glade (1967:252) has pointed out, 'the superior decision-making which springs from differential advantages in the organization of resources involves a manipulation of all relevant resources in the environment, not merely the conventional categories of land, labour, and capital accumulation'. Thus, depending on the context, and the types of decisions involved, the key resources may, as I have illustrated, be such things as information networks, political connections, or membership of a religious group. An entrepreneur may be characterized by reference to the way in which he disrupts existing patterns of production or distribution and combines resources in a somewhat unique manner. But in so doing, he inevitably becomes involved in choosing between the use of specific sets of interpersonal relations and in selecting certain normative frameworks within which obligations and rewards can be defined. A full analysis of entrepreneurial behaviour necessitates, then, a consideration of both transactional and decision-making elements.

CONCLUSION

As I indicated at the outset of this chapter, the discussion was not designed to offer yet another grand-theoretical interpretation of entrepreneurial activity. Nor was it my aim to present a systematic account of the many different types and scales of entrepreneurship found in the Third World. My interest has been far more circumscribed: to outline and evaluate recent anthropological contributions that stress the importance of analyzing the types of transactions, networks, and decision-making processes associated with entrepreneurship. Although analytically still underdeveloped, this perspective could lead to a more satisfactory understanding of the differential responses to change shown by different social categories within a population. The primary reason for this is that emphasis has shifted away from the identification of one or two so-called key factors, such as a particular value orientation or social background, to the study of the processes by which entrepreneurs attempt to deal with various internal and external organizational problems that arise in the establishment and development of their enterprises. Such an approach, it seems, would indicate more precisely than other types of analysis why certain categories or social groups are more strategically situated to take advantage of changing economic conditions. It also enables one to explore the ways in which entrepreneurs establish new channels for conversion, develop local and external networks, manipulate other persons and resources, and draw upon existing ideologies in order to legitimize their decisions or to further particular sets of relationships.

One weakness in the anthropological approach to entrepreneurship, however, is its failure to link the detailed study of micro-processes to a consideration of macro-structures. This is most noticeable in the tendency in some analyses to accord the individual too much independence of action and manipulative power, and concomitantly to give insufficient attention to the ways in which regional or national politico-economic structures determine the types and scales of entrepreneurship possible. [18] If, therefore, we are to exploit the full potential of transactional and decision-making models, we must give more consideration to the various frameworks within which entrepreneurs operate. These frameworks constitute the basic parameters within which entrepreneurial activities and decisions occur. While acknowledging the importance of the structure and functioning of the economy and polity, it is also necessary to take account of cultural and ideological frameworks, for these, too, may have a significant effect on the types of choices and relationships pursued.

This latter point is especially pertinent since entrepreneurial decisions, like other types, must be viewed as taking place in relation to actors' perceptions and understandings. Hence, the study of folk views and classifications, which has been a major preoccupation of anthropologists, must be developed to deal with problems of entrepreneurship and development. A basic reason for this, as Moerman (1968:187) comments, is that 'economic change occurs with the appearance of new standards for making economic decisions and not . . . when the outcomes of decisions take a modified distribution'. Interest in subjective understandings and ideology should not, however, commit one necessarily to giving priority to cultural and ideological factors. Above all else, the study of entrepreneurship emphasizes the complex interaction between material and non-material factors, and between the ideational and behavioural dimensions.

CHAPTER 6

Sociological Problems of Planned Social Change

An account of sociological and anthropological perspectives on development would not be complete without some discussion of planned change, for an understanding of the patterns of development and change necessarily involves understanding something about the types of approach used by governments and their agencies for initiating economic development and social change. This is especially the case with Third World countries where governments often play a dominant part in attempting to re-structure society in conformity with particular politico-economic goals. Moreover, while social and economic planning is also important in advanced industrial countries, in the less developed areas of the world there is often greater concern for centralized state planning, which is frequently backed by heavy inputs of foreign aid and assistance.

This chapter distinguishes broadly between two different approaches to rural planning in the Third World: the 'improvement approach' which aims to encourage agricultural development within existing peasant production systems; and the 'transformation approach' which attempts to establish new forms of agricultural and social organization, and which makes a radical break with existing peasant systems in terms of scale of operation, production techniques, and socio-legal structure. Thus, whilst the former concentrates upon improving the productivity and organization of production of peasant farmers, the latter may involve the implementation of new land tenure systems or the establishment of new types of settlements or farms, which necessitate very substantial capital outlay. By distinguishing between these two different approaches, I do not wish to suggest that the two cannot co-exist within a common national or regional framework. Indeed, in practice, as Feldman (1969) points out, most policies are based on a compromise of mixed strategies involving both types of approach. This chapter describes the characteristics and structural consequences of these planning approaches and illustrates the argument by reference to specific empirical studies dealing with their implementation and effects.

THE IMPROVEMENT APPROACH

In 1960 the World Bank described the 'improvement approach' as aiming at 'the progressive improvement in peasant methods of crop and animal husbandry by working on the peasant farmer on both the psychological and technical planes to induce an increase in his productivity without any radical changes in traditional social and legal systems'. This approach allows for the continuity of existing social institutions and land tenure arrangements. Development is to be initiated through improved extension work methods which, it is hoped, will encourage farmers to apply new crop varieties and new methods of production. This will enable them to produce more for the market, which, in turn, will probably require the development of new marketing organizations. It is envisaged that the development of better extension services, and the stationing of agricultural experts to tour farms and villages to give advice and to provide other services such as arranging loans, will establish new incentives that will lead to increased commercial production. The improvement of agricultural extension has frequently formed part of a more general programme of community development. The latter represents an integrated approach to the question of rural development aiming to initiate improvements not only in agriculture, but in health, sanitation, craft industries, and in the level of literacy. Such programmes, of course, require a number of trained personnel, technically qualified in agriculture or some such skill, who are placed at the local level to provide assistance.

The improvement approach was especially characteristic of the development policies pursued by British colonial government in Africa, India, and elsewhere. Under colonial rule extension work was often coupled with the enforcement of various administrative ordinances to prevent soil erosion or to encourage the cultivation of certain crops – e.g. famine crops, such as cassava in central Africa (Allan, 1965). Hence, - general economic incentives to production were combined with the principle of 'persistent persuasion', a polite term for enforcement. The implementation of regulations was supervised by officers of the Agricultural Department and cases of non-observance were generally reported to the local authorities for court action. The improvement approach during colonial rule led to much greater control over peasant and tribal populations and only in certain zones to increased commercial orientation. Various governments encouraged the marketing of cash-crops through either government agencies (e.g. marketing boards) or government-sponsored co-operative societies. These co-operatives were basically associations of small-holder farmers who grouped together for the specific purpose of marketing their produce. Thus colonial governments were willing to assist in developing an infrastructure concerned with distribution as well as production.

In most countries, the improvement approach was extended considerably after political independence. For example, India's first Five Year Plan (1952) stated that one of its aims was to increase agricultural production through the application of scientific knowledge and capital investment, and that this was to be achieved mainly through increased extension work among the peasant farming population. It was not until the second, third, and fourth National Plans that there was a significant stress upon the notion of co-operative farming and the possibility of effecting major structural change through land reform programmes. The same reliance on improvement strategies was found in most African countries during the early years of their independence (see, e.g. Ruthenburg, 1964) and one of the main reasons for this, it seems, was that they depended heavily on advice given by various world economic experts. The latter tended to argue, especially during the mid-1950s and early 1960s, that agricultural development problems were fundamentally caused by bad extension work, by the lack of skilled personnel, and by the poor economic attitudes of peasants. Similar views are expressed by De Wilde (1967) in his book on rural development in Africa where he suggests that 'the conservatism of peasants, unless closely supervised, is a major problem' (De Wilde, 1967:176–77); and by Schultz (1964) who argues for the need to educate peasants and to improve their levels of technical skills.

During the early stages of community development programmes, extension officers were frequently disappointed by the results.

Having trained carpenters, bricklayers, and other skilled craftsmen, it was often found that on receipt of their training certificates these men would leave for work in the cities instead of using their newly-acquired skills for the betterment of the local village population. Extension workers sometimes found it difficult to comprehend the economic rationality in leaving the home community to seek better-paid work in an urban and unfamiliar environment. Another problem was that priority was frequently given to cash-crop production and this led in some areas to a heavy investment of labour and time in such crops to the detriment of food production. Thus, people, who had been previously self-sufficient in their basic food supplies, were now forced to use some of their earnings from cash cropping to purchase basic foodstuffs. This proved serious in times of economic crisis when the demand or price for the export crop fell suddenly and the producer had to face the prospects of food shortage despite his commercial orientation. Further difficulties existed because of the use in colonial days of administrative compulsion to effect technological and agricultural innovation; for later when these regulations were removed it was sometimes found that agricultural techniques and methods suddenly became very inefficient and fell to a low level of productivity.

The spread of innovations was organized largely through a network of trained personnel. In addition to visiting farmers, these workers organized farmers' meetings, helped to set up radio listening groups, and ran demonstration farms to show the level of increased yields possible under new methods. Farming centres were also established to train selected local farmers in new methods of agriculture. An underlying assumption of much of this work was that in order to effect widespread change it was first necessary to create a group of so-called 'progressive' farmers through whom new ideas and techniques could be channelled. Thus, during colonial times emphasis was placed on developing a system of 'yeomen' or 'improved' farmers, who were given preferential treatment and offered credit facilities for the purchase of modern technology. The end result of such a policy was the formation of a rural farming elite with so-called 'progressive' attitudes. Where local co-operative societies were established these were frequently controlled by members of this group or by a local merchant class interested in monopolizing marketing and the provision of fertilizers and other services. This has been documented for many situations in Africa (Apthorpe, 1970b) and Latin America (Fals Borda, 1969).

Several writers have discussed the question of how to achieve optimal use of money and personnel within an improvement policy framework. Two general points emerge. First, extension work should be concentrated in densely populated areas where soil and climatic conditions are favourable and markets assured, but where there is already evidence of land shortage. Pressure on land, it seems, often features as the most effective forerunner of agricultural progress, for where no additional land is available the only alternative is to increase yields per acre. It is in situations of this type that we find a greater willingness to work with extension work agencies. The second point is that work should concentrate on peoples who have already shown themselves receptive. This means, in fact, the economically better-off areas, where educational levels are higher and where there is already some semblance of a rural capitalist class, or at least of some established group of commercially orientated farmers.

From an economic point of view, the improvement approach appears to have achieved a great deal. There have been rapid increases in peasant production in developing countries during the last twenty or thirty years and this is mainly due to improved smallholder agriculture (see, e.g. Griffin, 1968:75–80, for a comparison of smallholder and *latifundia* production; also Dorner, 1972:120–4). Moreover, working with peasant farmers is a relatively cheap way of stimulating economic growth since the level of inputs required is comparatively low. Such a policy, however, has two fundamental shortcomings. In the first place, it leads to the reinforcement or development of socio-economic inequality in the countryside, sometimes resulting in a widening of the gap between the commercial farmer and the poor peasant or landless categories. And second, it is a slow-moving process which cannot be expected to produce quick returns. These themes are explored in relation to the Indian case.

The Community Development Programme in India

During the early years following India's independence in 1947 two major policy decisions were taken in an effort to stimulate growth in the rural sector. The first constituted an attack on the problem of landlordism. Much of India was characterized by the Zamindar system whereby landlords acted also as collectors of taxes, standing between the government and the cultivator (see Mandelbaum, 1970). Although there were some difficulties in thoroughly eliminating this system, especially because of the variations existing in different parts of the country, by the mid 1960s it appears that a considerable improvement had been made and intermediaries and landlords were in fact less secure in their positions than they had been.

The other policy decision concerned the establishment of a Community Development Programme. This programme had two broad objectives: 'to provide for a substantial increase in the country's agricultural production, and for improvements in the system of communications, in rural health and hygiene, and in village education'; and second, 'to initiate and direct a process of integrated culture change aimed at transforming the social and economic life of the villages' (Dube, 1958:8). The idea of culture change was viewed as a primary objective by the planners who wished to stimulate 'in the Indian masses the burning desire for change, which, through progressive adaptation of modern techniques, will lead to their achieving higher standards of life' (Dube, 1958:102; see also Five Year Plan, 1951:82). This was to be achieved through an integrated programme aimed at progressive improvement of the existing socio-economic system. Little attempt was made to evolve new social and legal structures, and land tenure and distribution was in most areas left alone.

The intellectual origins and inspiration for the Community Development movement came from the success which extension work had had in other parts of the world, particularly in the USA. Another influence, according to Barrington Moore (1966:392), was 'the influence of British paternalism and more specifically movements for "village uplift"'. The general idea behind the approach was to develop programmes for mobilizing village populations so as to achieve fuller utilization of local human and natural resources. 'It was not a programme of outside charity and aid, but one of village self-help' (Dube, 1958:11).

In the year following the publication of India's first Five Year Plan, a number of pilot projects were inaugurated. Each of these consisted of a block of about 100 villages, containing a population of about 50,000. In these zones, development programmes of an intensive kind were to be initiated involving agricultural improvement with an emphasis on increasing food production, and also social, educational, rural health, and public work projects. Each group of villages was to be serviced by a village-level worker, who would be trained as a multi-purpose extension agent and also function as a social worker. The second Five Year Plan extended this programme with the aim of bringing every village in India under the scheme, 40 per cent of which would be developed as more intensive development projects. In total, some 3,800 additional extension service blocks were planned of which 1,120 were to be concentrated into community development schemes. Crash programmes were organized to cover a three-year period. It was envisaged that existing institutions and agencies, such as village councils (*panchayats*), co-operative societies, schools, and other voluntary associations concerned with rural development, should be incorporated into the scheme so that there was the widest possible representation of people and different local bodies. A series of advisory committees, consisting of persons with technical and other skills, were to be established and some re-organization of local administrative structures was planned.

An evaluation report of 1957 specifies various criteria for classifying the activities undertaken by community development projects (see Desai, 1969:Chapter XII). Programmes were divided into the following major categories: instructional programmes, agricultural and irrigational programmes, and institutional and other programmes. A complex bureaucratic structure was established to administer them. This was composed of four levels: the central administration, state (i.e. regional) administration, district organization, and the project committee. At each level there existed an executive functioning with the help of a development committee and aided by an advisory board. At the project level, a project officer equipped with a staff of some 120 supervisors and village-level workers was made responsible for the implementation of the local programme.

Several studies have attempted to evaluate the impact of the Community Development Programme on rural development and change in India (see Desai, 1969:614, for comprehensive references). However, one of the more detailed accounts is that by Dube (1958) who analyzes the effects of the programme in Uttar Pradesh in North-West India. The study focuses upon two main themes: the responses to change shown by different segments of the rural population, and the role of state officials and extension agents.

Dube concentrates his attention on two villages – one, a large settlement of some 5,142 people (Rajput Village) and the other, a small village of only 757 people (Tyagi Village). Despite their difference in size, both villages exhibit a roughly similar caste and religious structure. Each settlement contains both Hindu and Muslim families which are internally divided into caste or caste-like groupings; and each possesses a dominant caste that tends to control a substantial part of the economic and political resources of the village. The village population is divided into three socio-economic groupings: (1) A group of agriculturalists who are of high status and high income, that make up the dominant caste, together with certain individuals from other castes who have achieved a better economic status than their fellows; (2) A middle group of less wealthy agriculturalists, artisans, and members of the occupational castes; and (3) A group of individuals of low status and income made up of untouchables and poor agricultural labourers. In both villages there is a small but powerful segment that constitutes the elite'. This comprises people mostly of high social status and income who are better educated, have urban contacts, and who play an active part in village and inter-village politics.

Dube's study assesses the consequences of the Community Development Programme in relation to different fields of activity. With respect to agricultural extension, some progress had been made in diffusing the use of improved seeds for wheat and sugar cane, though these had in fact been first introduced into the area some ten years before. Greater success pertained for sugar than for wheat, since the former was a cash-crop and there were sugar mills in the region interested in buying better quality cane. Coupled with this increased commercial production, was an expansion in the sale of chemical and other fertilizers, although some people clearly considered fertilizers as problematic, or even harmful. Dube quotes the comments of villagers who argued that fertilizers sapped 'the fertility of the soil and burnt the crops'; one man complained that 'They [chemical fertilizers] are like a strong aphrodisiac – temporarily stimulating but harmful in the long run' (Dube, 1958:64).

Such factors as the size of landholding, conditions of draft animals available, and the financial position of individual farmers affected the adoption and use of improved agricultural implements. For example, most farmers who had smallholdings found that tractors were of little use. There were only two in operation in Rajput Village: one run by an individual farmer and the other jointly owned by a group of lineally-related families. The latter vehicle eventually developed mechanical troubles and became the source of disputes between kinsmen over its use. Other new implements introduced were iron ploughs and cultivators. These were quickly adopted.

The use of new agricultural methods was slow in gaining ground. Line sowing of cane was recommended because it made weeding easier and facilitated cutting. Yet its acceptance was hindered by the large landowners who did not wish to change the traditional method for organizing labour which this new technique apparently necessitated. There was also a reluctance to adopt the Japanese method of rice cultivation which, it had been proved, could produce very high yields. This method entailed transplanting rice and carefully regulating the water supply and appropriate soil conditions, and hence, required a major re-organization of labour. Another problem concerned the introduction of orchards which it was originally envisaged would be planted communally. Little interest was shown in the idea of communal control, and the orchards themselves required considerable initial outlay with no prospects of immediate return. They, therefore, appealed only to the larger landowners. A plan for the consolidation of holdings came to nothing and a scheme for the co-operative ownership of tractors had to be abandoned. Also, due to the enormous capital expenditure required, little work was done on improving existing irrigation facilities beyond the digging of new wells.

The emphasis of the programme was on the gradual improvement of smallholder agriculture through the dissemination of new seeds and fertilizers, and through the introduction of a limited range of new types of equipment. Few determined attempts were made to modify the patterns of landholding and control, or to introduce new forms of labour organization.

Alongside these attempts to improve agricultural production was the plan to develop a series of co-operatives to deal with marketing, servicing, and the provision of short-term credit. But, as Dube shows, many people were hostile to this idea as they regarded these co-operatives as official organizations imposed from outside. Moreover, where they were set up, membership, and especially the leadership positions, were monopolized by persons of high social and economic status. The general population found the complex rules and administrative procedures tiresome and feared getting involved in complicated legal issues. Furthermore, the credit societies proved less accommodating to poor peasants than the money lenders, since any money or grain obtained from the co-operative had to be returned by a specified date.

The introduction of better livestock (i.e. pedigree bulls and breeding buffalo) was generally well received but there were difficulties in eliminating poor-quality breeds because, for religious reasons, the animals could not be slaughtered or castrated. Similar sorts of problems arose with respect to the introduction of better sanitation and public health. For example, several compost pits were dug outside the villages for the depositing of manure and refuse. This was supported by the passing of regulations by local village councils making it obligatory for villagers to use these pits, and fines were to be imposed for default. Yet many of these pits remained unused. Although it was customary for women (even of high caste) to clean the household and to deposit rubbish in one corner of the yard near to the house, women of higher castes refused for reasons of status to carry it all the way to the compost pit. In order to comply with the new regulations; a few of the high caste families were even prepared to pay a servant to do the job.

Another project involved the attempt to pave the lanes in the villages. It was decided that the easiest way of financing this was through a levy on sugar production which, it was agreed, would be collected by the sugar mills, who would deduct it from the value of sugar cane they purchased. However, many farmers who supplied large quantities of cane to the mills but who had only small sections of lanes near to their houses, felt that their financial contribution was out of all proportion to the direct gain to themselves. They did not, that is, want to subsidize the non-sugar growing sections of the village. And, in addition, some families were more interested in growing wheat than sugar. At the other end of the social scale, the untouchables were not in a position to contribute, either in cash or labour, because that would have meant sacrificing earnings which they could ill afford. Hence, economic differentiation militated against finding a simple solution to this problem. The difficulties were especially marked in Rajput Village where there was a more substantial cash-crop sector and families with large houses, and a proportionately greater area of village lanes.

In the fields of education and youth work, the programme established adult classes for literacy and clubs for youths and children to be held at a newly-opened centre. Although the value of education was generally recognized, practical difficulties also arose in these fields. Two of the more important problems were: the apparent incompatibility of adult status with that of school attender, and the special difficulties facing women. A daughter-in-law, for example, was not customarily expected to leave the house frequently until she had achieved a comparatively responsible status within the family by becoming a mother of several children. Thus, so long as she remained subordinate in the mother-in-law's household, she was prevented from participating in public activities and in mixed classes; and, on the other hand, later, when adult with children, she faced additional responsibilities and found it equally difficult to get away.

In the case of public projects, like the building of roads and schools and the renovation of wells, the programme required the mobilization of voluntary labour. The state government of Uttar Pradesh laid great emphasis on this and authorized village councils to exact five days compulsory labour every year from residents, and to impose fines on defaulters. It also tried to stimulate an ideology based on 'the dignity of labour' and 'the cult of dirty hands', emphasizing *shramdan* (unpaid voluntary labour).

According to Dube, *shramdan* received different reactions from persons of different standing in the communities. The village elite and upper-status, higher-income groups welcomed this concept of voluntary labour, which was mainly directed to the improvement of road networks. A main reason for this was that it facilitated easier transportation of their export crops and afforded them the opportunity of reinforcing their positions of power through the organization of work parties, since it was the lower castes who did the manual work. Those of higher status assumed supervisory roles. These 'voluntary' work parties were usually inaugurated by speech making and ceremonial at which the local elite tried to win acclaim and praise from outside officials. The poorer groups received little visible gain. A few of them owned bullock carts but only a handful produced enough sugar cane to transport to urban markets for sale. Indeed, as Dube (1958:82) comments, many of them viewed *shramdan* 'as a revival of *begar,* a practice under which influential landowners and government officials compelled the poorer people to work without wages or at nominal rates and which is now prohibited by law'. Hence, the organization of work parties provided a means by which the dominant castes could assert their authority over their subordinates.

What, then, were the general results of this Community Development Programme? A first observation is that the best organized and most successful activities occurred in the field of agricultural extension, and that consequently it was the farmers who benefited most. However, about 70 per cent of these benefits went in fact to the more affluent farmers – poorer smallholders were often not in a position to take full advantage of the new methods. Another consequence was that the programme completely ignored the needs of the artisans and agricultural labourers, for no specific projects were initiated to help them. As a result of these deficiencies, conflicts arose between the poorer and wealthier members of the communities; and this was further exacerbated by the fact that the adoption of certain improved agricultural implements, such as cultivators and tractors, led to a reduction in the employment opportunities for labourers in the area.

The interest and acceptability of projects was affected, therefore, first by economic advantage and utility; and second by the kind of prestige and power that the project might offer to the social group concerned. Dube also mentions the question of curiosity value: some things were initially adopted because of their novelty, though they would be abandoned later if they offered no practical benefits. There was also the question of compliance with the wishes of government or influential village leaders. Dube found that there was a general attitude, especially among the poorest section of the population, of merely responding in a subservient way to the demands of government: 'If the government wants us to do a thing we should do it.'

General Consequences of the Improvement Strategy
The Indian Community Development Programme provides a good

example of the improvement approach to rural development (see Hunter and Bottrall, 1972, for details on Indian agricultural development policy). In evaluating this policy, it is important to emphasize that considerable progress was made in raising levels of production and technology, although, as Barrington Moore (1966:396) has shown, it did not lead to startling increases in the productivity of crops. Also, as the example aptly illustrates, it met with considerable opposition from various social groups. Nevertheless, in certain regions and with respect to certain classes, the programme did bring significant socio-economic benefits.

The Indian case exemplifies the typical effects of an improvement strategy. In the first place, the policy tends to reinforce existing economic differentiation or leads to the emergence of more marked patterns of stratification based on differential access to the new technology and facilities. For example, Dube's analysis shows how a rural elite, consisting mainly of big farmers and landowners, benefited most from 'community development'. A similar conclusion is drawn by Epstein (1962) in her study of Wangala.[1] This village, it will be remembered, received the advantage of improved irrigation which resulted in an increase in agricultural production, although it did not entail any re-allocation of productive resources. Her re-study of the same village, some ten years later, shows that the situation had possibly worsened: the magnates or larger landowners had by then entrenched themselves more effectively in the economic structure (Epstein, 1973).

A basic feature of the improvement approach is that it does not re-allocate productive resources. It merely provides more capital and equipment for farmers (usually the larger landowners). In certain situations this can lead to a polarization of classes: between, on the one hand, a dominant landowning group that has far greater access than others to credit, extension services, and technology, and who probably control the resources of the co-operatives and other local bodies, and, on the other hand, the mass of the poorer peasants who remain largely unaffected by the extension programme. Somewhat paradoxically, it is only in situations where important non-agricultural opportunities exist for earning cash, which can then be re-converted into land or productive assets, that the process is likely to work differently. In this case it may be possible for peasants from poorer families to buy or rent additional land so that they might develop commercial forms of agriculture. This is illustrated, for example, by the investments made by returning migrant workers from mining centres in areas like Zambia, or in the central highlands of Peru (Alberti and Sanchez, 1974; Long and Roberts, 1978). Another example is that of Bailey (1957) who shows how in one Mysore village[2] members of the Distiller caste of middle rank capitalized on their commercial and administrative expertise and invested their savings in village land. In this instance, the process was assisted by increasing pressure of population and rising expenditure on various contingencies and customary obligations, which resulted in some of the landowning families having to sell their land to raise cash. These plots were bought up by the Distillers who enhanced their economic status.

The phenomenon of bigger farmers reaping the economic benefits of improved technology has recently been interpreted as a consequence of the urban bias of Indian planning (Lipton, 1968a). Lipton argues that, whilst India's planners fully accept the abstract base for agricultural priority, they nonetheless exhibit an urban orientation in their formulations. This he attributes to many factors: the assumption that marketed surplus is primarily important for its role in providing resources for industrialization; the neglect of village power structures which funnel services and capital to those of higher politico-economic status; the close connection between the larger landowning class and the money lenders, who usually have property in town and who wish to protect their urban resources and power; the fact that planners themselves are under pressure from these and other groups; and the urban orientation of extension workers and others concerned with rural development. Agricultural development, then, tends to be geared to the bigger farmers with irrigated land and a marketable surplus in ways that often increase risk and reduce incentives for the other farmers. It is characteristically these bigger farmers who participate actively in regional politics and who have urban property and interests to protect. In contrast, it is the smaller farmer, who has little direct influence over administrative and planning matters, who lacks the basic resources and incentives. Hence, improvements in agricultural technology may lead to substantial increases in productivity and production, but not necessarily to any qualitative change in the socio-economic and power structure of rural areas.

Space does not permit us to discuss in detail other examples of the community development or extension-work approach to development in the rural sector. Studies from Africa, Latin America, as well as other parts of Asia, suggest that Dube's findings concerning economic differentiation and the growth of antagonistic relations between groups of unequal economic and political status could be more widely substantiated. One might also explore the same themes in relation to the structure and functioning of marketing and servicing co-operatives, which are often expected to play a central role in diffusing new technology and encouraging market-orientation among smallholder and commercial farmers. Indeed, it has been suggested that rural co-operatives in fact exacerbate the process of differentiation by creating new divisions based on the differential access and control over the resources of the co-operative institution itself.

THE TRANSFORMATION APPROACH

Although the improvement approach has produced tangible results in some areas and with respect to certain systems of production, dramatic changes have only infrequently taken place. The typical process is a gradual one of slowly increasing productivity and market orientation.

As I indicated in Chapter 3, several writers have attributed this slow and sometimes negative response to new economic opportunities to the essential conservativeness of peasants, who lack managerial ability and who are unaffected by economic incentives. Another line of interpretation is that a major constraint on growth is the high agricultural underemployment or surplus labour which is assumed to exist in peasant societies. According to this point of view, economic growth can only take place if there is a marked increase in the levels of inputs complementary to labour, or if a substantial part of the labour supply is siphoned off the land into urban-industrial employment; or alternatively, if major changes are introduced in the methods of production and cropping patterns so that the surplus can be more gainfully employed. Such changes, it is often argued, cannot be implemented thoroughly enough under an improvement programme. Similar arguments are advanced concerning the necessity of introducing new forms of land tenure and larger production units so that economies of scale might be achieved and more efficient, mechanized forms of cultivation adopted.

These are some of the arguments offered by economists and planners for making a break with the improvement approach and pursuing a policy based more on a transformation of existing social and economic structures. Such reasoning (much of which, in fact, seems erroneous),[3] coupled with certain socio-political objectives, such as the need to develop increased political control over populations in order to instill a greater commitment to national development goals, has led several governments to intervene more actively in development. They have sought, that is, to introduce new technical, social, and legal systems that allow for the development of modern agricultural techniques and a higher rate of capital investment, leading, it is hoped, to increased economic growth. The most visibly dramatic way in which this has been done has been through the setting up of new settlements which involve the large-scale movement of population to new centres, and through the implementation of land reform programmes.

Settlement and Re-Settlement Schemes

There are many different forms of settlement schemes but, as Chambers (1969) has shown in his study of African examples, they do in fact have two broad features in common: first, a geographical movement of population, and second, a large element of planning and control which is normally the responsibility of some kind of management board. In his review of colonial and post-colonial settlement programmes in Africa, Chambers documents how in the early colonial period the settlement or re-settlement of peoples living at subsistence or near subsistence level took place either for political reasons (e.g. in Rhodesia and Kenya, the African populations were moved into native reserve areas to make room for European settlement) or for humanitarian reasons, when people were moved from areas infested with sleeping sickness (e.g. along the coast of Lake Victoria in Uganda). However, settlement programmes of this type constituted induced migrations rather than organized settlement schemes, since minimal agricultural planning and services were provided.

The first major settlement project established in colonial Africa was the Gezira Scheme of the Sudan. This scheme was conceived and implemented by the administration in the early 1950s, in what has been described as 'a spirit of paternalism and a paramountcy of native interest'. It was a large-scale, irrigated, and mechanized project for the production of cotton for export (Gaitskell, 1959; Barnett, 1975). In other parts of Africa, colonial governments faced problems of over-population and resulting soil erosion. This led, for example, in Northern Rhodesia to a re-settlement of peoples in the Eastern Province under improved agricultural conditions (Allan, 1965).

Later, with the increased interest in encouraging co-operative modes of organization, several colonial governments ventured into group or co-operative farming experiments. These projects, like that of the peasant farming scheme of Northern Rhodesia (Coster, 1958), involved the re-settling of selected farmers on new farming plots that were administered by a manager or group of technicians. The farmers were offered a new technology and improved extension services, and required to collaborate in the performance of various work tasks. This, it was envisaged, would lead to economies of scale and higher levels of production. However, in most cases these schemes ran into administrative and financial difficulties. Tremendous debts were built up due to the provision of capital items on credit which it was impossible to repay if output was not constantly kept high or, if the return on crops dropped because of a fall in market prices. The organization of co-operative labour presented difficulties because of the differential degree of commitment shown by households of differing size and economic interest. There were also conflicts between the farmers and managers concerning decisions over production, cropping, and labour deployment. As these difficulties multiplied, so colonial regimes became more and more disillusioned with this approach and concentrated once again on piecemeal improvement through the use of better extension work and through the introduction of cash-crops into existing peasant farming systems. But the idea of using co-operative forms of organization was not completely abandoned. During the last decades of colonial government a large number of marketing, servicing, and credit co-operatives were set up to handle supply and distributional problems among small-holder farmers.

The idea of settlement schemes was revived during the early

years of independence, and in countries like Kenya, Uganda, Tanzania, and Zambia a great deal of attention was given to setting up new settlement projects under state control. Some of these projects, as Chambers shows, were forced on new governments by populations being displaced by political changes (e.g. the re-settlement of the southern Sudanese in Uganda, the peoples from Rwanda in Uganda and Tanzania). Refugee settlements, however, were basically formed with the objective of incurring a minimum of expenditure so that the displaced persons could as quickly as possible become self-supporting. In addition to these settlements, various governments devised ambitious plans to solve other sorts of problems. For example, in Western Nigeria, agricultural re-settlement programmes were implemented to counteract the drift of school leavers to towns (Olatunbosun, 1967), and there was also in Kenya the 'Million Acre' Settlement Scheme which was an attempt to re-distribute European farms to landless Africans. Uganda established mechanized farming schemes to bring larger areas under cultivation and to achieve higher levels of productivity. Tanzania initiated a villagization programme to re-group the population so that people could avail themselves more easily of various agricultural and other services (Cliffe and Cunningham, 1973). During these initial years of independence, a great deal of foreign aid and service was provided for the development of settlement projects. A popular model was that of the Israeli *moshav* which involved small, individual farms with centralized services for cultivation, marketing, and social welfare. The farm settlement programmes in Nigeria were explicitly based on this model; and Tanzania received assistance from Israeli advisors.

Most of these schemes were organized through direct intervention by the state. There are very few examples of them being initiated and organized from local level. A remarkable exception is that of the Ruvuma Development Association in southern Tanzania which, under the inspiration of local political party officials and with the collaboration of certain overseas aid agencies, established a number of collective settlements (Cunningham, 1966; Ibbott, 1966; Long, 1970b). These were small in scale and produced little in the way of crops for export. Their main features were that they opened up new land for production without depending on massive hired labour and mechanization, and that they attempted to establish socialist forms of production. This experiment later provided a blueprint for the *ujamaa* policy introduced by the national government which was extended to many other parts of the country (Nyerere, 1967; 1968; Long, 1970b).

Chambers's review of settlement schemes in Africa concludes that very few involved the establishment of communal forms of land tenure: most were organized in individual plots but provided for co-operation in certain farming tasks. Only in Tanzania was there a genuine attempt to socialize agriculture by shifting from individual exploitation of land towards a collective system based on communal ownership and control.[4]

Chambers distinguishes between four broad types of settlement schemes. A central feature of the first type is the planned organization of small individual holdings where farm decisions are taken independently by the settlers. Capital costs per settler are low and so, too, are operating costs. What co-operation that exists is largely of an *ad hoc* kind, since official controls are slight and limited to land transactions and soil conservation rules. The managerial style is advisory and has very few sanctions at its disposal.

The second type is characterized by having a mandatory marketing system which often extends to cover regulations concerning the cultivation of certain crops. There is also, in most cases, a reasonably developed system of credit for the purchase of equipment and/or land. Farm units are small and run independently, although some cash-crop decisions may be controlled by the management. Capital and operating costs are somewhat higher than the first type of scheme but still of moderate level. The organization of marketing is generally operated by a co-operative society; and official supervision is limited to the production of crops required for credit repayments or processing. The managerial style is both advisory and disciplinary; and a central body exists to ensure seasonal credit and/or regular supplies of a crop to a processing plant.

The third type is distinguished by having an organization of centrally controlled technical services (dealing, for example, with mechanization and irrigation) upon which cash-crop production on individual holdings is based. For convenience of operation, farm units are usually arranged in strips. Capital costs are high and frequently subsidized, although attempts are made to cover operating costs through deductions in the pay-outs. In order to ensure that repayments are made, marketing is organized through a central organization and farmers are required to market their crops through this channel. Considerable official control exists: there is a centrally determined schedule for the provision of technical services, and management is essentially technocratic and commercial. Sanctions can be operated through deductions made for the services performed by the management when the settlers fail to carry out farming instructions. There is also the possibility of witholding such services and of evicting defaulters. Official control generally lasts for a long period before any devolution of authority takes place enabling the settlers themselves to run their own affairs.

The last type of settlement scheme is one where, in addition to scheduled services, land and labour-use are communal and the rewards collectively shared. Even if settlers have small individually farmed plots, the main territorial unit is the scheme as a whole. High capital and operating costs are either subsidized or recouped by deductions before pay out from crop-sales takes place. Co-operative forms of organization predominate and strict controls are imposed to ensure that settlers perform set activities at particular times. Management varies but is often based on a strong ideological commitment of a political or religious nature, and sanctions are generally social and politico-economic, rather than simply legal. The marketing, production, and allocation of settler labour is centrally determined. Devolution of power within the settlement is normally planned for, but the scheme, if it survives, will remain a special entity.

Obviously there is considerable variation in the form of settlements within each of these categories but this typology gives some indication of the more dominant patterns. There is also the developmental aspect whereby settlement schemes may change in character from one type to the other. They may, for example, start off having close supervision but later move towards a more decentralized structure. An assessment of the viability of such schemes for promoting rural development is a complex problem requiring analysis of the interplay of economic, administrative, and socio-political aspects. In order to indicate broadly some of the dimensions involved, I intend to examine the recent experience of

Tanzania in attempting to establish new *ujamaa* settlements. These settlements are characteristically small-scale, involve a relatively low level of capitalization, and aim at establishing socialist forms of production.

Ujamaa Settlements in Tanzania

Having spent five or more years trying to make a financial and administrative success of large-scale settlement schemes of the kind described above, the Tanzanian Government decided in 1967, under the inspiration of President Nyerere, to commit itself to the implementation of a smaller scale and more locally-rooted policy which would concentrate upon the development of co-operative modes of organization. Nyerere (1967) argued that the heavy capital investment and concentration of extension workers and experts, which had been a feature of the earlier settlement programme, had proved a costly and administratively dubious exercise. He proposed as an alternative that Tanzania should develop production-based co-operatives which would require a relatively low capital input, would remain small in scale, and would be initiated primarily by local farmers. This programme he designated the '*ujamaa*[5] development scheme'. As I suggested earlier, this policy was partly stimulated by the experiments in socialism practised in southern Tanzania by the villages of the Ruvuma Development Association.

I cannot review here the large though somewhat scattered literature dealing with *ujamaa* development in different parts of the country. Instead I wish merely to outline the sorts of factors that should be considered when accounting for the success or otherwise of the *ujamaa* programme.

A primary commitment of *ujamaa* is to the notion of collective work. Although not all *ujamaa* villages at the present time are operated on a collective basis, the idea of moving towards a fully collective system with communal ownership and control of land and other resources is a central feature of the programme. The second important aspect is that these settlements should not be heavily dependent on government for aid and should be self-reliant in terms of labour and other basic resources. Linked to this is the view that labour should be fully employed if collectivism is to succeed.

The degree to which particular settlements approximate to these ideals is affected by a host of factors. In the first place, we have the influence of technology and the cropping system. Depending on the type of crops grown, the required labour supply will vary both in total amount and from month to month. Hence, it is important that the pattern of labour organization takes account of the demands of particular crops and devises a system whereby the labour force of the settlement is gainfully employed during the full agricultural cycle. The use of mechanization, as it has been practised for wheat cultivation in the north of Tanzania, creates special problems, since this reduces very considerably the amount of labour needed; whereas a crop like tobacco presents the opposite sort of difficulty. Tobacco requires heavy but fluctuating labour inputs. It is important, therefore, to arrange for sufficient labour to be available for tobacco production during its peak periods and for some of the labour to be employed on other tasks during the low seasons. The organization of labour also involves the problem of devising a satisfactory set of criteria by which the settlement rewards its workers; and it must do this in the face of considerable variations in the amount and type of labour provided by individual households due to differences in family size and age-sex composition. Hence, careful studies are required of the kinds of labour organization possible under different agricultural and demographic regimes (see Feldman, 1969).

In addition to these factors, which are directly concerned with the production process, there is a whole range of other social factors affecting the propensity and willingness of individuals and families to engage in co-operative forms of organization. Careful note must be taken of the types of external relationships maintained by members of the settlement. In many cases, especially during the early years, members are allowed to retain plots of land outside the settlement at their old villages. This is permitted so as to provide security during the early settlement phase. The existence of these individual plots in the villages of origin, however, tends to make certain individuals less inclined to engage in co-operative work for the settlement itself, especially during times when their own crops are ready for harvesting or planting. A second problem concerns the questions of whether or not people are orientated to seek employment outside the settlement. This sometimes arises from the need to acquire additional cash income for the purchase of clothing and consumer items. In some parts of Tanzania we find *ujamaa* settlements located close to commercial farms where seasonal or permanent wage employment is available. Some settlers take advantage of this and offer their labour during certain times of the agricultural cycle. This undoubtedly affects the smooth running of collective labour at *ujamaa* settlements, although under certain circumstances it may have the opposite effect of taking up slack when there exists a labour surplus (see, for example, the case of mechanized wheat production, Newiger, 1968; and Raikes, 1968). A third aspect concerning external relationships is that of migration due to improved educational standards. If *ujamaa* settlements encourage the education of children, as many of them do, this is likely in the long run to lead to a process whereby at least a proportion of the young men and women will leave in search of higher education and the hope of urban employment. This is a problem which has been endemic to the kibbutzim of Israel (Eisenstadt, 1968) and which some *ujamaa* villages are now beginning to face. The loss of a sizeable number of young, educated members can have a profound impact upon the organizational viability of *ujamaa* settlements.

A different type of factor is the overall social composition of the settlement. Differences in commitment to the collective enterprise tend to vary according to household structure and the stage of family development. It has been argued, for example, that *ujamaa* villages made up of households of young couples have the best chance of developing communal control of resources and collective labour organization, since fewer problems arise over labour inputs and the allocation of rewards (Feldman, 1969). Also age and sex differences are sometimes associated with differing socio-economic interests and perceptions of the value of collective work. Hence, it would seem that women who continue to cultivate gardens outside the settlement will tend to be less interested in communal production, and that younger members 'may show a higher degree of orientation towards the commercialization of agriculture and towards maximizing profits wherever possible, whilst the older men are concerned with achieving some satisfactory level of returns' (Long, 1970b:354). Divergence of opinions and interests, therefore, can disturb internal social relations and interfere with the attempts at establishing a collectivized system.

Other differences arise because of ethnic or cultural differentiation. Several *ujamma* settlements are composed of families from different and possibly conflicting tribal and cultural backgrounds. In certain circumstances this can lead to difficulties in the running of *ujamaa* institutions, although, as Feldman (1969) argues for the sisal settlements, this does not necessarily follow. The sisal example is particularly pertinent in that these *ujamaa* villages were established by persons of diverse tribal affiliation but who had a common work experience (i.e. they had worked together on the sisal plantations) and were all members of the Tanganyika African National Union (TANU) political party.

A final point of importance is the nature of the relationships of the leaders of the community to other members and to government or party officials, and the extent to which political ideology is a strong motivating force for collective endeavour. The establishment of an *ujamaa* settlement is, in effect, an attempt to institute a new form of democratic organization tied to a new political ideology; and its economic and organizational success depends in part upon how effectively this is done. It is for this reason that Cliffe (1970) and others (Luttrell, 1971; Awiti, 1972) stress the importance of political propaganda and the training of political cadres to go out into the countryside to convince peasants of the advantages of the *ujamaa* way of life.

Recent commentators (Huizer, 1971; Cliffe and Cunningham, 1973; Coulson, 1975; Raikes, 1975) on the policy of *ujamaa* have drawn attention to various ways in which the Tanzanian Government, in its bid to achieve a rapid and economically successful transition to socialism, has failed to live up to its original ideals. The move towards increased communal production has been slower than expected, due mainly it seems to the poor performance on existing communal plots (see, for example, Angwasi and Ndulu, 1973; and Boesen, 1972:37). *Ujamaa* members join these new settlements in order to acquire land when they have none or to extend their agricultural production; but very few of them seem convinced of the advantages of communal production and most are more interested in their individual household plots allocated for domestic cultivation. In some cases farmers have been known to join *ujamaa* villages solely to gain access to government credit facilities or machinery, whilst they retain their own main plots elsewhere (Raikes, 1975). In other examples we find *ujamaa* villages catering predominately for the poorer peasantry who have been moved out of areas of population congestion in order to relieve pressure on land for the cultivation of cash-crops, with the net result that the wealthier commercial farmers immediately improve their economic condition whilst the new *ujamaa* farmers must struggle to start afresh.

In the face of such difficulties and contradictions, the government has increasingly adopted more centralized and coercive measures. This process in fact was initiated only two years after the 1967 Arusha Declaration proclaiming *ujamaa* policy, when the Ruvuma Development Association lost its autonomy and was taken over by TANU and government (Cliffe and Cunningham, 1973). This led in other parts of the country to increased participation by bureaucrats and party officials in the planning and implementation of *ujamaa* development. According to Raikes (1975) and Huizer (1971), this signified a return to the villagization and settlement policy of the early 1960s and meant an end to the *ujamaa* ideals of democratic participation and self-determination. Hence, *ujamaa* villages were frequently the creation of government officials who saw the *ujamaa* model as a solution to various practical problems. In many parts of Tanzania the indigenous population lived in scattered homesteads and this posed major difficulties for the provision of services such as schools, health clinics, and agricultural extension. This problem could be partially solved by concentrating the population in larger settlements, close to existing roads; this would also, as in the early colonial days, facilitate the smooth running of administration and enable government to establish more effective control over the peasant population. Similar arguments were advanced for the conversion of the old settlement projects into *ujamaa* villages and for the settlement of peoples displaced by the 1962 and 1968 floods. Thus, whilst lip service was paid to the notion of *ujamaa* grass-roots development, the evidence indicated that in many areas of the country government had actively intervened in order to convince or force peasants into accepting the *ujamaa* model. This has gone hand in hand with the extension of political party control at local and regional levels. Williams (1975) quotes a most enlightening passage from a TANU document of 1972 which enunciates government policy and which indicates the role to be played by the party. It argues that:

' "Small farmsteads and hand implements cannot be expected to bring about modern development. It is difficult for individual farmers who do not exploit their fellow men farmers to get rid of their small farmsteads and hand implements. Therefore it is our responsibility to hasten them to join in Ujamaa villages so as to be able to till bigger farms and use modern farming techniques".' (Williams, 1975:46–7)

This shows that government now views problems of development in much the same way as it did in the days before *ujamaa*. Party officials and members are assigned the role of stimulating the spread of so-called better agricultural practices just as the 'progressive' farmers did in the colonial period (Williams, 1975); and rather less, it seems, is left in the hands of the peasants themselves.

These aspects are part of the general drift towards greater centralization and bureaucratization of the programme. Thus, as Williams (1975) comments,

'Frustrated by the lack of peasant enthusiasm for forming villages or settlements, or producing communally, *ujamaa* turned into a programme of compulsory villagization, without any element of communal production. "Operations" were expanded throughout the low-density areas of the country, and on 6 November, 1973, Mwalimu (the President) declared that "To live in villages is an order", to be implemented by 1976.'

It remains to be seen in detail what the effects will be of this re-orientation in *ujamaa* policy, and to compare the Tanzanian experience with other Third World attempts at socialist transformation.

The Role of Land Reform

Another strategy for effecting major re-organization of the socio-economic structure of rural areas is that of land reform. This policy entails direct intervention by the state in order to introduce major changes in the tenancy or ownership of land. The decision to opt for land reform as a development strategy results, it seems, from the recognition of a growing agrarian problem characterized by major disparities in the distribution and control of land by various rural groups, and by the political exigency of having to deal with a peasantry which has begun to initiate, or threatens to initiate, the seizing of land held by larger landowners.

Land reform programmes come in many shapes and sizes. Some, like that of Taiwan in the 1940s and 1950s, attempt a gradual introduction of measures aimed at the creation of an economically more equitable and more productive smallholder farming system (see Dorner, 1972:49). The Taiwan programme was carried out in three stages: first, the introduction of legislation to reduce farm rents; second, the sale of publicly owned lands; and third, the implementation of a ceiling on private land holdings. Other programmes offer more sweeping reforms, often under a single piece of legislation. These latter have frequently adopted a collectivist solution whereby land is jointly farmed and its usufruct shared either through some co-operative or state farming system.[6] Examples of the latter would include the Cuban programme of the early 1960s, and the land reform policies of Allende's Chile and of the present Peruvian government.

Analysis of the causes and consequences of land reform is a complicated matter which requires an assessment of the pre-reform situation and of previous attempts at initiating agrarian change, together with an account of the new legislation and new government agencies created by it to carry through the programme. In addition, it is important to document the ways in which land reform affects other facets of the socio-economic structure: for example, employment opportunities, marketing, and forms of peasant organization. Evaluation of the outcomes of specific programmes necessitates a longitudinal approach since most reforms require between five and ten years before their full effects can be measured, by which time, of course, certain basic economic and political parameters may have changed.

In order to explore these and other dimensions, I intend to discuss the recent attempts by the Peruvian Government to implement a widespread programme of land reform. The Peruvian case is especially interesting because it represents one of the more recent examples of a collectivist type, and because there is considerable disagreement among observers as to the basic aims and effectiveness of the policy.

Land reform in Peru. When the military *junta* came to power in October 1968, it faced serious problems in the rural sector and in the economy generally. On top of the serious balance of payments crisis inherited from the Belaunde regime, there was unrest among peasants and agricultural workers due primarily, it seems, to the poor tenancy and work conditions that prevailed. During the 1960s this had led to an increase in the unionization of agricultural workers on the coastal plantations and to various political movements in the highlands which aimed at improving peasant access to basic economic and political resources. Indeed, the latter occasioned several successful occupations of hacienda land by peasants (see Craig, 1968; Hobsbawm, 1974; Smith, 1975). Clearly aware of this mounting pressure, President Belaunde had himself introduced, in 1964, a land reform which sought to expropriate the larger haciendas and place them under peasant control, though the more productive sugar and cotton estates on the coast were specifically excluded. However, Belaunde was unable to acquire the necessary political support in government and at regional level to implement this policy. It was left, therefore, to the military to issue a new, though basically rather similar, law which aimed at expropriating all large-scale agricultural enterprises both on the coast and in the highlands.

The legislation is very complex and covers a wide range of different aims. These include the following: to increase agricultural production and productivity; to create more extensive rural markets for Peruvian manufactured goods; to abolish certain tenancy share-cropping arrangements that involve systems of payment based on personal services of various kinds; to consolidate small and medium sized holdings; to stimulate the formation of co-operative organizations and collective systems of production; and finally, to achieve a more just income distribution in the agricultural sector, thus eliminating major inequalities due to differential control over the means of production. The law details various land ceilings above which expropriation can take place. These vary according to ecological zone.[7] For example, on the coast all directly managed holdings are expropriable if in excess of 150 irrigated hectares or 1500 hectares of natural pasture. In the highlands, the ceiling for irrigated arable land varies from 15–55 hectares, depending upon soil type and location, and for livestock holdings the limit is established by reference to the amount of pasture necessary to support 5000 head of sheep or the equivalent in other animals. The new law makes all livestock and machinery liable to expropriation and, unlike the 1964 law, specifically includes the sugar plantations and their associated processing mills. Indeed, these latter were some of the first commercial estates to be taken over by the government in 1969.

In order to carry out the necessary expropriations, government organized the setting up of a number of Agrarian Reform Zones. These zones are now divided into smaller areas called PIARS (Projects of Integrated Rural Settlements) consisting of a number of expropriated enterprises[8] which are grouped together to take advantage of supposed economies of scale in production, marketing, extension work, and credit facilities. A central aspect of the new legislation is that the owners of expropriated properties can be compensated. The amount received is determined by reference to existing property tax lists which, because owners desire to lessen their tax commitments, will generally undervalue the real commercial value of the holdings. Compensation is payable with a minimum cash payment and the rest in the form of government bonds. As an incentive to ex-landlords, bondholders are given the option of offering their bonds for industrial investment and, providing this constitutes 50 per cent or more of their total holdings and the scheme is acceptable to the Industrial Bank, then the investor will receive the cash value for the remaining bonds as well. This, it has been suggested, is a subtle way of encouraging the flow of capital into the developing industrial sector (see Quijano, 1970).

At the time of first issuing the new agrarian law, the government apparently did not have clear plans on what kind of organizational framework it wished to develop on the newly expropriated farms. However, in the months that followed, it emerged that co-operative modes were to be a preferred form and that the large haciendas and plantations were not to be split up among peasants and agricultural workers. These new large co-operative-type enterprises were to be of two different kinds: Production Co-operative (CAPS) and Agrarian Societies of Social Interest (SAIS). Several reasons were advanced for this strategy. It was argued that it was important to maintain the unity of pre-existing large-scale farms so as to minimize disruption of production. Also large-scale units, it was supposed, provided economies of scale in production, marketing, finance, and administration; and would be expected to create new employment opportunities through economic diversification. The costs of improving social conditions, such as housing, education, medical care, etc., would be correspondingly less; and peasants and workers alike would play a more effective part in the socio-political system through their participation in, and control of, the co-operatives.

Yet, like many similar formulations, this policy appears to have been based upon several questionable assumptions. In the first place, as I have indicated before, it does not necessarily follow that larger units are more productive; indeed the bulk of empirical evidence suggests that the productivity per hectare is greater on smaller farms. Similarly, the maintenance of large production units does not necessarily imply that the population will be concentrated in a small number of settlements where welfare and educational services can be easily supplied. The livestock haciendas of the highlands are, for example, characterized by a highly dispersed settlement pattern. Also, as I have shown in my discussion of the Tanzanian *ujamaa* policy, co-operatives often result in increased centralization and state control. They do not always entail greater peasant and worker participation at local or national level.

The creation of the two types of large-scale units – the CAPs and SAIS – constitute in fact the Peruvian government's attempt to deal with two quite distinct contexts. The Production Co-operatives (CAPs) represent a solution to the expropriation of very large-scale and commercially viable estates, such as the sugar and cotton plantations on the coast; whereas the formation of Agrarian Societies (SAIS) is a response to a mainly highland situation where the original haciendas were bordered by peasant communities that had for many years disputed the ownership of hacienda territory and had fought to secure additional land for themselves.

According to government legislation, a CAP is an indivisible production unit in which the ownership and utilization of assets is collective; and where individual production is prohibited, although in practice several co-operatives allow members to retain small plots for household consumption. Members receive wages or salaries and a share in the profits of the enterprise. Division of profits is either determined by the number of days worked by the members in question, or on the basis of a simple equal division. A General Assembly, consisting of the entire membership, or of a number of delegates if there are more than 500 members, is the body responsible for internal policy matters; and day-to-day administration is undertaken by an appointed professional manager who is assisted by various member committees. The Administrative Committee (*Consejo de Administración*) works in close association with the manager whose operational decisions it is normally expected to approve; and the Vigilance Committee (*Consejo de Vigilancia*) has the job of overseeing the running of the co-operative so that the decisions taken conform to both internal regulations and government legislation. The Agrarian Law requires that funds be allocated to deal with specific aspects like education, social services, and investment. The latter category makes up the largest of these obligatory contributions and must amount to at least 15 per cent of annual profits. In addition, each co-operative has to make annual payments to the state over a twenty-five year period to cancel the agrarian debt incurred on acquisition of the property. This is a considerable financial burden and can account for as much as 50 per cent of gross income in any one year. The remaining balance, after these various deductions have been made, is then divided up amongst the membership and paid in the form of cash or kind.

Co-operative membership is determined initially by the Agrarian Reform agency. A standard rule of thumb used is that all workers who have been employed on the estate for at least six months of the preceding year qualify. The rest, mostly seasonal workers, do not. This has led in many coastal co-operatives to a situation wherein ex-permanent workers receive a share in the co-operative whilst temporary labour, which continues to be used for specific tasks, is recruited and rewarded in exactly the same way as labourers are on privately owned farms. Indeed, according to one calculation, the volume of labour contributed by non-members on sugar co-operatives is far in excess of that provided by the members themselves, and is often employed all the year round for such tasks as cane cutting (Scott, 1972:279).

Several of these Production Co-operatives are extremely large. For example, Casagrande is reputed to be the largest sugar estate in the world, consisting of some 30,487 hectares, of which 23,195 were under sugar cane in 1974, with a membership of 4,855. Units of this size produce major organizational problems. In an attempt to solve some of these, the state has taken a firm hand in the appointment of delegates and managers: according to Zaldivar (1974:34), it is laid down that at least 25 per cent of delegates must be engineers or technicians. This enables government to intervene in management, since most of these are also members of the government-sponsored Central Organization of Sugar Co-operatives of Peru (CECOAAP). Moreover, of the twenty-eight managers (*interventores*) directly appointed by government, the majority, it seems, were formerly employed by the American Company of Grace Ltd., that controlled three of the largest plantations (Zaldivar, 1974:31).

In many cases, government has gone a good deal further than the suggested level of 25 per cent: in 1970, only one of six co-operative assemblies was made up of a majority of elected sugar workers; the other five had a clear majority, and in some cases, a three-quarter's majority of appointed members. Another implication is that the old earnings differential between management and technical staff and workers is perpetuated so that the former receive salaries that are considerably higher than those of the best paid workers, and in some cases, double the amount they had received during the days of private ownership.

The increasing role of the state in the running of these Production Co-operatives has created difficult relations with the trade unions. During the early days of the reform, government used the legislation to try to suppress the unions and prohibited union members from holding official positions on the co-operative committees. This sparked off several strike actions organized by workers in support of their union leaders (Scott, 1972:280), and forced government to rescind the ruling so as to allow a number of union members to be elected to office.

The main aim of government, then, appears to have been to retain the basic units of production and type of administrative control found on the plantations. It has only moved a short distance towards the co-operative ideals of democratic participation and equal profit-sharing. In addition, through the land tax and agrarian debt, the state is able to extract a sizeable proportion of the surplus generated by these enterprises. Thus, in 1971 the Tuman sugar co-operative, for instance, had to pay some 118,000 *soles*[9] in taxes and agrarian debt out of its total income of 228,000 *soles* (Zaldivar, 1974:37). Yet despite this, the evidence suggests that substantial improvements have been made in the earnings of members and in various types of essential services, such as education and housing. Horton (1973) concludes from a study of coastal co-operatives that between 1968 and 1970 there was an overall growth of about 64 per cent in wages and expenditure on infrastructure; although he points out that, at the same time, employment diminished due to increasing mechanization of cane production. This, coupled with the income disparities between seasonal and permanent workers, and between the latter and the management class, has exacerbated the socio-economic divisions existing in the zone, which, in some cases, have manifested themselves politically, as unions, associations of smallholders and medium-sized farmers, peasant organizations, and other interest groups have sought to protect or improve their members' livelihoods.

The Agrarian Societies (SAIS) are a form of organization designed to deal with a rather different situation. SAIS has been established in highland regions where ex-haciendas are bordered by freeholding peasant communities that had, in many instances, disputed the territorial limits and legal title of hacienda land. The main objective of SAIS has been to preserve the physical and administrative unity of the existing livestock units (ex-haciendas), whilst at the same time distributing some of the profits amongst neighbouring peasant communities, so as to reduce the possibility of land invasion and to promote social and economic development. Under the law, a SAIS is made up of the workers of the ex-hacienda (now named a production unit) and of a number of peasant communities that are designated as beneficiaries. Workers on the production unit are organized into a service co-operative which is regarded as making up one member of the SAIS. Each community also counts as a member. This marks an important difference between SAIS and the Production Co-operatives, for, whereas in the case of the latter, it is the individual members who constitute the membership, in a SAIS the membership is composed of a number of legally recognized organizations, not individuals. Hence, we find, for example, in SAIS Cahuide, which is situated in the central highlands, that there are seven production units and some 29 member communities. The ex-haciendas add up to some 269,115 hectares and, in addition, the communities themselves control a further 13,618 hectares. The total complex is populated by 17,800 persons.

Another distinction between a CAP and a SAIS is that in a SAIS the land and labour of the ex-haciendas and communities is not integrated for collective production. Land belonging to one particular production unit is worked by ex-hacienda permanent workers, supplemented at peak periods by outside labour. Community members (*comuneros*) work the lands of their own communities quite separately and are not supposed to pasture their herds on ex-hacienda land, even though they may have previously held such grazing rights. However, although *comuneros* do not work in the production units, they do share in the distribution of profits, which is so organized that it is the poorest communities, as measured by a pre-reform economic valuation, that receive the biggest shares. For example, in SAIS Pachacutec, studied by Fonseca (1975:361), we find that the service co-operative, representing the permanent workers, receives only a medium share in the distribution of profits, whereas nearly half of the member communities each receive up to 6 per cent more of the total.

The organizational structure of SAIS closely resembles that of the Production Co-operatives. Each member of SAIS has representation on SAIS's General Assembly of delegates, but since there are several community members and frequently only one service co-operative, the communities will predominate not only in the sharing of profits but also in management decisions. Thus, in SAIS Cahuide the service co-operative has only two delegates on the General Assembly as against 58 representatives for the communities. This has the curious consequence that those persons who in fact produce the wealth upon which the development of SAIS depends, can easily be outvoted and their interests disregarded. Serious tensions and conflicts have arisen, and in this particular case it has led to the formation of a labour union by the workers so that they might better protect their own interests (Roberts and Samaniego, 1973:13). In most SAIS we also find a division between workers and administrative staff. The latter are appointed by central government and are often engineers or administrators left over from the hacienda days. Thus, like the CAPs, SAIS are effectively controlled by a technical elite. Also, since SAIS are expected to pay off their agrarian debt in annual instalments, government can justify its intervention in management and planning until the debt is fully recovered.

Most of the profits that communities receive is earmarked for social welfare of various kinds. There in fact exists a statutory requirement to set aside part of SAIS's profits for re-investment, education, and social services, totally some 45 per cent (Roberts and Samaniego, 1973). The extent of these obligations, including that of debt repayment, is such that only a relatively small percentage of profits in any one year is available for other purposes. In the case of SAIS Cahuide, the total available for distribution amounts to about 300,000 *soles*, that is an average of just over 10,000 *soles* per village. The use of these funds is supervised by the Development Division. It has been invested mostly in village projects such as schools, roads, bridge construction, and transport.

The SAIS model represents, as Roberts and Samaniego (1973:5) put it, 'a middle of the road reform: it does not represent the decentralized working economy of a co-operative nor is it a state run enterprise. It is in theory a gradualistic instrument by which its members slowly take over more control and receive greater benefits from the enterprise', though, for the time being, government continues to play a major decision-making role. The formation of SAIS has, it seems, enabled government to create a sense of social and economic participation, while retaining under its close control the productive organization of the ex-haciendas. Eventually, however, government (so it claims) expects that the SAIS will evolve into fully-fledged co-operatives and that the villages themselves will become more organized around co-operative institutions leading to a more diversified economy, containing agro-industrial, consumer, service, and distribution co-operatives.

But a major obstacle to such a plan is the highly differentiated nature of the membership, which is not only reflected in the division between permanent workers and community members but also in the composition of the villages themselves. Roberts and Samaniego's study of SAIS Cahuide demonstrates, for example, how the *comuneros* are internally differentiated in terms of their basic socio-economic interests and this, they suggest, hinders the formation of co-operative institutions.[10] According to them, many of the more entrepreneurially minded community members are involved in economic activities that link them with the lowland valley region rather than the ex-hacienda pastoral zone. These activities often involve trading ventures (e.g. in livestock and agricultural products) or migration for work in mining or administration centres. A similar point is made by Fonseca (1975: 362) who records that several member communities of SAIS Pachacutec are closely integrated with the mines: in one community some 80 per cent of registered *comuneros* work as miners in nearby mining towns; and in one year they devoted their share of the SAIS income to the building of a road to link the community with the mine town of Collqui.

All this indicates, then, that some villagers have become less concerned with the opportunities available in pastoral farming and more oriented towards outside possibilities. Hence, communities are divided between locally and extra-locally oriented members, which makes it difficult for them to identify common economic interests and to come together to form village co-operatives as recommended by the Development Division. This process of internal differentiation is not peculiar to SAIS communities, but has been widely commented upon for highland Peru. Indeed, it has also proved to be a major hindrance to the successful application of the new Statute for Peasant Communities aimed at the development of production co-operatives based on the joint exploitation of existing communal lands (for details, see Long and Winder, 1975).

Although it is probably far too early to judge the success or otherwise of the reform from an economic point of view – there is a dearth of data anyway – a recent report suggests that since 1968 total agricultural production and per capita food production have increased significantly (Horton, 1974:9, Chart 1). It also shows that over 80 per cent of a sample of 27 reform enterprises had earned profits in 1972–73. In half of them, output and employment had risen, and in over two-thirds investment as well (Horton, 1974: 108–109). Other data are provided by Harding (1974:16) who argues that with one exception (Cayalti), the sugar co-operatives 'have been highly successful economically and their members are relatively privileged members of the Peruvian working class'. The co-operatives of Tuman and Pucala received 100 per cent wage increases in 1972 and, in 1973, at Casagrande, the share out amounted to 11,700 *soles* per individual, which was a reasonable extra bonus.

It is difficult on the basis of such scanty information to generalize for the whole of Peru. However, there does appear to be some indication of a gradual increase in performance, at least among the technologically and commercially more developed estates of the coast. For example, Horton's report shows that enterprises previously operating with a system of wage labour were more successful than those that had tenancy and sub-tenancy arrangements. On the negative side, of course, there is the flow of resources from the reform sector due to the payment of agrarian debt and taxes. This places considerable financial strain on the smaller, less productive co-operatives.

The political dimensions of the reform can be more clearly delineated. As I suggested earlier, the idea of land reform and its swift implementation was in part dictated by political considerations. The immediate application of the policy to the sugar estates was partly designed, it seems, to undermine the political support of the APRA (*Alianza Popular Revolucionaria Americana*) party, which had, since the 1930s, established a strong base within the unionized proletariat (see Klaren, 1973) and which constituted the only visibly organized opposition to the military. The expropriation of the livestock estates in the highlands was likewise related to political troubles in the peasant sector.

Nevertheless, the land reform programme has generated its own brand of political problems. One major factor has been the massive role allocated to the state in the total process. The state was responsible for redistributing the expropriated land, for setting up the new enterprises, for drawing up the production plans for the various zones, and for co-ordinating the plans for particular production units; it also organized the supply of credit through the government Agricultural Development Bank. The only area where the new enterprises have relative autonomy is in the recruitment and use of labour. Political control by the state has been aided in recent years by the creation of a new institution named SINAMOS (*Sistema Nacional de Apoyo a la Mobilización Social*), which has been given the job of co-ordinating regional development and bringing together the various types of economic enterprise, associations of landowners, peasant unions, and community associations characteristic of particular regions. A basic motive here, it seems, is that government wishes to assume greater control at local and regional levels. However, SINAMOS has the mammoth and probably impossible task of reconciling conflicting interest groups and basic social contradictions in Peruvian society. These oppositions have been exacerbated by the land reform policy. Its implementation has set off a whole series of social conflicts: conflicts between poor peasants and landless agricultural labourers, between the direct beneficiaries and the non-beneficiaries of land reform, between the unions and the production co-operatives and the government (in the sugar industry particularly), and between APRA and other political groups. In the Agrarian Societies (SAIS), major antagonism exists between the ex-wage labourers and the members of peasant communities. There has also been confrontation between government and various organizations protecting the interests of middle peasants and landowners whose properties are threatened with expropriation under the new law. Most of the complaints made by the latter (e.g. by the Peruvian Stockbreeders Association, and other agricultural associations in Cañete, Ica, and other coastal valleys) were phrased in terms of the difficulties which farmers faced in the 'the climate of uncertainty and mistrust which discourages investment', and were not presented as direct attacks upon the programme itself (Harding, 1974:7).

Whether or not the Peruvian Government will be able to resolve these various difficulties and achieve its twin goals of increased production and a more equitable distribution of resources in the agricultural sector remains to be seen. Comparison with other rural development policies suggests that a programme of this size and extent is inevitably fraught with a multitude of uncertainties and unintended consequences which may in fact produce only moderate improvements. Other commentators take a more extreme view of the situation, arguing, like Quijano (1970) and Cockcroft, Frank, and Johnson (1972:141–5), that the Peruvian 'social revolution' was never really intended as a radical measure. It was essentially aimed at persuading capitalists to transfer their wealth from agriculture to industry and at developing more effective state control over the economy. The relative validity of these views requires further systematic testing. Sociological and economic research on the impact of the programme in different regions of the country is as yet in its infancy.

CONCLUSION

As the preceding cases show, the discussion of rural development policies raises a number of complex problems for analysis. These include such aspects as the content of the policy itself (i.e. is it coherent, what are its underlying assumptions, and how do its objectives relate to planning in other economic sectors?), the types of administrative means devised for its implementation, and the likely outcomes of the strategy in particular regions and their feedback effects at national level.

A major difficulty in identifying the precise economic and socio-political objectives of policies is that governments seldom spell out clearly, without ambiguities, what they intend; nor do they indicate the exact priorities for the goals they set. A primary reason for this, of course, is that they need to retain a degree of flexibility so that they may modify or scrap their plans if these appear to be creating more problems than they actually solve. This process is illustrated by the shift towards increasing centralized control in the Tanzanian *ujamaa* programme after it was found that grass-roots development based on the principle of self-reliance was slow in making headway. Yet modification in the programme did not require much change in the rhetoric of development, which was still tied to the idea of creating socialist villages, though it did lead to changes in policy presentation and in the role of administrative and political staff at regional level.

The examination of development policies, then, requires an appreciation of the kinds of language and concepts employed, how these may change over time, and the varying interpretations offered by power-holders and by various interest groups at national and regional level. Policies in effect represent ideological devices for the making of political statements as well as being instruments by which governments attempt to solve their social and economic problems. However, it is equally important to analyze the ways in which policies are being implemented and the effects they are having, since an understanding of the 'practice of development' often reveals more about socio-political attitudes and interests than do policy documents *per se*. This, of course, raises the difficult issue of distinguishing between the intended and unintended consequences of policy.

These are intricate problems which I have only been able to touch upon in this chapter. They are further complicated by the fact that governments normally formulate a number of distinct policies aimed at dealing with different sectors and types of problems. These policies may conflict or contain elements that are contradictory in their outcomes. Hence, the Peruvian example shows that whilst attempts were made to implement structural change in certain fields (e.g. the land reform programme), in others, the government sought to protect the interests of established classes (e.g. it allowed for considerable private enterprise and speculation to continue in marketing and finance). The net result of this, it seems, was to reduce the impact of those reforms ostensibly aimed at achieving a more equitable distribution of productive resources, so that goods and capital could continue to flow relatively freely.

The main theme of the chapter has been to distinguish between two contrasting rural development policies and to illustrate these with particular empirical examples. The two approaches are broadly differentiated in terms of their socio-economic goals: the improvement approach aims to bolster up existing patterns of economic growth and to promote increased production in the peasant sector, whilst the transformation approach seeks to bring about structural change through making a radical break with existing systems. As the examples show, the latter has frequently involved the implementation of new settlement schemes and pro-grammes of land reform.

Underlying these two types of policy are different conceptions concerning the nature and problems of socio-economic develop-ment in the Third World. Improvement policies rest fundamentally on a modernization view of change, and stress the importance of the diffusion of modern technology, skills and resources to the 'traditional' sector, which for various reasons has lacked the motivation and opportunities to develop economically. This strategy, it is hoped, will lead to the emergence of a 'progressive' group of farmers who use improved techniques and produce for the market, and who eventually, through a 'demonstration effect', will encourage others to do likewise. This policy contrasts with the transformation approach which tends to draw its inspiration from a more radical tradition of social research. This tradition empha-sizes the necessity of making a break with existing systems of peasant production and of eliminating neo-colonial patterns of exploitation. Several governments that have recently adopted a transformation approach have, in fact, legitimated their position by direct reference to some kind of dependency critique of Third World development problems. For example, the Peruvian National Development Plan for 1971–5 opens with a paragraph devoted to describing the underdeveloped nature of the Peruvian economy caused by its satellite status in the international scene, and then affirms the government's intention to carry out a series of major social and economic reforms so as to ameliorate this condition.

Nevertheless, as the various case studies have stressed, there is no one-to-one relationship between policy commitment and the actual consequences of policy. This is most strikingly the case with the attempts at implementing a transformation approach, which generally spawns a large number of apparently unintended consequences. One of the reasons for this is that such a policy requires complicated planning involving different economic sectors and an elaborate administrative structure.

Analysis of the social consequences of rural development policies entails consideration of many dimensions: the relation between the particular policy and other government measures affecting the rural population; the patterns of political control and economic differentiation in the areas of implementation; the organization and styles of leadership characterizing the promotion agencies and government departments involved; the struggles occurring within the government bureaucracy for control of particular programmes and scarce resources; and the expectations and interests of the local population itself. A further crucial aspect concerns how different local groups interpret the general objectives and feasibility of government-sponsored schemes, and how far the policy itself favours the interests of particular social sectors at the expense of others. These are complex issues which necessitate focusing upon various structural, ideological, and organizational factors. This chapter offers a preliminary exposition of some of the more significant sociological dimensions.

CHAPTER 7

Conclusions

The foregoing review of literature has ranged widely over a number of theoretical and empirical issues. It is now time to take stock of these so that we might identify major themes and suggest lines for future research.

A central theme of many of the studies has been the relation between local-level processes and national development. This relation has been conceptualized from different theoretical standpoints. Modernization theorists tend to interpret the issues in terms of the ways in which so-called 'traditional' (and largely rural) social structures become incorporated into larger scale political and economic systems and in so doing gradually acquire the accoutrements of 'modernism'. A study of how this takes place requires documenting the processes by which societies become more differentiated institutionally and achieve new modes of structural integration. It is also necessary to examine the transfer of technical, social, and cultural items from the more 'modern' (or urban) to the more 'traditional' sector; and to diagnose the socio-cultural factors that facilitate or impede this process.

In contrast, dependency theorists visualize the effects of national development in terms of the setting up of vertically-organized patterns of dependency between metropolitan centres and various regional and local satellites. According to this model, the mass of the rural population remains subordinate to the more powerful interests of the urban bourgeoisie, who are aligned or conspire with foreign capitalists to siphon off economic surplus at successive points in the hierarchy of control. This process forms part of the phenomenon of 'under-development', which signifies the unequal relation between Third World economies and the advanced industrial nations, and which generates patterns of internal exploitation as well. Later writers suggest that at certain stages dependent capitalism allows for the maintenance of existing non-capitalist forms of production and associated institutions. Hence, rural social structure of a 'traditional' kind may persist and become functionally adapted to the requirements of capitalist markets for labour and products. The erosion or transformation of rural structures, therefore, can best be analyzed in terms of a socio-historical study of the penetration of capitalist forms of organization and of the kinds of exchanges that occur between capitalist and non-capitalist modes of production.

Although theoretically and ideologically opposed, modernization theory and the dependency model exhibit certain common tendencies. Both formulate a generalized linear model of socio-economic development which accords analytical priority to the role of exogenous factors in promoting change. Modernization approaches are based on a Western model of growth which posits that Third World countries will follow a similar developmental path. But whereas the Western experinece was of an industrial revolution from within, the Third World experiences a 'revolution' from outside brought by the impact of Western technology and by the transfer of social and cultural skills. Third World countries are characteristically composed of two sectors, the traditional-rural and economically backward sector, which is frequently the source of delays or obstacles to the path of modernization, and an urban-industrial, more modernized sector which provides the dynamic for change. Although certain formulations admit the existence of traditional institutions that are compatible with modern political and economic systems and that sometimes provide the essential pre-conditions for the rapid modernization of the society, the main emphasis is on changes that emanate from the modern urban centres or from the introduction of modern technology and commercial agriculture.

Early dependency theorists adopt a similar stance, although they would argue that the economic backwardness of Third World economies and of the rural sector results from the process of colonization and expansion of capitalism and is not inherent in the nature of non-capitalist institutions themselves. Nevertheless, they too stress the importance of external forces in promoting change and in determining local and provincial structures. They also tend to adopt a uni-directional view since under-development is seen as the logical outcome of the development of European capitalism and follows a broadly similar pattern in various Third World contexts. This is manifest most strikingly in the work of Frank, who argues that international capitalism has a disintegrating effect on existing traditional structures leading to the emergence of dependent forms of capitalism. Only in later dependency theorists do we find attention given to the problem of accounting for the persistence and apparent vitality of traditional, non-capitalist modes of organization.

Both types of analysis, then, tend towards a centralist view of development and interpret changes in the organization and activities of local populations as responses to externally-initiated change. Neither approach, it seems, gives sufficient attention to the ways in which local groups and processes can contribute and indeed modify the patterns of regional and national development. Hence, they tend to take too deterministic a view of socio-economic change and do not allow sufficiently for the interplay of local and national forces.

A corrective to this view is provided by anthropological work on socio-economic change. Anthropologists have been particularly interested in the question of differential responses to change and have analyzed the emerging patterns of entrepreneurship at village level. This has been combined with an interest in developing actor-oriented models of behaviour which identify the social strategies used by different individuals and households. The main contribution of this type of research is that it focuses upon the variations in response to broadly similar external circumstances shown by different social groups and categories; and it examines how local economies are articulated with the wider system through the activities of brokers of different types. Moreover, a detailed analysis of local structures highlights the differentiated and multi-structured nature of rural societies and this counteracts the tendency to regard peasants or rural people as a homogeneous class which merely reacts to forces impinging upon it from outside. This approach enables one to appreciate how the opportunity structure, which shapes the general pattern of aspirations and expectations, is, in fact, manipulated by particular households in accordance with their needs and in order to develop new economic and social strategies. The seizing of new opportunities is often facilitated by the use of existing sets of relationships and resources, and by the reinterpretation of traditional norms and values. An actor-oriented approach entails an understanding of the structural and ideological frameworks that limit peasant action, whilst also focusing on the process by which particular individuals and groups evolve ways of dealing with their changing environment. This leads to a closer consideration of the sets of interpersonal relationships involved, to a study of social networks and interpersonal exchanges, and to an account of how particular categories of peasants and entrepreneurs attempt to legitimate their decisions and courses of action through an appeal to values and ideologies.

A major implication of this type of analysis is that it emphasizes the need to view the significance of economic development and change from the actors' or recipients' perspectives, i.e. from 'below' rather than 'above'. It also offers the prospect of relating local-level processes and decisions to national structures, since it treats the peasant and local entrepreneur as active elements in the process by which rural transformation takes place and allows for the possibility that provincially-based groups may directly or indirectly influence the direction and outcomes of national development and policy. This is illustrated most dramatically by the way in which peasant political mobilization has in some instances led to radical changes in agrarian policy. Yet, even if peasants do not organize to oppose the state in this way but instead collaborate with government-sponsored programmes, this itself is evidence that they perceive some advantage in helping to reinforce a pattern of change already initiated.

The kinds of transactional and decision-making models discussed in Chapter 5, however, are limited by their tendency to concentrate upon individual decisions and interactional processes at the expense of comprehending the transformations occurring in the broader political and economic framework and how these affect choice and entrepreneurship at local level. Moreover, as Van Velzen (1973) argues, interest in problems of leadership (e.g. in entrepreneurs and brokers) leads to the neglect of the factors that determine the allocation of resources and the extraction of surplus by groups outside the immediate arena of the village.

This raises a further difficulty. Much anthropological work is restricted to the internal workings of a single residential unit such as a peasant village or hacienda, or of a relatively small district within a region; and only marginal treatment is given to the ways in which the local system forms part of a regional and national structure. It is precisely because of this that the articulation of the local system with the wider structure is frequently conceptualized in terms of the activities of individual brokers rather than seen as a structure of inter-related parts represented by different systems of production or levels of political control, or by social groupings of various kinds. Another consequence is the tendency to regard the behaviour of brokers or village migrants in external contexts as falling outside the main purview of the study. This, I believe, has militated against a more adequate analysis of the inter-relations of rural and urban groups and of the exchanges between different sectors of the economy. On the other hand, the consideration of such dimensions is also crucial for a fuller understanding of the nature and problems associated with village and household organization and development.

This suggests that actor-oriented approaches might be of much greater utility for the study of rural development if they were applied to social groups situated analytically within a regional rather than merely a local community context. One could then isolate varying economic and political strategies and perspectives on change from the point of view of actors occupying different social locations within the economic or geographical structure of the region. The success of this method of analysis would depend upon it being combined with a systematic historical and structural account of the characteristics of the regional economy; its links with the national system and its changes over time. Such a study would require giving close attention to the process of market penetration and to the development of new types of production and exchange relations, whilst at the same time documenting the ways in which existing forms of organization have been creatively adapted to meet the demands of new circumstances. It would also be necessary to examine at successive points in time the interaction between rural and urban groups, the types and magnitude of transfers or flows of value between different economic sectors (the agricultural, commercial, and industrial), and the interconnections between different modes of production.

It should then be possible to focus upon particular groups and individuals who control critical points of linkage in the regional socio-economic structure and to describe the differentiated nature of economic activities at the level of the household, enterprise, and social group. Such an approach aims to integrate both micro and macro levels of analysis, and to give equal attention to horizontal and vertical patterns of co-operation and control. It also recognizes the importance of explaining the variations in response to similar types of macro factors and of identifying the flexibilities in the pattern of pre-existing relationships and values.

As I have already emphasized, such an analysis must be set within the context of an historical study of the evolving economy and political structure of a specific region so that various stages in the process might be isolated. Only in this way is it possible to show how local groups have responded to changes in the regional and national economy and to explore how local-level organization and activities have influenced development at the broader level. This, I believe, can lead to a more meaningful treatment of the interplay of local and national development processes, and of the specific role played by the agricultural sector. In addition, it enables one to explain the persistence of certain traditional institutions as well as the emergence of new patterns of differentiation and social inequality, without adopting either a simple modernization or dependency approach to the problem.

A crucial dimension to take into account is that of the changing nature and policies of the state. This aspect, as I demonstrated in Chapter 6 when dealing with the problems of planned change, is central to any attempt to analyze the processes of rural development in the Third World.

The consideration of state intervention at regional and local level raises complex analytical issues which can only be dealt with briefly. In the first place, state policies are intimately related to the developing character of the national economy, which will vary according to the relative importance of the urban-industrial, mining, commercial, and agricultural sectors; and to the interests of the social groups or classes who control the governmental machinery and who therefore formulate these policies. A second aspect concerns the types of organization and development agencies set up to implement specific programmes and the nature of their relationships to central and local government bodies. A third range of problems relates to the question of determining the precise objectives and feasibility of specific policies and of documenting their intended and unintended consequences.

Each of these aspects is significant for studying the changing opportunities and dilemmas that form part of the process of socio-economic change at regional or village level, although, of course, no one such study can hope to do more than deal cursorily with national economic and political parameters. The best that can be expected is that those particular programmes and policies impinging upon the locality or region in question be examined in detail in order to determine their effectiveness in promoting certain kinds of structural and organizational change. This involves giving careful attention to how particular local groups interpret the aims of government and its programmes; how they participate in them and how they may utilize the newly-available resources in pursuit of their own goals. Such an analysis clearly links up with problems of entrepreneurship and socio-economic differentiation: the injection of additional organizational and material resources by government frequently results in increased opportunities for leadership and social manipulation, and often benefits only a small (and mostly already privileged) sector of the rural population. Moreover, changes in government policy can have important repercussions on the inter-relations between various social groups (e.g. between rural and urban populations or between different economic classes) and can in some cases lead to a reinforcement of 'traditional' institutions or, alternatively, to the development of new patterns of organization and levels of social consciousness. This process occasionally produces the unanticipated and contradictory outcome whereby local groups actively subvert government programmes in order to achieve their own sectional interests. In other cases, it leads to the state assuming more centralized control, resulting in a consequent loss of local autonomy.

The exploration of these problems, I suggest, is best tackled within a regional framework of analysis since this allows one to examine the effects of national politico-economic processes on different localities and social groups. Differences in outcomes may then be explained in terms of differences in ecology, resource-base, and degree of social differentiation, and by reference to existing external social networks and differing socio-cultural resources. Such an approach also isolates the socio-economic interdependencies of rural and urban groups and charts the pattern of exchanges (e.g. economic transactions and migration flows) characteristic of the region. Hence, it shifts emphasis away from the study of social groups defined primarily by physical location or by administrative and cultural units, towards the examination of social organization across spatial boundaries. This facilitates an understanding of the basic structure of the region and of how it articulates with other parts of the national system; and brings together an historical-structural account of regional inter-relations with that of an actor-oriented study of specific groups and individuals.[1]

Yet, despite the large body of literature on questions of regional development, there are few sociological studies of this kind.[2] The main emphasis, it seems, has been upon the study of regional integration from the point of view of 'growth poles', 'urban hierarchies', and 'centre-periphery' relations (see Brookfield, 1975: 105–23). Although certain of these concepts might be useful for unravelling complex spatial and economic patterns, most of this work fails to give sufficient weight to historical and situational dimensions. For example, there is no detailed discussion of the ways in which particular groups and social categories conceptualize and operate in terms of specific 'regions' or 'fields of activity', nor of how their definitions and interactions may change over time in response to transformations in the wider political economy.[3] Such questions I believe to be of critical importance for comprehending the changing nature of regional systems. Furthermore, when complemented by a structural analysis of the relations between different modes of production and of the linkages between different economic and social sectors, we have the beginnings of a sounder basis for the explanation of socio-economic change. This approach offers a 'middle-range' analysis which neither aims to formulate a grand theoretical schema for depicting patterns of development or underdevelopment, nor concentrates exclusively upon problems at the village or actor level. Instead, it represents an intermediate level of analysis which can best be developed through the comparative study of differing regional contexts. Such an approach, I believe, provides a necessary framework for the analysis of the processes of rural development.

Notes

CHAPTER 2

1. Compare Smelser's treatment of changes in the political system with Easton's more elaborate typology of political systems based on the degree of role differentiation (Easton, 1959).
2. Briefly put, Parsons was interested in the value patterns governing the behaviour of one actor towards another. Thus 'universalism' is paired with 'particularism' meaning by this that an actor has the choice between treating individuals as individuals ('particularism') or regarding them in the roles they play as members of classificatory groups, e.g. as producers, political leaders, etc. ('universalism'). He can choose between 'ascription' (responding to an individual because of his given attributes) or 'achievement' (because of what he has achieved); and between 'diffuseness' and 'specificity' (regarding him as the provider of many services or of specialized services only). For a fuller explanation of Parsonian theory see Rex (1961), especially pp. 105–9. For another application of the pattern variables to economic development see Thoedorson (1953).
3. See Preface to Smelser (1959) where he presents a formal model of structural differentiation in terms of Parsonian pattern variables. This study analyzes the social changes that accompanied the Industrial Revolution focusing on the Lancashire cotton industry. His later papers on developing countries are a further elaboration of this original idea.
4. Epstein's restudy fifteen years later shows that the break-up of the joint family was most marked among the middle–farmers where competition between family members was fierce, and its survival most evident among the wealthier village elite who used it to benefit from certain economies of scale. She also documents the emergence of a new pattern, 'the share family', which, like the joint family, operates as an economic unit, though its members no longer live under one roof. See Epstein (1973:200–11).
5. See W. E. Moore (1963:Chapter 1) for a fuller discussion of these and related problems.
6. See her discussion of the part played by 'progressive' and 'conservative' factions in both villages (Epstein, 1962:129–40, 284–90).
7. Another interesting study of the adaptations required to introduce a new commercial crop, in this case cocoa in Nigeria, is S. S. Berry (1975). See also P. Hill (1963).
8. This view of social change can of course be traced back to the work of

194 *Introduction to the Sociology of Rural Development*

Spencer who constructed an evolutionary typology of societies exhibiting varying degrees of structural complexity analogous to organisms, to Tonnies' distinction between *Gemeinschaft* (community) and *Gesellschaft* (society), to Durkheim's treatise on the division and increasing specialization of labour, and to Maine who wrote of the shift from 'status' to 'contract' societies.

9. In his discussion on development in Central and Eastern Europe and in the Middle East he distinguishes another pattern which he calls 'split-up' modernization. This denotes the process by which 'the push to modernization was split up between different groups or institutional focuses in society, among which a greater degree of incompatibility and conflict with regard to their modernization tendencies developed' (Eisenstadt, 1966:68).

10. See Van Velsen, 1967, for a more extensive critique of British structural anthropology.

11. For a discussion of this and other conceptual issues, see Smith, 1973: 61–79; Nettl and Robertson, 1968:42–57; and Desai, 1971.

12. Redfield later abandoned the notion of a folk-urban continuum in favour of an analysis of peasant societies in terms of what he called the 'Great' and 'Little' traditions (see Redfield, 1956, and Redfield and Singer, 1954). However he never lost interest in the study of urban-rural relations, which he examined from both a structural and cultural perspective.

13. See, for example, the extensive literature on the developmental cycles of domestic and village groups (Goody, 1958; Mitchell, 1956). The method has been justified by Gluckman (1968) as a sound procedure for the examination of certain types of problems.

14. For two recent critiques of dualism see Weeks (1971) who exposes the inadequacies of Lewis's original model of labour transfer; and Mafeje (1973) who draws upon African examples to demonstrate the difficulties of a dualist interpretation.

CHAPTER 3

1. Bennett (1966) suggests that Foster's model conforms to the 'zero-sum' situation of game theory, where 'the sum of one player's gains offsets exactly the second player's losses' (McGuire, 1964: 141). It is important to add the rider, however, that Foster does not take the view that a particular world view or cognitive orientation will always be consciously articulated by members of the society. On the contrary, he describes it as 'an unverbalized, implicit expression of their understanding of the "rules of the games" of living' (Foster, 1965: 293).

2. Foster's discussion is limited to what he calls 'classic' peasant societies, i.e. the village communities of the Mediterranean, Near East, India, China, and Latin America; and he describes negro Africa as semi-peasant (Foster, 1965:396). His characterization bears little relation to the problems of peasantization in Africa or more recently colonized areas. For a discussion of peasantries in twentieth century Africa see Post (1972).

3. Foster suggests that patron-client relationships may be regarded as extending beyond the natural to cover the supernatural order as well:

peasants supplicate the saints for specific acts of mercy or assistance and offer allegiance to them in a similar way as they do to their political patrons.

4. Attempts were also made to establish carpentry and weaving co-operatives in Tzintzuntzan, but these also failed. A main reason, it appears, was because they could not market their goods profitably (Foster, 1967:336–37).

5. There is an extensive literature on the Indian joint family, much of which assumes that it will break down, under the impact of industrialization, urbanization, and commercialization, and be replaced by the nuclear family. The persistence of joint family organization in some contexts is then interpreted as constituting an important barrier to socio-economic development (see, for example, Lannoy, 1971; Kaldate, 1962; Bailey, 1957). This view has been effectively challenged by a number of writers who argue that the joint family shows considerable adaptability in the face of change and in fact can play a positive role in mobilizing and organizing resources for development (see Singer, 1968; Epstein, 1973:200–11).

6. Like that of other founding fathers, Weber's work is surrounded by a massive body of exegetical writings aimed at elucidating his central ideas and presuppositions. However, some of this literature has oversimplified or misconstrued his arguments. This is most noticeably the case with the Protestant Ethic essay. Several writers, for example, have attributed to the Protestant sects a central causative role in the rise of western capitalism rather than seeing Weber's analysis in terms of the 'correlations between forms of religious belief and practical ethics' which, indirectly, influence socio-economic behaviour (Weber, 1904:91). Another group of writers (e.g. McClelland, 1961; Hagen, 1962) has reformulated Weber's argument in psychological or social-psychological terms; and have hypothesized that certain attitudinal or personality changes are closely associated with the evolution of modern forms of capitalism. I cannot here demonstrate the erroneousness of such interpretations of Weber, nor avoid sometimes giving the impression, when quoting other writers, that I accept their views. I have tried instead to indicate when ideas are derivative of Weber, but not necessarily in accord with what he actually says, by labelling them 'neo-Weberian'.

7. Geertz also recognizes the significance of organizational and social network factors. For example, he draws attention to the importance of being involved in a framework of extra-local ties: the Moslems as itinerant market traders throughout the region, and the Hindu aristocrats as part of a sophisticated court culture linked into regional and national capitals. See also his discussion of the organizational problems facing entrepreneurs (Geertz, 1963:121–27).

8. Gerschenkron (1962) challenges the widely-held view (see Rostow, 1953; Geertz, 1963) that times of rapid industrial progress were preceded by a more or less protracted period during which the preconditions of modern industrialization were created. He also points out that writers often confuse the notion of 'preconditions' with that of 'conditions', where the latter is essentially a definitional problem not a matter of historical sequence. An example of this is W. E. Moore (1963:93–7) whose argument and terminology oscillate between both concepts.

CHAPTER 4

1. A major exception to this is the recent monopoly over oil production exercised by the Middle Eastern oil states which gives them increasing economic and political power in international affairs.
2. Throughout the book the notion of 'plural' society is used rather loosely and there is no discussion of the sociological literature on the topic.
3. Cotler's analysis assumes the existence of marked regional inequality between highland and coastal areas of Peru which is shown by the imbalances in trade and capital flows, and rationalized in terms of certain social and cultural stereotypes of Indian versus *mestizo* culture. The imbalance in inter-regional trade between the highlands and the coast is documented by Griffin (1968:63–5). Cotler (1967–8) gives evidence of the types of social inequality that exist. See also Bourricaud (1967).
4. They are also used by F. Lamond Tullis (1970) in a study of the factors affecting the rise and success of peasant movements in central Peru.
5. It is debatable of course whether the workers have much effective control under the present system since decision-making tends to rest in the hands of small groups of government technocrats appointed to supervise the running of these co-operatives. For more details on recent land reform policy and its effects, see Hobsbawm 1971; Quijano, 1970; Scott, 1972; and Roberts and Samaniego, 1973.
6. A review of this work is found in Chapter 5.
7. An excellent theoretical discussion of the concept of mode of production is contained in Balibar (1970). There remain, however, certain analytical difficulties in applying a mode of production analysis, as Marx developed it, to non-capitalist systems. Not least of these is the problem of avoiding a Western ethnocentric bias when we attempt to specify the structures pertaining to 'the ownership' of the means of production, or what Balibar has called 'the property connexion', when dealing with non-Western societies, especially those of a tribal organization. Louis Dumont makes a similar point when he questions the application of Marxist ideas and Western sociological concepts to the study of Indian society and history (Dumont, 1970). Sayer (1974) has offered a solution to this problem by suggesting that Marx frequently uses the notion of property interchangeably with the concept of 'production relation'. This, he argues, indicates that by property relation Marx 'means any social relation between Man and his conditions of production, through which the latter are experienced as "belonging to him"' (Sayer, 1974:20). This may not entail the concept of property in the Western capitalist sense. Sayer also provides an interesting methodological critique of the dichotomy between forces and relations of production.
8. While in formal legal terms this is true, Martinez-Alier (1973) and Cotler (1970:548) have shown that under certain circumstances *colonos* can acquire considerable influence over the forms of land use and labour relations. For example, Martinez-Alier cites several cases where *colonos* were able to bargain for better working conditions and improve their labour 'contracts'. Moreover several groups were also

successful in resisting the introduction of wage-labour systems which were designed to eliminate usufructuary rights to land and pasture (Martinez-Alier, 1973:32). According to Martinez-Alier one strong motive for such resistance was that in many instances in the central highlands of Peru the annual income of *colonos*, derived primarily from their own production of agricultural and livestock goods, was far superior to that of the landless wage labourers employed by the haciendas and of smallholders living outside (1973:18).

9. These economic ties were sometimes extended to cover debt relationships that were established by *colonos* being allowed credit at the hacienda shop or through the acquisition of loans directly from the hacendado. The latter often took the form of advances on produce to be sold later in the season.

CHAPTER 5

1. Various authors have suggested different criteria for defining entrepreneurship. Some have stressed risk-taking, others innovation, and others the management function. See Kilby (1971) for a summary of these viewpoints. For the purpose of the present discussion I use the notion of entrepreneur to mean someone or category of persons who, through the manipulation or transformation of existing sets of relationships, values, and resources, pursues an expansive economic policy (see Belshaw 1965:115–6). Depending on the context, the role of entrepreneur will also be combined with that of socio-economic innovator (see Long, 1968:5), or with that of 'broker' i.e. someone who controls crucial sets of relationships between different social, economic, or political levels (see Boissevain, 1974:Chapter 6).

2. A neo-Weberian argument has been developed by McClelland and associates to suggest that the 'achievement motive' functions as the crucial mediating social-psychological mechanism (McClelland 1961). He tries to demonstrate that child rearing practices emphasizing standards of excellence, self-reliance, and low father dominance contribute to the development of high achievement motivation. Eisenstadt (1963:420–31) exposes the methodological and logical errors of such an interpretation. See also Schatz (1965).

3. See Hoselitz (1964) on socio-cultural minorities (e.g. the Jews in Europe, the Lebanese in West Africa, the Chinese in South-east Asia); and Hagen (1962) who argues that withdrawal of status respect leads eventually to the emergence of a more creative personality type and thus to entrepreneurship. Hagen's highly speculative theory has been challenged by numerous writers. See Kunkel (1965) who proposes as an alternative a behavioural theory based on the principles of operant conditioning; Higgins (1968: Chapter 12); and Kasdan (1965) who offers a reinterpretation of Hagen's explanation for the Basque contribution to economic development in Colombia.

4. Obviously other considerations besides monetary gain enter into the decision whether or not to work for the Forestry Department, such as the loss of independence or time on other activities.

5. Successful capital accumulation by this method depends of course on land being available for cash-crop cultivation and on the willingness of workers to work under such an arrangement. The fact that the original entrepreneur was an Arab outsider may have made it easier to

deploy labour on the tomato crop since he had no land under millet cultivation and was not involved in reciprocal labour arrangements with neighbours, etc.

6. The quantitative data provided by Klausen are derived very largely from the official statistics of the project itself. Differences in patterns of house and land ownership are deduced from a census in which some 50 per cent of the population gave no reply (see Klausen, 1968:86, Table 17). It is also claimed that the Latin Catholics form a diverse and heterogeneous group on the grounds that the 732 employed Catholics are engaged in a total of 31 different professions, while the 270 employed Arayas encompass only 18 different professions. These data are contradictory since there are 0.067 different professions per employed Araya as against only 0.043 per employed Latin Catholic. In addition, an almost identical percentage of the two groups is still engaged in the traditional occupation of fishing. These comments highlight the serious inadequacies of Klausen's quantitative material and analysis. I am grateful to Dr A. Good who drew my attention to the inconsistencies in his argument.

7. One can distinguish two different exchange approaches. The first derives from what Ekeh (1974) calls the 'collectivist' tradition and focuses upon the identification of customary or institutionalized patterns of exchange in a society. See for example, Malinowski (1922) and Mauss (1925) on ceremonial exchange; Levi-Strauss (1949) on marriage systems; and Bohannan (1955), Polanyi, Arensberg, and Pearson (1957), and Dalton (1961) on primitive and peasant economies. The other is the 'individualist' or 'interactionist' approach represented by Homans (1961), Blau (1964), and Thibaut and Kelley (1959). For two interesting recent applications see Kapferer (1972) and Anderson (1971).

8. See Mitchell (1969: Introduction) where he differentiates between structural aspects like anchorage, reachability, and density, and interactional indices such as exchange content, directedness, durability, intensity, and frequency. Boissevain (1974:24–48) gives a similar breakdown.

9. In his discussion of brokers Boissevain (1974:147–69) stresses that 'a broker is a professional manipulator of people and information who brings about communication for profit' (1974:148). In contrast to the patron who controls 'first order resources', like land, capital, jobs, and technology, the broker specializes in 'second order resources' that constitute the strategic networks leading to persons of power or influence.

10. But see Leeds (1964) who analyzes Brazilian career patterns and isolates the conditions under which individuals are able to pursue professional and entrepreneurial careers. Also Adams (1970) who examines the problem in relation to power brokers. My own study (Long, 1968:218–36) on Jehovah's Witness in Zambia analyzes the relation between religious conversion and socio-economic mobility and presents life histories for detailed discussion.

11. Decision-making models have been used for the analysis of a wide variety of empirical problems. See Ortiz (1967, 1973), Moerman (1968), Lipton (1968b), Long (1968, 1970a), Cancian (1972) on peasant and commercial farming; Howard (1970) and Monberg (1970) on adoption patterns; Howard (1963) on ecological exploitation; and

Garbett and Kapferer (1970) on labour migration in Southern Africa.

12. For general theoretical statements on decision-making see Howard and Ortiz (1971), Simon (1959), Robinson and Majak (1967), and Rosenau (1967).

13. Simon (1959) introduces the notion of 'satisficing' in order to get away from the usual assumption of maximization used in economic theory. He writes: 'We must expect the firm's goals to be not maximizing profit, but attaining a certain level or rate of profit, holding a certain share of the market or certain level of sales. Firms would try to 'satisfice' rather than to maximize' (1959:263). For further discussion of the problem of maximization see Cancian (1966) who distinguishes between maximization as a societal norm which may or may not be present, and maximization as a general strategy for comprehending social behaviour (i.e. we assume that every individual in choosing a course of action is attempting to maximize something).

14. She also mentions a third category, 'gambling decisions'. She comments (1973:269) that it was typically the poorer families, who had enough land planted with subsistence crops, who did not mind gambling some of their cash on risky ventures, such as pig breeding.

15. The two terms used by Ortiz in fact derive from two vernacular concepts: *indios cerrados* (meaning by this an unwillingness to accept anything new), and *indios racionales* (rational Indians).

16. My discussion here has tended to focus upon the ideological dimension. Other important differences (e.g. in social characteristics, such as age and migration experience; in assets, such as capital and equipment; and in the availability of kinship and other networks) are explored elsewhere. See Long (1968, 1970a).

17. Strickon (1972) presents an interesting case study of a family firm in Argentina, showing how resources were shifted between different economic fields. In a recent paper (Long, 1975) I have tried to develop this kind of analysis and have discussed the phenomenon of multiple enterprise in highland Peru.

18. Van Velzen (1973) provides a most convincing criticism of what he calls the 'big-man paradigm' in anthropology which, over the last decade or so, has been a dominant orientation in the study of local politics. One of his criticisms is that the stress on leadership problems and on so-called pivotal persons (i.e. 'leaders' and 'entrepreneurs') has led to the neglect of 'the whole subject of resource allocation and drainage by superior political fields' (Van Velzen, 1973:598).

CHAPTER 6

1. The villages in Epstein's study fell outside the designated blocks of the Community Development Programme and therefore were not subject to an intensive multi-pronged extension programme. However, the introduction of improved technology had the same differential impact as that described by Dube.

2. Although at the time of the study the village lay outside the Community Development Programme, it was nonetheless affected by developments in the regional economy that extended the economic frontier into the heart of the village.

3. See Feldman (1969) and Williams (1975:11–16) for critiques of these various propositions.
4. Communal ownership was not so radical a departure as it might seem for in many parts of Tanzania a tribal system of land tenure continued to persist. Under this system the chief acted as custodian of the land for the people of his chiefdom and individual households or extended families had usufructuary access for domestic production. But whilst land rights were held communally, production itself was organized by individual households (see Gluckman, 1965:Chapter II: 36–8).
5. The term *'ujamaa'* was chosen to emphasize the specific Tanzanian content of the socialism to be developed. Its literal meaning is 'family-hood' and thus suggests parallels with notions of the 'traditional' extended family system. Nyerere makes this clear in various writings (see Nyerere, 1968:2; and Nyerere, 1967).
6. Lipton (1974:270) contrasts this with what he calls 'distributivist' reform when the state divides up large estates or farms into smaller units for private cultivation.
7. The jungle region lies outside the scope of the reform law, although certain of the newly-formed production co-operatives are expected to promote colonization schemes in order to provide work for excess labour (see Harding, 1974:16, 26).
8. The law originally made it possible for the sub-division of expro-priable holdings to take place under private initiative, thus avoiding state intervention. This led to the parcelling out of land among the landowner's relatives and friends. Later, under pressure from well-organized protest by agricultural workers from the Cañete valley and the estates near to Lima, the government suppressed this part of the law and annulled various sub-divisions that had already occurred (see Harding, 1974:7–9, for details). Another difficulty concerns the fact that within a particular Agrarian Reform Zone there will exist farms that legally are not subject to expropriation. Here the legislation maintains that on such farms, workers must share a certain proportion of the farm's profits and participate in management, although the means by which this is to be achieved or enforced are left unspecified.
9. In 1971 there were approximately 104 *soles* to £1 sterling.
10. Similar observations have been made about other peasant commu-nities in the highlands of Peru. See Long and Winder (1975), and Long and Roberts (1978).

CHAPTER 7

1. For a discussion of how structural and actor-oriented types of analysis might be combined to deal with regional development problems see Long and Roberts (1974).
2. A useful, but to my mind theoretically deficient, attempt to develop a regional perspective in anthropology for analyzing problems of development is Pelto and Poggie (1974). Their paper also includes a brief review of previous research, with particular reference to Latin American studies.
3. The nearest one gets to an actor perspective is Friedmann's general discussion of how the entrepreneur organizes economic space through his location and investment decisions, thus stimulating the rise of

urban places and integrating an area economically. See Friedmann and Alonso (1964). Also the development of cognitive models in geography, which have been used to explore how individuals perceive and categorize their spatial and ecological environments (see Downs and Stea, 1973), could perhaps be directed more specifically towards the discussion of regional development problems.

References

ABEGGLEN, J. G. 1958. *The Japanese Factory*. Glencoe: The Free Press.
ACHESON, J. M. 1972. Limited Good or Limited Goods? Response to Economic Opportunity in a Tarascan Pueblo. *American Anthropologist* 74 (4):1152–69.
ADAMS, R. 1970. Brokers and Career Mobility Systems in the Structure of Complex Societies. *Southwestern Journal of Anthropology* 26 (4): 315–27, Winter.
ALBERTI, G. and SANCHEZ, R. 1974. *Poder y Conflicto Social en el Valle del Mantaro*. Lima: Instituto de Estudios Peruanos.
ALLAN, W. 1965. *The African Husbandman*. Edinburgh: Oliver and Boyd.
ALTAMIRANO RUA, T. 1971. *El Cambio del Sistema de Hacienda al Sistema Comunal en Un Area de la Sierra Sur del Perú: el Caso de Ongoy*. Unpublished thesis. University of San Marcos, Lima.
ANDERSON, M. 1971. *Family Structure in Nineteenth Century Lancashire*. Cambridge: Cambridge University Press.
ANGWASI, J. and NDULU, B. 1973. An Evaluation of Ujamaa Villages in the Rufiji. Paper presented to East African Universities' Annual Social Science Conference.
APTHORPE, R. 1970a. *People, Planning and Development Studies*. London: Frank Cass.
———— 1970b. *Rural Cooperatives and Planned Change in Africa: Case Materials*. Geneva: United Nations Research Institute for Social Development.
AWITI, A. 1972. Class Struggle in Rural Society of Tanzania. *Maji-Maji* (7).
BAILEY, F. G. 1957. *Caste and the Economic Frontier*. Manchester: Manchester University Press.
BALIBAR, E. 1970. The Basic Concepts of Historical Materialism. In L. ALTHUSSER and E. BALIBAR, *Reading Capital*. New York: Pantheon Books.
BANFIELD, E. C. 1958. *The Moral Basis of a Backward Society*. Glencoe: Free Press.
BARAN, P. 1957. *The Political Economy of Growth*. New York: Monthly Review Press.
BARNETT, T. 1975. The Gezira Scheme: Production of Cotton and the Reproduction of Underdevelopment. In I. OXAAL, T. BARNETT, and D. BOOTH (eds.), *Beyond the Sociology of Development*. London: Routledge and Kegan Paul.
BARTH, F. 1963. *The Role of the Entrepreneur in Social Change in Northern Norway*. Bergen: Norwegian University Press.
———— 1966. *Models of Social Organization*. London: Royal Anthropological Institute.

———— 1967. Economic Spheres in Darfur. In R. FIRTH (ed.), *Themes in Economic Anthropology*. London: Tavistock Publications Ltd.

BELLAH, R. N. 1957. *Tokugawa Religion*. Glencoe: The Free Press.

BELSHAW, C. S. 1955. *In Search of Wealth: A Study of the Emergence of Commercial Operations in the Melanesian Society of South Western Papua*. Memoir No. 80. American Anthropological Association.

———— 1965. *Traditional Exchange and Modern Markets*. Englewood Cliffs, New Jersey: Prentice-Hall Inc.

BELSHAW, M. 1967. *A Village Economy. Land and People of Huecorio*. New York and London: Columbia University Press.

BENNETT, J. W. 1966. Further remarks on Foster's 'Image of the Limited Good'. *American Anthropologist* 68:206–10.

BENNETT, J. W. 1967. *Hutterian Brethren: The Agricultural Economy and Social Organization of a Communal People*. Stanford, California: Stanford University Press.

BERNA, J. J. 1960. *Industrial Entrepreneurship in Madras State, India*. Bombay: Asia Publishing House.

BERNSTEIN, H. (ed.) 1973. *Underdevelopment and Development. The Third World Today*. Harmondsworth: Penguin Books Ltd.

BERRY, B. J. L. 1967. *Geography of Market Centres and Retail Distribution*. Englewood Cliffs, New Jersey: Prentice-Hall Inc.

BERRY, S. S. 1975. *Cocoa, Custom and Socio-economic Change in Rural Western Nigeria*. Oxford: The Clarendon Press.

BIRNBAUM, N. 1953. Conflicting Interpretations of the Rise of Capitalism: Marx and Weber. *British Journal of Sociology* 4 (41):125. Reprinted in N. J. SMELSER (ed.), *Readings on Economic Sociology*. Englewood Cliffs, New Jersey: Prentice-Hall, Inc.

BLAU, P. 1964. *Exchange and Power in Social Life*. New York: John Wiley and Sons.

———— 1968. Interaction: Social Exchange. In D. L. SILLS (ed.), *International Encyclopedia of the Social Sciences*, Vol. 7. New York: Macmillan and the Free Press.

BOEKE, J. H. 1953. *Economics and Economic Policy as Exemplified by Indonesia*. New York: Institute of Pacific Relations.

BOESEN, J. 1972. Development and Class Structure in a Smallholder Society and the Potential of Ujamaa. Copenhagen: Institute for Development Research.

BOHANNAN, P. 1955. Some Principles of Exchange and Investment among the Tiv. *American Anthropologist* 57:60–70.

———— 1959. The Impact of Money on an African Subsistence Economy. *The Journal of Economic History* 19:491–503. Reprinted in G. DALTON (ed.), *Tribal and Peasant Economies*. New York: The Natural History Press.

BOISSEVAIN, J. 1974. *Friends of Friends. Networks, Manipulators and Coalitions*. Oxford: Basil Blackwell.

BOSWELL, D. 1973. Labour Migration and Commitment to Urban Residence. In M. DRAKE, R. FINNEGAN, A. LEARMOUTH, D. BOSWELL, and N. LONG, *The Process of Urbanization*. Bletchley: The Open University.

BOURRICAUD, F. 1967. *Power and Society in Contemporary Peru*. London: Faber and Faber. Translated from French by P. Stevenson.

BROOKFIELD, H. 1975. *Interdependent Development*. London: Methuen & Co. Ltd.

BUECHLER, H. C. 1970. The Ritual Dimensions of Rural-Urban Networks: The Fiesta System in the Northern Highlands of Bolivia. In w. MANGIN (ed.), *Peasants in Cities: Readings in the Anthropology of Urbanization*. Boston: Houghton Mifflin Company.

BUNZEL, R. 1952. *Chichicastenango: A Guatemalan Village*. Seattle and London: University of Washington.

BURGOS, H. 1970. *Relaciones Interétnicas en Riobamba*. Mexico: Instituto Indigenista Interamericano. Ediciones Especiales, 55.

BUSIA, K. A. 1951. *The Position of the Chief in the Modern Political System of Ashanti*. London: Oxford University Press.

CANCIAN, F. 1966. Maximization as Norm, Strategy, and Theory: A Comment on Programmatic Statements in Economic Anthropology. *American Anthropologist* **68**:465–70.

——— 1967. *Economics and Prestige in a Maya Community. The Religious Cargo System of Zinacantan*. Stanford: Stanford University Press.

——— 1972. *Change and Uncertainty in a Peasant Economy. The Maya Corn Farmers of Zinacantan*. Stanford: Stanford University Press.

CARDOSO, F. H. and FALETTO, E. 1970. *Dependencia y Desarrollo en America Latina*. Mexico: Siglo XXI Editores.

CASTILLO, ARDILES, H. 1970. *Pisac*. Mexico: Instituto Indigenista Interamericano. Ediciones Especiales, 56.

CHAMBERS, R. 1969. *Settlement Schemes in Tropical Africa*. London: Routledge and Kegan Paul.

CHENERY, H., AHLUWALIA, M. S., BELL, C. L. G., DULOY, J. H., and JOLLY, R. 1974. *Redistribution with Growth*. London: Oxford University Press.

CLIFFE, L. 1970. The Policy of *Ujamaa Vijijini* and the Class Struggle in Tanzania. In L. CLIFFE and J. S. SAUL (eds.), *Socialism in Tanzania*. 2 Vols. 1972. Dar-es-Salaam: East African Publishing House.

CLIFFE, L. and CUNNINGHAM, G. 1973. Ideology, Organization and Settlement Experience in Tanzania. In E. A. BRETT and D. G. R. BELSHAW (eds.), *Politics and Agriculture*. London: Frank Cass.

COCKCROFT, D., FRANK, A. G., and JOHNSON, D. L. 1972. *Dependence and Underdevelopment*. New York: Doubleday and Company Inc.

COHEN, A. 1969. *Custom and Politics in Urban Africa*. London: Routledge and Kegan Paul.

COOK, S. 1975. Economic Anthropology: Problems in Theory, Method and Analysis. In J. J. HONIGMAN (ed.), *Handbook of Social and Cultural Anthropology*. Chicago: Rand McNally and Co.

COSTER, R. N. 1958. *Peasant Farming in the Petauke and Katete Areas of the Eastern Province of Northern Rhodesia*. Lusaka: Government Printer.

COTLER, J. 1967–8. The Mechanics of Internal Domination and Social Change in Peru. *Studies in Comparative International Development* **III** (12).

——— 1970. Haciendas y Comunidades Tradicionales en un Contexto de Movilización Politica. In R. KEITH (ed.), *El Campesino en el Perú*. Lima: Instituto de Estudios Peruanos.

COULSON, A. C. 1975. Peasants and Bureaucrats. *Review of African Political Economy* (3): 53–8.

CRAIG, W. 1968. *El Movimiento Campesino en la Convención, Peru*. Lima: Instituto de Estudios Peruanos.

CUNNINGHAM, G. L. 1966. Ruvuma Development Association – An

Independent Critique. *Mbioni* **III** (2):44–55. Dar-es-Salaam.

CYERT, R. M. and MARCH J. G. 1963. *A Behavioural Theory of the Firm.* Englewood Cliffs, New Jersey: Prentice-Hall Inc.

DALTON, G. 1961. Economic Theory and Primitive Society. *American Anthropologist* **62**:483–90.

———— 1971. Theoretical Issues in Economic Anthropology. In G. DALTON (ed.), *Economic Development and Social Change*. The Modernization of Village Communities. New York: The Natural History Press.

DE WILDE, J. C. 1967. *Experiences with Agricultural Development in Tropical Africa*. Vol. I. *The Synthesis*. Baltimore: The John Hopkins Press.

DEGREGORI, C. I. and GOLTE, J. 1973. *Dependéncia y Desintegración Estructural en la Comunidad de Pacaraos*. Lima: Instituto de Estudios Peruanos.

DESAI, A. R. 1969. *Rural Sociology in India*. Part II, Section XII: 599–626. Community Development Projects. Bombay: Popular Prakashan.

———— 1971. *Essays on Modernization of Underdeveloped Societies*. Vol. I. Bombay: Thacker and Co. Ltd.

DIAZ, M. N. 1966. *Tonalá: Conservatism, Responsibility and Authority in a Mexican Town*. Berkeley and Los Angeles: University of California Press.

DORNER, P. 1972. *Land Reform and Economic Development*. Harmondsworth: Penguin Books Ltd.

DOS SANTOS, T. 1969. The crisis of Development Theory and the Problem of Dependence in Latin America. *Siglo* **21**. Reprinted in H. BERNSTEIN (ed., 1973), *Underdevelopment and Development*. Harmondsworth: Penguin Books Ltd.

DOUGHTY, P. L. 1970. Behind the Back of the City: 'Provincial' Life in Lima, Peru?. In W. MANGIN (ed.), *Peasants in Cities*. Boston: Houghton Mifflin.

DOWNS, R. M. and STEA, D. (eds.). 1973. *Image and Environment: Cognitive Mapping and Spatial Behaviour*. Chicago: Aldine Press.

DUBE, S. C. 1958. *India's Changing Villages: Human Factors in Community Development*. London: Routledge and Kegan Paul Ltd.

DUMONT, L. 1970. The Individual as an Impediment to Sociological Comparison and Indian History. In L. DUMONT, *Religion, Politics and History in India: Collected Papers in Indian Sociology*. Paris: Mouton.

DUPRÉ, G. and REY, P. P. 1973. Reflections on the Pertinence of a Theory of the History of Exchange. *Economy and Society* **2**:(2):131–163, May.

EASTON, D. 1959. Political Anthropology. In B. J. SIEGEL (ed.), *Biennial Review of Anthropology*. London: Oxford University Press.

EKEH, P. P. 1974. *Social Exchange Theory: The Two Traditions*. London: Heinemann.

EISENSTADT, S. N. 1963. Need for Achievement. *Economic Development and Cultural Change* **XI**:420–31, July.

———— 1966. *Modernization: Protest and Change*. Englewood Cliffs, New Jersey: Prentice Hall Inc.

———— 1968. *Israeli Society*. New York: Basic Books Inc.

———— 1970. Social Change and Development. In E. N. EISENSTADT, *Readings in Social Evolution and Development*. Oxford and London: Pergamon Press

EPSTEIN, T. S. 1962. *Economic Development and Social Change in South*

India. Manchester: Manchester University Press.
———— 1968. Capitalism, Primitive and Modern – Some Aspects of Tolai Economic Growth. Canberra: Australian National University Press.
———— 1973. South India: Yesterday, Today and Tomorrow. London: Macmillan.
FALLERS, L. 1955. The Predicament of the Modern African Chief: an instance from Uganda. American Anthropologist 57(2):209–305.
FALS BORDA, O. 1969. Estudios de la Realidad Campesina: Cooperación y Cambio. Geneva: United Nations Research Institute for Social Development.
FELDMAN, D. 1969. The Economics of Ideology. In C. LEYS (ed.), Politics and Change in Developing Countries. Cambridge: Cambridge University Press.
FIVE YEAR PLAN. Planning Commission, Government of India. The First Five Year Plan. Delhi, 1951.
FONSECA, C. M. 1975. Comunidad, Hacienda y el modelo SAIS. America Indigena XXXV (2):249–66, April–June.
FORMAN, S. and RIEGELHAUPT, T. F. 1970. Market Place and Marketing System: Towards a Theory of Peasant Economic Integration. Comparative Studies in Society and History. 12:188–212.
FOSTER, G. M. 1962. Traditional Cultures: The Impact of Technological Change. New York and Evanston: Harper and Row.
———— 1965. Peasant Society and the Image of the Limited Good. American Anthropologist 67:293–315.
———— 1967. Tzintzuntzan: Mexican Peasants in a Changing World. Boston: Little, Brown and Company.
FRANK, A. G. 1967. Sociology of Under-development and Under-development of Sociology. Catalyst (3):20–73. Buffalo: University of New York. Reprinted in Frank, 1969b.
———— 1969a. Capitalism and Under-development in Latin America. New York and London: Monthly Review Press.
———— 1969b. Latin America: Underdevelopment of Revolution. New York and London: Monthly Review Press.
FRANKENBERG, R. 1967. Communities in Britain. Harmondsworth: Penguin Books Ltd.
FRIEDMANN, J. and ALONSO, W. (eds.). 1964. Regional Development and Planning: A Reader. Cambridge, Mass.: The M.I.T. Press.
FUENZALIDA, F., VILLARAN, J. L., GOLTE, J. and VALIENTE, J. 1968. Estructuras Tradicionales y Economía de Mercado: La Comunidad de Indigenas de Huayopampa. Lima: Instituto de Estudios Peruanos.
GAITSKELL, A. 1959. Gezira: A Study of Development in the Sudan. London: Faber and Faber.
GARBETT, K. and KAPFERER, B. 1970. Theoretical Orientations in the Study of Labour Migration. The New Atlantis 2 (1):179–97.
GEERTZ, C. 1956. Religious Belief and Economic Behaviour in a Central Javanese Town. Economic Development and Cultural Change. IV (2):134–58.
———— 1963. Peddlers and Princes: Social Development and Economic Change in Two Indonesian Towns. Chicago and London: The University of Chicago Press.
GERSCHENKRON, A. 1962. Economic Backwardness in Historical Perspective. New York: Harvard University Press.
GLADE, W. P. 1967. Approaches to a Theory of Entrepreneurial Formation. Explorations in Entrepreneurial History 2nd Series, 4 (3).

GLUCKMAN, M. 1955. *Custom and Conflict in Africa.* Oxford: Basil Blackwell.
———— 1965. *Politics, Law and Ritual in Tribal Society.* London: Basil Blackwell.
———— 1968. The Utility of the Equilibrium Model in the Study of Social Change. *American Anthropologist* **70**:219–37.
GLUCKMAN, M., MITCHELL, J. C., and BARNES, J. 1949. The Village Headman in British Central Africa. *Africa* **XIX** (2):89–106.
GODELIER, M. 1972. *Rationality and Irrationality in Economics.* Translated from French by B. Pearce. London: New Left Books.
GONZALEZ, N. L. 1972. Patron-Client Relationships at the International Level. In A. STRICKON and S. M. GREENFIELD (1972).
GOODY, J. (ed.). 1958. *The Developmental Cycle in Domestic Groups.* Cambridge: Cambridge University Press.
GRAY, J. 1974. Mao Tse-Tung's Strategy for the Collectivization of Chinese Agriculture: An Important Phase in the Development of Maoism. In E. DE KADT and G. WILLIAMS (eds.), *Sociology and Development.* London: Tavistock Publications.
GRIFFIN, K. 1968. *Underdevelopment in Spanish America.* London: George Allen and Unwin.
GUESSOUS, M. 1967. A General Critique of Equilibrium Theory. In W. E. MOORE and R. M. COOK (eds.), *Readings in Social Change.* Englewood Cliffs, New Jersey: Prentice-Hall Inc.
HAGEN, E. 1962. *On the Theory of Social Change.* Homewood, Illinois: Dorsey Press.
HARDING, C. 1974. Agrarian Reform and Agrarian Struggles in Peru. *Latin American Centre Working Paper,* (15) Cambridge.
HAUSER, P. M. 1965. Observations on the Urban-Folk and Urban-Rural Dichotomies as Forms of Western Ethnocentrism. In P. M. HAUSER and L. F. SCHNORE (1965).
HAUSER, P. M. and SCHNORE, L. F. (eds.). 1965. *The Study of Urbanization.* New York: Wiley.
HAZELHURST, L. W. 1966. *Entrepreneurship and the Merchant Castes in a Punjabi City.* Durham N. C: Duke University.
HIGGINS, B. 1956. The Dualistic Theory of Underdeveloped Areas. *Economic Development and Cultural Change* **4**:99–115.
———— 1968. *Economic Development: Problems, Principles and Policies.* New York: Norton. First edition 1959.
HILL, P. 1963. *Migrant Cocoa Farmers of Southern Ghana.* Cambridge: Cambridge University Press.
HOBSBAWM, E. 1971. Peru: The Peculiar Revolution. *New York Review of Books.* December 16:29–36.
———— 1974. Peasant Land Occupations. *Past and Present* (62) February: 120–52.
HOMANS, G. C. 1961. *Social Behaviour, its Elementary Forms.* New York: Harcourt, Brace and World.
HORTON, D. E. 1973 Haciendas and Cooperatives: A Preliminary Study of Latifundist Agriculture and Agrarian Reform in Northern Peru. Research Paper No. 53, Land Tenure Centre, Madison, Wisconsin: University of Wisconsin.
———— 1974. *Land Reform and Reform Enterprises in Peru.* Report submitted to the Land Tenure Center and the International Bank for Reconstruction and Development. Madison, Wisconsin: University of Wisconsin.

HOSELITZ, B. F. 1960. *Sociological Factors in Economic Development.* Chicago: Free Press.
——— 1964. A Sociological Approach to Economic Development. In D. NOVACK and R. LEKACHMAN (eds.), *Development and Society.* New York: St. Martin's Press.
HOWARD, A. 1963. Land, Activity Systems, and Decision-making Models in Rotuma. *Ethnology* 2:407–440.
——— 1970. Adoption in Rotuma. In V. Carroll (ed.), *Adoption in Eastern Oceania.* Honolulu: University of Hawaii Press.
HOWARD, A. and ORTIZ, S. 1971. Decision Making and the Study of Social Process. *Acta Sociologica* 14:213–26.
HUIZER, J. 1971. The *Ujamaa* Village Programme in Tanzania. The Hague: Institute of Social Studies.
HUNTER, G. and BOTTRALL, A. F. (eds.). 1972. *Serving the Small Farmer: Policy Choices in Indian Agriculture.* London: Croom Helm and the Overseas Development Institute.
IBBOTT, R. 1966. Ruvuma Development Association. *Mbioni* III (2): 3–43. Dar-es-Salaam.
JOHNSON, A. W. 1971. *Sharecroppers of the Sertao.* California: Stanford University Press.
KALDATE, S. M. T. 1962. Urbanization and Disintegration of Rural Joint Family. *Sociological Bulletin* II Nos. 1 and 2.
KAPFERER, B. 1972. *Strategy and Transaction in an African Factory.* Manchester: Manchester University Press.
KAPLAN, B. A. 1960. Mechanization in Paracho: A Craft Community. *Alpha Kappa Delta* 30:59–65. Reprinted in D. B. HEATH and R. N. ADAMS (eds., 1965), *Contemporary Cultures and Societies of Latin America.* New York: Random House.
KAPLAN, D. and MANNERS, R. A. 1972. *Culture Theory.* Englewood Cliffs, New Jersey: Prentice-Hall, Inc.
KAPLAN, D. and SADLER, B. 1966. Foster's Image of the Limited Good: An Example of Anthropological Explanation. *American Anthropologist* 68: 202–6.
KASDAN, L. 1965. Family Structure, Migration, and the Entrepreneur. *Comparative Studies in Society and History* VII (4):345–57. Reprinted in P. KILBY (1971).
KENNEDY, J. G. 1966. Peasant Society and the Image of the Limited Good. *American Anthropologist* 68:1212–25.
KENNEDY, R. F. 1962. The Protestant Ethic and the Parsis. *American Journal of Sociology* 68 (1):11–20.
KILBY, P. (ed.). 1971. *Entrepreneurship and Economic Development.* New York: The Free Press.
KLAREN, P. F. 1973. *Modernization, Dislocation and Aprismo Origins of the Peruvian Aprista Party: 1870–1932.* Austin: University of Texas Press.
KLAUSEN, A. M. 1968. *Kerala Fishermen.* London: Allen and Unwin Ltd.
KUHN, T. S. 1962. *The Structure of Scientific Revolutions.* Chicago: University of Chicago Press.
KUNKEL, J. H. 1965. Values and Behaviour in Economic Development. *Economic Development and Cultural Change* 13:257–77, April. Reprinted in P. KILBY (1971).
LACLAU, E. 1971. Feudalism and Capitalism in Latin America. *New Left Review* (67):19–38.
LAMOND TULLIS, F. 1970. *Lord and Peasant in Peru.* Cambridge, Massachusetts: Harvard University Press.

LANNOY, R. 1971. *The Speaking Tree: A Study of Culture and Society*. London: Oxford University Press.

LEEDS, A. 1964. Brazilian Careers and Social Structure: An Evolutionary Model and Case History. *American Anthropologist* **66**:1321–47.

LERNER, D. 1958. *The Passing of Traditional Society: Modernizing the Middle East*. Glencoe: Free Press.

LÉVI–STRAUSS, C. 1949. *Les Structures Elémentaires de la Parenté*. Paris: Presses Universitaires de France. Translated into English 1969. London: Eyre and Spottiswoode.

LEWIS, O. 1951. *Life in a Mexican Village: Tepoztlán Restudied*. Urbana, Illinois: University of Illinois Press.

———— 1952. Urbanization without Breakdown. *Scientific Monthly* **1**:(75)31–41.

———— 1953. Tepotzlan Restudied: A Critique of the Folk-Urban Conceptualization of Social Change. *Rural Sociology* **18**(2):121–34.

———— 1965. Further observations on the Folk-Urban Continuum and Urbanization with Special Reference to Mexico City. In HAUSER and SCHNORE (1965).

LEWIS, W. A. 1954. Economic Development with Unlimited Supplies of Labour. *The Manchester School* (22), May. Reprinted in A. N. AGARWALA and S. P. SINGH (eds.), *The Economics of Underdevelopment: A Series of Articles and Papers*. Bombay: Oxford University Press 1958; and New York: Oxford University Press, 1963.

LEYS, C. 1975. *Underdevelopment in Kenya. The Political Economy of Neo-Colonialism*. London: Heinemann.

LIPTON, M. 1968a. Strategy for Agriculture: Urban Bias and Rural Planning. In P. STREETEN and M. LIPTON (eds.), *The Crisis of Indian Planning: Economic Planning in the 1960s*. London: Oxford University Press.

———— 1968b. The Theory of the Optimizing Peasants. *The Journal of Development Studies*. **4** (3).

————. 1974. Towards a Theory on Land Reform. In D. LEHMANN (ed.), *Agrarian Reform and Agrarian Reformism*. London: Faber and Faber.

LONG, N. 1968. *Social Change and the Individual. A Study of the Social and Religious Responses to Innovation*. Manchester: Manchester University Press.

———— 1970a. Rural Entrepreneurship and Religious Commitment in Zambia. *Internationales Jahrbuch für Religionssoziolgie* **VI**:142–157.

———— 1970b. Cooperative Enterprise and Rural Development in Tanzania. In R. APTHORPE (1970b).

———— 1972. Kinship and Associational Networks among Transporters in Rural Peru: the Problem of the 'Local' and the 'Cosmopolitan' Entrepreneur. Paper presented to seminar on *Kinship and Social Networks* at the Institute of Latin American Studies, London University.

———— 1973. The Role of Regional Associations in Peru. In M. DRAKE, R. FINNEGAN, A. LEARMOUTH, D. BOSWELL and N. LONG, *The Process of Urbanization*. Bletchley: The Open University.

———— 1975. Multiple Enterprise in the Central Highlands of Peru. Paper presented to Advanced Seminar, School of American Research, Santa Fe, New Mexico.

LONG, N. and ROBERTS, B. R. 1974. Regional Structure and Entrepreneurial Activity in a Peruvian Valley. Final Report to Social Science

Research Council. Mimeo. Available through British Lending Library.
———— (1978). *Peasant Cooperation and Capitalist Expansion in Central Peru*. Austin: Texas University Press.
LONG, N. and WINDER, D. 1975. From Peasant Community to Production Co-operative: An Analysis of Recent Government Policy in Peru. *The Journal of Development Studies* 12 (1): 75–94, October.
LUTTRELL, W. J. 1971. Villagization, Cooperative Production, and Rural Cadres. *Economic Research Bureau Paper*. (11). University of Dar-es-Salaam.
MAFEJE. A. 1973. The Fallacy of Dual Economies Revisited. In *Dualism and Rural Development in East Africa*. Copenhagen: The Institute for Development Research.
MALINOWSKI, B. 1922. *Argonauts of the Western Pacific*. London: Routledge.
MANDELBAUM, D. 1970. *Society in India. Vol. 2: Change and Continuity*. Berkeley and Los Angeles: The University of California Press.
MANGIN, W. 1959. The Role of Regional Associations in the Adaption of Rural Population in Peru. *Sociologus* 9 (1):23–35.
MARTINDALE, D. 1971. Foreword to B. NEVASKAR, *Capitalists without Capitalism*. Westport, Connecticut: Greenwood Publishing Corporation.
MARTINEZ–ALIER, J. 1973. *Los Huachilleros del Peru*. Paris: Ruedo Iberico.
MATOS MAR, J. 1967. *Las Haciendas del Cuzco*. Lima: Instituto de Estudios Peruanos.
MATOS MAR, J., WHYTE, W. F., COTLER, J., WILLIAMS, L. K., ALERS, J. O., FUENZALIDA, V., and ALBERTI, G. 1969. *Dominación y Cambios en el Peru Rural*. Lima: Instituto de Estudios Peruanos.
MAUSS, M. 1925. *The Gift: Forms and Functions of Exchange in Archaic Society*. New York: Free Press. 1954 edition.
MCCLELLAND, D. C. 1961. *The Achieving Society*. New York: Free Press.
MCGUIRE, J. W. 1964. *Readings of Business Behaviour*. Englewood Cliffs, New Jersey: Prentice-Hall Inc.
MEIER, G. M. (ed.). 1964. *Leading Issues in Development Economics*. New York: Oxford University Press.
MEILLASSOUX, C. 1972. From Reproduction to Production. *Economy and Society* 1 (1):93–105, February.
MELLOR, J. W. 1966. Toward a Theory of Agricultural Development. In H. M. SOUTHWORTH and B. F. JOHNSTON (eds.), *Agricultural Development and Economic Growth*. Ithaca: Cornell University Press.
MILLER, S. 1967. Hacienda to Plantation in Northern Peru: The Process of Proletarianization of a Tenant Farmer Society. In J. H. STEWARD (ed.), *Contemporary Change in Traditional Societies. Vol. III: Mexican and Peruvian Communities*. Chicago and London: University of Illinois Press.
MINES, M. 1972. *Muslim Merchants. The Economic Behaviour of an Indian Muslim Community*. New Delhi: Shr Ram Centre for Industrial Relations and Human Resources.
MITCHELL, J. C. 1956. *The Yao Village*. Manchester: Manchester University Press.
———— 1960. *Tribalism and Tribal Society*. London: Oxford University Press.
———— 1969. *Social Networks in Urban Situations*. Manchester: Manchester University Press.

MOERMAN, M. 1968. *Agricultural Change and Peasant Choice in a Thai Village*. Berkeley and Los Angeles: University of California Press.

MONBERG, T. 1970. Determinants of Choice in Adoption and Fosterage on Bellona Island. *Ethnology* 9:99–136.

MONTOYA, R. 1970. *A Propósito de Caracter Predominantemente Capitalista de la Economía Peruana Actual*. Lima: Ediciones Teoria y Realidad; Serie: *Formación Social y Estructura Económica*, No. 1.

MOORE, B. 1966. *Social Origins of Dictatorship and Democracy. Lord and Peasant in the Making of the Modern World*. Harmondsworth: Penguin Books Ltd.

MOORE, W. E. 1963. *Social Change*. Englewood Cliffs, New Jersey: Prentice-Hall, Inc.

MOSHER, A. T. 1966. *Getting Agriculture Moving*. New York: Praeger.

NAFZIGER, E. W. 1971. Indian Entrepreneurship: A Survey. In P. KILBY (ed.), *Entrepreneurship and Economic Development*. New York: The Free Press.

NASH, M. 1958a. *Machine Age Maya*. New York: The Free Press.

———— 1958b. Political Relations in Guatemala. *Social and Economic Studies* 7:65–75.

NETTL, J. P. and ROBERTSON, R. 1968. *International Systems and the Modernization of Societies*. London: Faber.

NEVASKAR, B. 1971. *Capitalists without Capitalism: The Jains of India and the Quakers of the West. Contributions to Sociology*. No. 6. Westport, Connecticut: Greenwood Publishing Corporation.

NEWIGER, N. 1968. Village Settlement Schemes: The Problems of Cooperative Farming. In H. RUTHENBERG (ed.), *Smallholder Farming and Development in Tanzania*. München: IFO-Institut, Weltforum Verlag.

NISBET, R. A. 1969. *Social Change and History: Aspects of the Western Theory of Development*. London: Oxford University Press.

NYERERE, J. 1967. *Socialism and Rural Development*. Dar-es-Salaam: Government Printer.

———— 1968. *Freedom and Socialism*. London: Oxford University Press.

OCAMPO, J. F. and JOHNSON, D. L. 1972. The Concept of Political Development. In J. D. COCKCROFT, A. G. FRANK, and D. J. JOHNSON (eds.), *Dependence and Underdevelopment: Latin America's Political Economy*. New York: Doubleday and Company, Inc.

OLATUNBOSUN, D. 1967. Nigerian Farm Settlements and School Leavers' Farms. East Lansing and Ibadan: CSNRD No. 9.

ORTIZ, S. 1967. The Structure of Decision-making. In R. FIRTH (ed.), *Themes in Economic Anthropology*. London: Tavistock Publications Ltd.

———— 1970. 'The Human Factor' in Social Planning in Latin America. In R. APTHORPE. (1970a).

———— 1973. *Uncertainties in Peasant Farming. A Colombian Case*. London: The Athlone Press.

PAHL, R. 1966. The Rural-Urban Continuum. *Sociologia Ruralis* IV: 299–329. Reprinted in R. PAHL (ed.), 1968. *Readings in Urban Sociology*. Oxford: Pergamon Press.

PAINE, R. 1963. Entrepreneurial Acitivity Without its Profits. In F. BARTH (1963).

PALACIO, G. 1957. Relaciones de Trabajo entre el patron y los Colonos en los fundos de la Provincia de Paucartambo. *Revista Universitaria del Cuzco* XLVI (112).

PARKIN, D. J. 1972. *Palms, Wine, and Witnesses. Public Spirit and Private*

Gain in an African Farming Community. London: Intertext Books.

PELTO, P. J. and POGGIE, J. J. 1974. Models of Modernization: A Regional Focus. In J. J. POGGIE, JR., and R. N. LYNCH (eds.), *Rethinking Modernization.* Westport, Connecticut: Greenwood Press.

PIERIS, R. 1969. *Studies in the Sociology of Development.* Rotterdam: Rotterdam University Press.

POLANYI, K., ARENSBERG, C. M., and PEARSON, H. W. (eds.). 1957. *Trade and Markets in the Early Empires.* Glencoe, Illinois: The Free Press.

POST, K. 1972. Peasantization and Rural Political Movements in West Africa. *Archives Européennes de Sociologie* **XIII** (2) 223–54.

PRATTIS, J. I. 1973. Competing Paradigms and False Polemics in Economic Anthropology. *Anthropological Quarterly* **46** (4):278–96, October.

PRESTON, D. 1972. Internal Domination: Small Towns, the Countryside and Development. *Working Paper No. 11.* Department of Geography, Leeds University.

QUIJANO, A. 1970. *Nationalism and Capitalism in Peru: A Study of Neo-Colonialism.* London: Monthly Review Press.

RAIKES, P. 1968. Wheat and Ujamaa Villages: Some Proposals. Mimeo. Dar-es-Salaam: Rural Development Committee, University College.

————— 1975. Ujamaa Vijijini and Rural Socialist Development. *Review of African Political Economy* (3):33–52.

REDFIELD, R. 1941. *The Folk Culture of the Yucatan.* Chicago: University of Chicago Press.

————— 1947. The Folk Society. *The American Journal of Sociology* **52**:292–308.

————— 1956. *Peasant Society and Culture: An Anthropological Approach to Civilization.* Chicago: University of Chicago Press.

REDFIELD, R. and SINGER, M. B. 1954. The Cultural Role of Cities. *Economic Development and Social Change* **3**:53–73. Reprinted in T. SHANIN, 1971, *Peasants and Peasant Societies.* Harmondsworth: Penguin Books Ltd.

REX, J. 1961. *Key Problems of Sociological Theory.* London: Routledge and Kegan Paul.

ROBERTS, A. 1966. Migration from the Congo (A.D. 1500 to 1850). In B. M. FAGAN (ed.), *A Short History of Zambia.* Nairobi: Oxford University Press.

ROBERTS, B. R. 1973. Migración Urbana y Cambio en la Organización Provincial en la Sierra Central de Peru. *Ethnica Revista de Antropologia.* (6):237–61. Barcelona.

————— 1974. The Interrelationships of City and Provinces in Peru and Guatemala. In W. A. CORNELIUS and F. M. TRUEBLOOD (eds.), *Latin American Urban Research Vol. 4.* Beverly Hills, California: Sage Publications.

ROBERTS, B. R. and SAMANIEGO, C. 1973. The Significance of Agrarian Reform in the Highlands of Central Peru. Paper presented at the Institute of Development Studies, Sussex University. Published in N. LONG and B. R. ROBERTS (1978).

ROBINSON, J. A. and MAJAK, R. R. 1967. The Theory of Decision-making. In J. C. CHARLESWORTH (ed.), *Contemporary Political Analysis.* New York: The Free Press.

ROGERS, E. 1962. *The Diffusion of Innovations.* Illinois: Free Press.

————— 1969. *Modernization among Peasants — The Impact of Commu-*

nications. New York: Holt, Rinehart and Winston.

ROSENAU, J. N. 1967. The Premises and Promises of Decision-making Analysis. In J. C. CHARLESWORTH (ed.), *Contemporary Political Analysis*. New York: The Free Press.

ROSTOW, W. W. 1953. *The Process of Economic Growth*. London: Oxford University Press.

RUBEL, A. J. and KUPFERER, H. J. 1968. Perspectives on the Atomistic-Type Society: Introduction. *Human Organization* **27** (3): 189–99.

RUTHENBERG, H. 1964. *Agricultural Development in Tanganyika*. Berlin: Springer-Verlag.

SALISBURY, R. F. 1962. *From Stone to Steel*. London: Cambridge University Press.

————— 1970. *Vunamami: Economic Transformation in a Traditional Society*. Berkeley and Los Angeles: University of California Press.

SAUL, J. and ARRIGHI, G. 1973. *Essays on the Political Economy of Africa*. New York and London: Monthly Review Press.

SAYER, D. 1974. *Method and Dogma in Historical Materialism*. Working Paper No. 8. Department of Sociology, University of Durham. Reprinted in *Sociological Review,* **23** (4):779, 810, November, 1975. New Series.

SCHATZ, S. P. 1965. Achievement and Economic Growth: A Critical Appraisal. *Quarterly Journal of Economics* **79** (2):234–41, May. Reprinted in P. KILBY (1971).

SCHULTZ, T. W. 1964. *Transforming Traditional Agriculture*. New Haven, Connecticut: Yale University Press.

SCHURMANN, F. 1966. *Ideology and Organization in Communist China*. Berkeley and Los Angeles: University of California Press.

SCOTT, C. 1972. Agrarian Reform, Accumulation and the Role of the State: The Case of Peru. In *Dependance et Structure de Classes en Amerique Latine* IVe Seminaire Latino Americain, CETIM (AFJK) October.

SIMON, H. A. 1959. Theories of Decision-making in Economics and Behavioural Science. *American Economic Review* **49** (3):253–83, June.

SINGER, M. 1968. The Indian Joint Family in Modern Industry. In M. SINGER and B. S. COHN (eds.), *Structure and Change in Indian Society*. Chicago: Aldine Publishing Co.

SIVERTS, H. 1969. Ethnic Stability and Boundary Dynamics in Southern Mexico. In F. BARTH (ed.), *Ethnic Groups and Boundaries*. Boston: Little, Brown and Company.

SKINNER, G. W. 1964. Marketing and Social Structure in Rural China (Part I). *The Journal of Asian Studies* **XXIV** (1), November. Reprinted in J. M. POTTER *et al* (eds.), *Peasant Society: A Reader*. Boston: Little, Brown and Company.

SMELSER, N. J. 1959. *Social Change in the Industrial Revolution*. London: Routledge and Kegan Paul.

————— 1963. Mechanism of Change and Adjustment to Change. In B. F. HOSELITZ and W. E. MOORE (eds.), *Industrialization and Society*. The Hague: Mouton in collaboration with UNESCO. Reprinted in G. DALTON (ed.), 1971. *Economic Development and Social Change*. New York: The Natural History Press.

SMITH, A. D. 1973. *The Concept of Social Change: A Critique of the Functionalist Theory of Social Change*. London: Routledge and Kegan Paul.

SMITH, G. A. 1975. *The Social Basis of Peasant Political Acitivity: The Case of the Huasicanchinos of Central Peru.* D.Phil. Thesis University of Sussex.

SMITH, W. G. 1966. *The People of La Pacanda: Social Organization and Social Change in a Tarascan Village.* Ph.D. dissertation. University of California, Berkeley.

SRINIVAS, M. N. 1969. *Social Change in Modern India.* Berkeley and Los Angeles: The University of California Press.

STAVENHAGEN, R. 1965. Classes, colonialism, and acculturation. *Studies in Comparative International Development* 1 (6):53–77.

——— 1969. Seven Erroneous theses about Latin America. In I. L. HOROWITZ (ed.), *Latin American Radicalism.* New York: Random House.

STRICKON, A. 1972. Carlos Felipe: Kinsman, Patron, and Friend. In A. STRICKON and S. M. GREENFIELD (1972).

STRICKON, A. and GREENFIELD, S. M. (eds.) 1972. *Structure and Process in Latin America.* Albuquerque: University of New Mexico Press.

SZENTES, T. 1973. *The Political Economy of Underdevelopment.* Budapest: Akademiai Kiado.

TAX, SOL 1941. Culture and Civilization in Guatemalan Societies. *Scientific Monthly* 43:22–42.

——— 1958. *Penny Capitalism: A Guatemalan Indian Economy.* Washington D.C.: Smithsonian Institution. Institute of Social Anthropology. Publications No. 16.

TERRAY, E. 1969. *Le Marxisme devant les Sociétés Primitives: Deux Etudes.* Paris: Maspero. 1972. New York/London: Monthly Review Press. Translated by M. Klopper.

THIBAUT, J. W. and KELLEY, H. H. 1959. *The Social Psychology of Groups.* New York: John Wiley.

THOEDORSON, G. A. 1953. Acceptance of Industrialization and Its Attendant Consequences for the Social Patterns of Non-Western Societies. *American Sociological Review* 18 (5):477–84.

ULYANOVSKY, R. and PAVLOV, V.1973. *Asian Dilemma: A Soviet View and Myrdal's Concept.* Moscow: Progress Publishers.

VAN DEN BERGHE, P. L. 1963. Dialectic and Functionalism: Toward a Theoretical Synthesis. *American Sociological Review* 28:695–705.

VAN VELSEN, J. 1967. Situational Analysis and the Extended-Case Method. In A. L. EPSTEIN (ed.), *The Craft of Anthropology.* London: Tavistock Publications Ltd.

VAN VELZEN, T. H. U. E. 1973. Robinson Crusoe and Friday: Strength and Weakness of the Big Man Paradigm. *Man* 8 (4):592–612, December. New Series.

VAN ZANTWIJK, R. A. M. 1967. *Servants of the Saints: The Social and Cultural Identity of a Tarascan Community in Mexico.* Assen: Van Gorcum.

WATSON, W. 1958. *Tribal Cohesion in a Money Economy.* Manchester: Manchester University Press.

WEBER, M. 1904. *The Protestant Ethic and the Spirit of Capitalism.* Translated by Talcott Parsons, 1930. London: George Allen and Unwin.

WEEKS, J. 1971. The Political Economy of Labour Transfer. *Science and Society* 35 (4):463–80.

WEINER, M. 1966. *Modernization: The Dynamics of Growth.* New York and London: Basic Books, Inc.

WERTHEIM, W. F. 1971. The Way towards 'Modernity'. In A. R. DESAI (ed.), *Essays on Modernization of Underdeveloped Societies* Vol. I. Bombay: Thacker and Co. Ltd.

WILLIAM, S. G. 1975. Taking the part of Peasants: Rural Development in Nigeria and Tanzania. Seminar paper. Political Economy Group, University of Durham. Also in P. C. W. GUTKIND and I. WALLERS-TEIN (eds. 1976), *The Political Economy of Contemporary Africa*. Beverly Hills: Sage.

WILSON, B. R. 1973. Jehovah's Witnesses in Africa. *New Society* 25 (562):73–5.

WOLF, E. R. 1955. Types of Latin American Peasantry: A Preliminary Discussion. *American Anthropologist* 57:452–71.

WOLF, E. 1956. Aspects of Group Relations in Complex Societies. *American Anthropologist*. 58:1065–76.

WOLF, E. and MINTZ, S. 1957. Haciendas and Plantations in Middle America and the Antilles. *Social and Economic Studies* VI:380–412.

WOLPE, H. 1972. Capitalism and Cheap Labour-power in South Africa: From Segregation to Apartheid. *Economy and Society* 1 (4):425–56.

——— 1975. The Theory of Internal Colonialism: The South African Case. In I. OXAAL, T. BARNETT, and D. BOOTH (eds.), *Beyond the Sociology of Development*. London and Boston: Routledge and Kegan Paul.

ZALDIVAR, R. 1974. Agrarian Reform and Military Reformism in Peru. In D. LEHMANN (ed.), *Agrarian Reform and Agrarian Reformism*. London: Faber and Faber.

Author Index

Subject Index